DATE			

PLAYS for MODERN TEEN-AGE ACTORS

PLAYS FOR MODERN
TEEN-AGE ACTORS

*A collection of one-act comedies, farces, dramas,
and melodramas*

By HAROLD CABLE

Publishers   PLAYS, INC.   *Boston*

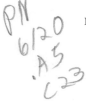

Library of Congress Catalog Card Number: 73–166340
ISBN: 0–8238–0126–8

MANUFACTURED IN THE UNITED STATES OF AMERICA

CONTENTS

THE WAY-OUT CINDERELLA   1
     A sophisticated satire

A DEPUTY FOR BROKEN BOW   25
     A comic melodrama of the Old West

THE FAIREST PITCHER OF THEM ALL   42
     A spoof on "Snow White"

PEACE, PILGRIM   69
     An improbable guided tour

LAST STOP   94
     An eerie drama

ANOTHER MAN'S FAMILY   120
     Two-way generation gap

BAILEY, GO HOME   144
     A Caribbean comedy

WAY, WAY DOWN SOUTH   165
     A mod melodrama

YOUNG FOREVER   185
     A comedy about the Fountain of Youth

THE RELUCTANT COLUMBUS   209
    History as it might have been

THE BEST OF SPORTS   232
    A minor battle of the sexes

LITTLE JACKIE AND THE BEANSTALK   256
    A television star climbs to new fame

THE REFORM OF STERLING SILVERHEART   282
    A ghoulish melodrama

BIG RED RIDING HOOD   302
    Beating the wolf at the door

PLAYS for MODERN
TEEN-AGE ACTORS

The Way-Out Cinderella

Characters

ELLA   MYRNA, *her fairy godmother*
MITZI ⎫   KING OF MICROVANIA
GRETA ⎬ *her stepsisters*   PRINCE OF MICROVANIA
STEPMOTHER (*Katrina*)   TWO PALACE GUARDS

SCENE 1

SETTING: *Ella's cottage in Microvania, a tiny kingdom lost in the mountains of Europe.*

AT RISE: ELLA *is washing windows while* STEPMOTHER *paces floor.* GRETA *and* MITZI *are sewing.*

STEPMOTHER: Please, Ella. Please! You've washed those windows twice this afternoon. All you do is clean and scrub, wash and iron, dust and mop.

ELLA: I like to see things looking nice.

STEPMOTHER: We do, too, don't we, girls?

GRETA *and* MITZI: Yes, Mama.

STEPMOTHER: But you're working yourself to death, child.

GRETA: You never sit down.

MITZI: Except in the corner. With your pile of cinders.

ELLA (*Stopping work and turning to girls, with a smile*):

1

This morning I made a cinder castle. It was real cute.

STEPMOTHER: A girl your age should be thinking of other things.

ELLA (*Fearfully*): You're not going to take my cinders away from me, are you?

STEPMOTHER: Yes, Ella. And I'm going to lock up all the brooms and feather dusters and hire a maid.

ELLA: Nobody loves me!

STEPMOTHER: Ella, I love you as if you were my own child. Greta and Mitzi love you, too.

GRETA: We love you, Ella.

MITZI: We love you lots.

STEPMOTHER: That's why we can't stand to see you working yourself to a nubbin and taking no time to make yourself look pretty.

ELLA: I don't want to look pretty.

STEPMOTHER: But you must, Ella. Every girl in Microvania wants to look pretty.

GRETA: Especially now.

MITZI: With the Prince back from school in America.

GRETA: And about to tour the kingdom in search of a bride.

ELLA: He won't be searching for me. I'm plain, and I'm drab, and I like it that way. Excuse me, I haven't cleaned the oven in three hours. (ELLA *starts toward oven, but* STEPMOTHER *bars her way.*)

STEPMOTHER: Leave that oven alone! Even the strudel and the sauerbraten are beginning to taste like ammonia and detergent.

ELLA: You're scolding me again.

STEPMOTHER (*Impatiently*): I'm not scolding you, child!

ELLA: Oh, yes, you are.

GRETA: We only want you to have some fun out of life.

MITZI: You've never even been to the teen canteen.

ELLA: You're scolding me because I have big feet.

GRETA: All the better to waltz with.

MITZI: And all the girls in Microvania waltz.

GRETA: Except you.

ELLA: I hate waltzing. I hate all that music and all those violins.

STEPMOTHER: But you can still make yourself look pretty.

ELLA: I like myself the way I am. I like my cinder box, and I like to clean and wash dishes. Why can't you let me be myself?

STEPMOTHER: It's for your own good, isn't it, girls?

GRETA *and* MITZI: Yes, Mama.

ELLA: No, it isn't. You're ashamed of me.

STEPMOTHER: Well, people *do* talk.

ELLA (*Pouting*): I don't care what they say. (*She stalks over to table and sits down.*)

STEPMOTHER: Then have pity on me! Everywhere I go people are gossiping about me. Everywhere the ladies are laughing behind their fans, and the gentlemen are snickering behind their dueling masks. And do you know why? They think I'm a wicked, fiendish step-mother who's giving Greta and Mitzi all the advantages while I turn you into a dismal drudge. Why can't you come out of the kitchen and the cinder pile and be like the other girls?

GRETA: And waltz?

MITZI: And sing?

GRETA: And flirt with the officers of the palace guard?

ELLA (*Whimpering*): You *are* scolding me!

STEPMOTHER: We mean it for your own good.

ELLA: No wonder they gossip. The only thing you want to do is make me miserable.

STEPMOTHER: We want you to go to parties and have fun.

ELLA: And flirt with all those tin soldiers and have my big

feet stepped on by a lot of waltzing clowns! (*Crying loudly*) I'm going to my room and wash the curtains! (ELLA *runs off.*)

STEPMOTHER: That child! What are we going to do with her?

GRETA (*Lightly*): Maybe she's sick.

MITZI: We can't worry about it now.

GRETA: We have to get ready for the ball.

MITZI (*To audience*): The ball at the palace.

GRETA (*Also to audience*): To celebrate the Prince's home-coming from school in America. (*Faint sound of waltz music is heard from offstage.*)

MITZI: Listen! Oh, I love these celebrations!

GRETA: Mother, is it true that Microvania is famous for its waltzes?

STEPMOTHER: Yes, dear. When I was a girl, we used to waltz in the streets all night long. That's why the cobble-stones of Microvania are so flat. And my feet, too. Better wear your arch supports, girls.

GRETA: Come on, Mitzi. It's time to make ourselves even prettier than we are.

MITZI: I wish Ella would come with us.

STEPMOTHER: I'm afraid nothing short of Ella's fairy god-mother will be able to blast her out of this house.

GRETA: What ever happened to Ella's fairy godmother, anyway?

STEPMOTHER: I haven't heard from her in years. Not since she packed up her violin and sailed away to the New World. She must be very old by now.

GRETA: Maybe she's dead.

MITZI: Fairy godmothers never die.

GRETA: If she isn't dead, she ought to realize her responsi-bility and come back here to help Ella pull herself to-gether.

MITZI: Why don't you send her a wire, Mama?

STEPMOTHER: If I knew where to find her, my dears, I think I would.

GRETA: Poor Mama.

MITZI: You're almost at the end of your rope, aren't you?

GRETA: We'll leave you alone now so you can worry in peace.

MITZI: Listen to the music, Mama. It may take your mind off things.

GRETA *and* MITZI (*Joining hands and waltzing offstage*): One two three, one two three, one two three. . . . (*Waltz music fades.*)

STEPMOTHER (*Reciting in a mournful voice*):

My daughters, my daughters, my two lovely girls,
Hear not your mother's faint cry.
May life speed you on with its three-quarter whirl,
See not the tear in my eye.

My heart is apart; is there no dawn in sight?
Ella won't change and won't go.
She should play and be gay and should waltz through
  the night,
And not fill my life with such woe.

It's awful, it's awful to face future years
Here in this spotless old shack,
With Ella—still single—just wiping my tears . . .
Won't she get off of my back?
(*Curtain*)

*   *   *

SCENE 2

SETTING: *The throne room in the palace of the King of Microvania. The throne is up right.*
AT RISE: PRINCE *is slumped on throne, looking bored.* KING *stands down right.*

PRINCE: Man, this place has bad vibes.

KING: Son, I sent you to school in America for an education. I did not expect to have you shipped back home a . . . a . . . a hippie!

PRINCE (*Pleased*): Thanks, man.

KING: You have a duty to your country.

PRINCE (*Sitting up*): Country! Man, this place is nowhere! And I have news for you. Nobody in the big outside world ever heard of Microvania. It isn't even on the map.

KING (*With dignity*): We have a noble tradition, a noble culture, a noble history.

PRINCE: We have nothing but waltzes—um-pah-pah, um-pah-pah. And you know something? Nobody even knows we gave that to the world. They all think it came from Vienna.

KING: Vienna? Where's that?

PRINCE: In Austria, man, a country so big it dwarfs this rock the way an elephant dwarfs a mosquito. (*Rises and walks downstage*) Now, I have a mission, see? I'm going to bring this hole up-to-date. First thing that has to go is the music.

KING: But you can't do that! Our subjects wouldn't stand for it. The world wouldn't stand for it.

PRINCE: I told you—the world doesn't know we exist.

KING (*Deflated*): So you did. I guess that explains why all my efforts to establish world trade have been thwarted.

Nobody answers my letters. The treasury is almost bare, son.

PRINCE (*Walking toward* KING): O.K. So something has to be done about it. When something has to be done, you do something.

KING: But you don't do just any old thing. You don't throw out beautiful tradition and replace it with a lot of crude new fads.

PRINCE: Don't go blowing your top. Little princey will fix up everything. First, the party tonight is off. We can't afford it, and we can't use credit cards if nobody ever heard of us.

KING: You can't mean it. Our people would revolt!

PRINCE: And what would they use for weapons—apple tarts and gumdrops?

KING: Did you ever get hit with a gumdrop? I did once. Right in the eye. It hurt!

PRINCE (*Ignoring him*): And I'm not searching the kingdom for a bride. These days there's only one thing for a prince of an unknown little country to do. He has to marry a celebrity. A rock singer! (KING *winces*.)

KING: I'll make a deal with you. You can marry anybody you want. But search the kingdom for a bride first. It's expected of you. In fact, we've already announced a date for the beginning of your tour.

PRINCE: I've seen all the birds in the realm already. They don't groove. You show me one who doesn't look like a little dumpling with ribbons and curls.

KING: Have it your way. But I will not cancel the party tonight, and that's final. If you expect to make any changes around here, you'll have to win the people to your side. Depriving them of a chance to waltz all night is not the way.

PRINCE: O.K., O.K.

KING: And I want you to appear in your full-dress uniform, looking like a prince.

PRINCE: You're not getting me into one of those gold and scarlet straitjackets.

KING: I'm still the King around here!

PRINCE: Big deal.

KING: And I'm still giving the royal commands. This is a royal command!

PRINCE: O.K., O.K. Cool it! But I'm not marrying any dumpling.

KING: That is quite enough out of you, young man. I shall see you at the ball—conducting yourself in the manner of a prince of Microvania. Is that clear?

PRINCE: I hear you, man.

KING (*Holding his head and turning away from* PRINCE): My son. My own son!

PRINCE: Can I bring my records to the party?

KING (*Quickly turning back*): What records?

PRINCE: The ones I brought from America. I have a cool one of the Skin-Divers doing "You're My Teen-Age Sunfish." (PRINCE *sings, snapping his fingers.*)

> You're my teen-age sunfish, yeh, yeh, yeh—
> You're my teen-age sunfish, yeh, yeh, yeh—
> You're my teen-age sunfish, yeh, yeh, yeh—
> You're my teen-age sunfish, yeh, yeh, yeh—
> You're my swimmin' baby, you're my swimmin'
>   baby—
> I flip when you flap your fins. *Baby!*

KING (*In despair*): My very own son! (*He exits hurriedly.*)

PRINCE (*To audience*): I can see I'll have to do some adult education around here. (*Curtain*)

*   *   *

Scene 3

SETTING: *Ella's cottage. There is a coffeepot on the stove, and a plastic or paper pumpkin on the table.*

AT RISE: STEPMOTHER *is wringing her hands and crying. Knock on door is heard.*

STEPMOTHER (*Calling*): Enter. Enter if you must this house of sadness. (MYRNA *opens door and enters, carrying violin case.*)

MYRNA: Anybody home? (*She sets down violin case.*) Of course, you're home. I see you right there. What are you bawling about, Katrina?

STEPMOTHER (*Embracing* MYRNA): Myrna! Oh, I'm so happy to see you!

MYRNA: Good to see you, too, sweetie. Why the tears?

STEPMOTHER: Oh, nothing, nothing. (*Walks to stove*) Let me fix you some coffee. Some cake? Some strudel?

MYRNA: No, thanks, dearie. Have to watch my figure.

STEPMOTHER (*Pouring herself a cup of coffee*): You've aged, Myrna.

MYRNA: I know. You're a honeybun to mention it, too. One thing I can promise you, though—I'm sick of grey hair. How would I look as a redhead?

STEPMOTHER: Try being a blonde. All girls in Microvania are blonde. (*She sits at table.*)

MYRNA: I'll be a redhead. Shake 'em up a little bit.

STEPMOTHER: Sit down, Myrna. (MYRNA *picks up violin case and sits on chair near door.*) Really you are heaven-sent. Where have you been all these years?

MYRNA: In New York City. That's in the United States of America. Had a ball. (*Pats violin case*) Found a job playing gypsy violin in a swanky restaurant. Looked real snazzy as a gypsy, I did. Read palms and crystal balls on the side. You need to pick up a little extra change in New York. But—you'll never believe this, Katrina—I became very civic minded. Yes. I've been passing out pamphlets in front of the United Nations Building. (*Rises, placing violin case on floor*) I tell you, Katrina, I was flabbergasted when I found that people over there have never even heard of Microvania. And do you know what? They think the waltz came from another country altogether. I wasn't going to let that kind of thing go on. Not this kid.

STEPMOTHER (*Going to cupboard and cutting herself a piece of strudel*): Are you sure you won't have some strudel?

MYRNA: Those pamphlets of mine were circulated coast to coast. I was even interviewed on television. Everybody knows where the waltz came from now. I have a big organized tour coming over here next week to see our music festival.

STEPMOTHER (*Sitting at table*): But we've never had a music festival here.

MYRNA: Well, we'd better get one going, don't you think? These people expect to see something—costumes and uniforms—something out of a corny operetta. Now, if this festival comes off well, we ought to be able to do a roaring tourist business just by being ourselves.

STEPMOTHER (*Excited*): And we can dance and sing all the time! What does the King think of the idea?

MYRNA: Haven't told him yet. I'll see him at the ball to-night. Plenty of time. (*Sits at table*) Say, how's Ella?

STEPMOTHER (*Sadly*): Oh. I'd almost forgotten about her.

MYRNA: Bet she's a real beauty by now.

STEPMOTHER: She's nice looking, Myrna, but you'd never know it.

MYRNA: Doesn't make much sense, dearie.

STEPMOTHER: She goes out of her way to make herself look plain and unattractive. She wears herself out cleaning and cooking. Myrna, she gives this place a spring cleaning three and four times a day! And if she isn't working, she's sitting and playing in her cinder pile.

MYRNA: Cinder pile!

STEPMOTHER: She never goes out. She hates music and waltzing.

MYRNA: My, what a dreary state of affairs! Sick, sick, sick!

STEPMOTHER: Do you think you can do something for her?

MYRNA: Don't know, dearie. I can try.

STEPMOTHER: Could you wave your magic wand and send her to the ball tonight?

MYRNA: You want her to marry the Prince, I suppose.

STEPMOTHER: Oh, yes!

MYRNA: Don't be too ambitious for the child, Katrina. Do her a world of harm. Now, let's see. (*Rises and walks as she thinks*) Princes go for girls who look like princesses, I guess.

STEPMOTHER (*Rising and joining* MYRNA): With a tiara of diamonds and (*Gesturing*) a gown with flounces way out to there!

MYRNA: It's a tough order. I haven't been doing much wand-waving lately. Plays in a cinder pile, you say?

STEPMOTHER: It's some sort of complex. She has rather big feet.

MYRNA: Big feet. I'll try to correct that. What else?

STEPMOTHER: Dancing. She has to dance. And the attitude is so important.

MYRNA: O.K. I'll do the job. But you must help me prepare for the festival. Chair my committee, will you?

STEPMOTHER: Anything! Anything you say!

MYRNA: Shake. (*They shake hands.*) Now, I ought to have a look at Ella. Where is she?

STEPMOTHER: She's in her room, taking down the curtains so she can wash them.

MYRNA: Good heavens! It's pretty bad, isn't it? Better give me a few minutes to think.

STEPMOTHER: It will probably take me an hour to pry her out of her room.

MYRNA: Tell her the kitchen floor needs scrubbing.

STEPMOTHER: Yes! On hands and knees. That should send her flying. (*Crosses to door*) Good luck, Myrna.

MYRNA: Thanks, dearie. I'll do my best. (STEPMOTHER *exits.*) Promises, promises. I shouldn't make them. Not when I'm so rusty. Doesn't like waltzes. That's the strangest thing of all. Why, even at my age, I'd waltz 'til dawn—that is, if somebody would waltz with me. (*Waltz theme from "Die Fledermaus" is heard softly in background.* MYRNA *waltzes briefly around room. She stops, out of breath, as music fades.*) Oh, limitations, limitations. I could do with a fairy godmother myself. Now, let me see. (*She crosses to violin case, opens it, and takes out her magic wand.*) Ella has to go to the ball. She has to dance. And she has to appeal to the Prince more than any other girl there. All right. (*Waves magic wand*) One. Two. Three. (*She chants.*)

> Ella, leave your housework all;
> Tonight you're going to the ball.
> Be the girl the Prince desires;
> Dance and kindle love's young fires.
> From your ankles to your hair
> Be the girl the Prince finds fair.
> Pumpkin, alter and be suitable
> To transport a maid so beautiful.

Bring her back at twelve's last chime
For then my spell runs out of time.

I guess that ought to do it. (*She puts wand on table. Pumpkin on table is pulled through window, and sudden roar of motorcycle is heard.*) Gracious sakes alive! What kind of racket is that? (ELLA *saunters in, wearing goggles, helmet, and hippie clothes. She speaks in a deep voice.*)

ELLA: It's my motorcycle, Granny. My coach, to you. Hi. Long time no see.

MYRNA (*Staring at* ELLA): No, it's impossible! I couldn't be that rusty.

ELLA: Rusty at what? You mean the magic spell bit? Am I ever relieved. I thought you were going to turn me into some kind of clod.

MYRNA: A princess—that's what you were supposed to be.

ELLA: Well, here I am! Ready for the party!

MYRNA: Oh, what have I done? I'll be thrown out of the country. I'll be disgraced in my profession.

ELLA: Don't pop your hair net, Granny. Say, where did I put my electric guitar?

MYRNA: What electric guitar? Oh, dear me!

ELLA: *My* electric guitar. Thought I'd beat out a few numbers for the Prince. (*She snaps her fingers.*)

MYRNA: Help! Please, somebody help!

ELLA: Don't wait up, Granny. Things may really swing tonight.

MYRNA: You'd better be back by twelve.

ELLA: O.K., if that's the way it goes. You should have changed my feet, though. They're as big as ever.

MYRNA (*Remembering*): Ankles. I said ankles instead of toes! Well, it's too late now.

ELLA: That's O.K. You can't have everything. Away to

my motorcycle. (*Crosses to door and looks back*) Be more considerate next time, though, will you, Granny? You can't get parties swinging if you leave by midnight. It's not fair. Well, so long!

MYRNA (*Weakly*): Have a good time.

ELLA: Good time? Granny, this party's going to be wild! (ELLA *exits quickly and the motorcycle roars loudly as the curtain falls.*)

*   *   *

SCENE 4

SETTING: *Ballroom of the royal palace.* NOTE: *This scene is optional. It may be quite brief, or it may be expanded if the director desires. It may take place before the curtain, and should be a pantomime version of some of the events described by Stepsisters in Scene 6. Scene should include Ella's dropping the shoe and leaving when the clock strikes twelve.*

*   *   *

SCENE 5

TIME: *The morning after the ball.*

SETTING: *Throne room in the royal palace.*

AT RISE: KING *is sitting on his throne, talking with* PRINCE.

KING: I'm ashamed. Ashamed! Never in my life have I seen such dancing and goings-on. Never!

PRINCE: Relax. We were just moving with the beat.

KING: Swinging yourselves around like that?

PRINCE: Swinging! Now you've got it, man.

KING: And that crazy, crazy music?

PRINCE: Crazy! You have got it, man.

KING: It isn't even music. It's nothing but a beat.

PRINCE: The beat. That's it. You gotta get the beat.

KING: It's savage, that's what it is.

PRINCE: Savage, man, savage!

KING (*Pounding arm of his throne*): We'll find that girl and send her out of the country.

PRINCE: We'll find her, and she'll be my bride.

KING (*Rising*): Never!

PRINCE: I have the palace guards searching for her now.

KING: She's probably hiding out in some cave.

PRINCE: They have her shoe. She dropped it when she left last night. The guards have orders to bring me the girl who can wear the shoe.

KING: I only hope somebody acceptable fits into the shoe before they find that monster.

PRINCE: Not likely, man. It was a size twelve triple E.

KING: Good night!

PRINCE: The craziest dancing feet you ever saw.

KING (*Walking toward exit*): We're going after those guards right now. We're going to stop them before this thing goes any further.

PRINCE: But I thought you wanted to find her and throw her out of the country.

KING: Let her find her own way out. After the terrible things she said about our waltzes, she probably won't be staying around long, anyway. She's certainly not a Microvanian. She's from far off, (*Gesturing*) from way out there somewhere.

PRINCE: Way out. Yeh!

KING: We're going to find those guards. Come with me!

PRINCE: Now look, man, just because you don't dig this kind of chick—

KING: Come with me! (*He grabs* PRINCE *by the ear.*) Or it will be the strap!

PRINCE: Yes, Father. Yes, sir. Right away, sir. Ow! Ow! (*They exit. Curtain.*)

*   *   *

SCENE 6

SETTING: *Ella's cottage.*

AT RISE: STEPMOTHER *is sitting at the table.* ELLA *is trying to clear away the dishes.* ELLA *now speaks in her normal, high-pitched voice, and she wears her work clothes.*

STEPMOTHER: Ella, my darling child, please don't take that plate away yet. I'm still eating.

ELLA: I only wanted to wash the dishes. I have so much to do this morning. The whole house needs scrubbing.

STEPMOTHER: But I would like to finish my coffee cake, if you don't mind.

ELLA: You'll throw me off schedule—all off schedule. After I clear the table, I have to clean the whole upstairs, and I think the curtains in my room need washing again. And then—

STEPMOTHER (*Handing plate to* ELLA): Here! Take the plate!

ELLA (*Taking plate and clearing rest of table*): Thank you, Mother. Thank you, thank you. (*She crosses to corner of room, puts down dishes, picks up broom, dustpan, and feather duster and exits.* GRETA *and* MITZI *enter.*)

STEPMOTHER: Well, good morning, girls.

GRETA *and* MITZI: Good morning, Mother.

GRETA: I see Ella has already cleared the table, so I guess we don't get any breakfast.

STEPMOTHER (*Going to cupboard*): Here, have some strudel. And tell me about the dance. (STEPMOTHER *puts strudel on table.*)

GRETA: It was awful, Mama. Everybody was waltzing around and having such a lovely time, and in walked the weirdest girl.

MITZI: The Prince was sitting on his throne, as proper as you please, and she walked up to the orchestra . . .

GRETA: And then she grabbed the microphone and a guitar and started singing the strangest music.

MITZI: The Prince leaped across the floor. We thought he was going to throw her out. But he kissed her right in front of everybody.

STEPMOTHER: No! (*She sits in chair at table.*)

GRETA: Then he made the orchestra learn the song she was playing. And they played it all night long.

MITZI: Over and over.

GRETA: Until midnight, when she went sailing out of the room as if she were pulled by an invisible rope.

MITZI: And the dancing they did!

GRETA: The King had to be revived with smelling salts and escorted to his private chambers.

STEPMOTHER: The Prince certainly has changed!

GRETA (*Thoughtfully*): You know, though, we can't very well fight progress.

MITZI (*Inspired*): Greta, how do you think I'd look dressed like that girl?

GRETA: I'd look better, and I can dance that dance better than you.

MITZI: I can play the guitar. It wouldn't take me long to learn that song.

GRETA: And if that's the type of girl the Prince likes . . .

MITZI (*Singing*): "You're my teen-age sunfish, yeh, yeh, yeh . . ."

STEPMOTHER: Stop that this instant! (MYRNA *enters.*)

MYRNA: Yes, do stop it. I have a terrible headache.

GRETA *and* MITZI: Oh, hello, Myrna.

MYRNA: Katrina, it was distinctly a disaster! Thank goodness it's all over. Ella's all right, isn't she?

GRETA: Of course, she's all right. What can happen to you in a pail of sudsy water?

MITZI (*Singing again*): "You're my swimmin' baby . . ."

STEPMOTHER: Stop it! (*Thoughtfully*) Myrna, what happened with Ella last night?

GRETA *and* MITZI (*Singing together*):
"You're my swimmin' baby—
I flip when you flap your fins. *Baby!*"

MYRNA: Aspirin. I need some aspirin. (*Knock on door is heard.*)

PALACE GUARDS (*From offstage*): Open! Open in the name of the Prince of Microvania!

GRETA *and* MITZI: Oh, what fun!

STEPMOTHER: We'll be hanged.

MYRNA: Calm yourself, dearie. They'll never know.

STEPMOTHER (*Calling*): Come in. (TWO GUARDS *enter.* 1ST GUARD *carries* ELLA's *shoe.*)

1ST GUARD: The Prince has ordered a search.

GRETA (*To* MITZI, *indicating* GUARDS): They're cute.

2ND GUARD: A search of the entire kingdom.

MITZI (*To* GRETA, *pointing*): I like that one.

1ST GUARD: To find a fair maiden—

2ND GUARD: With the biggest foot you ever saw.

GRETA: My feet are huge.

MITZI: Mine, too.

1ST GUARD (*Showing shoe*): Whoever can wear this shoe—

2ND GUARD: Will become the princess of Microvania.

MITZI: That's a pretty big shoe.

GRETA: You said it.

MITZI: It's no use, guards. It's too big for us.

GRETA: But tell the Prince we can dance the way she did.

MITZI: And we can sing the way she did.

STEPMOTHER: What?

GRETA: And we're good Microvanians through and through.

1ST GUARD: You and all the other fair maidens in the land.

2ND GUARD: They're groovin' all the way from the palace gate down to Blitzer's Delicatessen.

MYRNA: Oh, no! (KING *and* PRINCE *enter.*)

KING: Oh, yes!

ALL (*Bowing or curtsying*): Your Highnesses.

PRINCE: Hi, cats.

KING: Call off the search.

PRINCE (*Taking* GUARDS *aside*): You heard it, boys. Sorry. The old man's putting his foot down.

1ST GUARD: We're finished, anyway. These are the last girls in the last house.

GRETA: You left us till last?

MITZI: Why, you jerk!

GRETA: You think you know so much. We're not the last girls at all.

MITZI: There's another girl here—our stepsister. (*Calling*) Ella! (ELLA *runs in, wiping her hands on apron.*)

ELLA: Yes, dear sisters, what can I do for you?

GRETA (*Pushing* ELLA *into a chair*): You can try on this shoe. (*Grabs shoe from* 1ST GUARD, *and hands it to* ELLA, *who puts it on*)

1ST GUARD: His Highness ordered us to stop trying on the shoe.

GRETA: Oh, he won't mind, will you, King? Just for us?

MITZI: Then you'll know every girl in the land has had a chance.

KING: And my son will know that the creature he seeks is not among us.

PRINCE (*Disgustedly*): Come on, Pop. This chick's from hunger.

2ND GUARD (*Pointing to shoe on* ELLA's *foot*): But the shoe, Your Highness—it fits perfectly.

PRINCE: Aw, come on. This mousy, frumpy girl?

KING: I must say she looks nothing like your creature.

ELLA: But we are one and the same, kind sirs.

PRINCE: Get that voice. Sugar and honey! Let's go, Pappy. This is some kind of joke.

ELLA: No. I *am* the girl. I *am*. Listen. (*She sings in a quavering, high-pitched voice.*) "I'm your teen-age sunfish, yeh, yeh, yeh."

PRINCE (*Laughing*): A voice like Minnie Mouse!

ELLA: Fairy godmother, tell them who I am!

PRINCE (*Gesturing to* MYRNA): Fairy godmother? This old hag?

MYRNA: Watch your tongue, or I'll put a pox on you.

PRINCE (*Weakly*): Did you hear what she said, Daddy?

ELLA: Please change me back the way I was last night. Please!

STEPMOTHER: But Ella, darling, I thought you liked being plain and drab.

GRETA: And playing with your cinders.

ELLA: But last night, for the first time in my life, I had a real groovy time. I mean, man, it was cool! This Prince is too much!

STEPMOTHER: Myrna? This was all your fault to begin with.

MYRNA: You're the one who asked for help. I guaranteed you nothing.

ELLA: But I dig this Prince the most!

MYRNA: The answer is no. I will not turn you back into a . . . a hippie. And that is that.

ELLA (*Crying and running off*): Oh, I hate you. How could you be so wretched and so cruel? Oh-h-h. . . . (*Exits*)

MYRNA (*To* STEPMOTHER): Sorry, Katrina. It was all an accident. I didn't know she'd turn out that way. You weren't at that wingding last night. You didn't see what happened. Little Ella turned that beautiful ball into a rock fest.

PRINCE: So what's it to you?

MYRNA: Prince, my dear young prince, the waltz to me is sacred. It's sacred to all the people of Microvania.

KING: Good for you. That's just what I've been telling him.

MYRNA: And we need to preserve it. It's our most valuable asset. Why, just before the King fainted last night, I was about to tell him that the waltz is going to put Microvania in the black again.

KING: And what do you mean by that?

MYRNA: I've been publicizing our waltzes in America. Publicity is everything these days, dearie, and I've started organized tours of Microvanian music festivals featuring the waltz and nothing but. Oh, you'll believe me next week when the Americans start arriving by the busload. And how are you going to feel when all those people with all that money to spend find there isn't any waltz festival at all?

KING: But there must be a festival. There must!

MYRNA: At this rate there won't be any waltzes left. Everybody will be groaning and twisting. Who's going to come from America to see that, I ask you?

KING: That settles it. (*To* STEPMOTHER) Your daughter, madam, will remain here, and my son will renounce any claim to her.

PRINCE: It's not the same bird, man. So who cares?

MYRNA: She's the same bird, sonny, and I'm tempted to wave my magic wand just to prove I'm right. But I'm not sacrificing my principles for vanity, no siree.

STEPMOTHER: She is the same bird, Your Highness.

PRINCE: Then you must change her. I want my teen-age sunfish back again!

MYRNA: Not on your life! Long live the waltz!

KING: Long live Microvania!

MYRNA: With a growing treasury, too. You'll see.

PRINCE: All right, you can have your waltz.

MYRNA: I don't believe a word you say, Prince. Sorry.

PRINCE: *You* can have your waltz if *we* can have our music, too.

MYRNA: The answer is still no.

STEPMOTHER: But you brought them together—these two young people—Myrna. And they fell in love. (MYRNA's *face brightens.*) You must do it. For love, Myrna. For love!

MYRNA: Love! Ah, love. All our most beautiful waltzes are about love.

STEPMOTHER: So you must do it, Myrna.

MYRNA: Is it a promise, Prince? I mean, for real?

PRINCE: A promise. Yes.

KING: I must bow to your wishes in the matter, madam. If you're able to build up the treasury single-handed. . . .

MYRNA: And I am. . . .

KING: Then the rest is up to you.

STEPMOTHER: Please do it, Myrna. If you knew what it was like to live with that simpering child all the time. And the cleaning. And the piles of cinders everywhere. Please do it, Myrna.

MYRNA (*Chanting*):

Magic, magic, work your spell,
But this time change her feet as well.
Change the girl just as before,
But add this note of what's in store:

Should the Prince his promise break . . .
Change the girl into a snake!

PRINCE: Long live the waltz!
ALL: Long live the waltz! (ELLA *runs in, wearing hippie clothes.*)
ELLA: And long live my fairy godmother! Look at my little feet!
MYRNA: Too much, Ella baby. I dig your vibes, too. Say, do you suppose we could work out an arrangement of "Teen-Age Sunfish" in waltz time?
GRETA *and* MITZI: Great!
PRINCE: I'll take the beat! Um-pah-pah, um-pah-pah . . . (MYRNA *begins singing, and all join in.* ELLA *dances with* PRINCE; GRETA *and* MITZI *then dance with* GUARDS, *and finally* MYRNA *waltzes with* KING.)
ALL:

You're my teen-age sunfish, yeh, yeh, yeh.
You're my swimmin' baby, you're my swimmin' baby—
I flip when you flap your fins. *Baby!*
(*Curtain falls.*)

THE END

Production Notes

THE WAY-OUT CINDERELLA

Characters: 4 male; 5 female.

Playing Time: 35 minutes.

Costumes: Greta, Mitzi, Myrna and Stepmother wear frilly dresses. Ella wears oversized shoes, and drab apron and work clothes; at dance and at end of play she wears motorcycle helmet, goggles, and hippie clothes. Prince wears guru shirt, bell bottoms, chain with pendant or beads, headband, and small crown. At dance, he wears uniform. King and Guards wear appropriate costumes. Stepsisters and Guards should be made up to look as doll-like as possible.

Properties: Sponge, bucket of soapy water for washing windows, sewing materials, coffeepot, coffee cup and saucer, strudel, plate, magic wand, violin case, plastic or paper pumpkin on a string, breakfast dishes, plate with coffee cake, cardboard box labeled "Cinders," mops, brooms, dustpan, feather dusters, large shoe.

Setting: Scenes 1, 3, and 6 are set in main room of Ella's cottage. Up left is a table, with chairs, near the windows. Oven is at left, near door to rest of cottage. There is a chair by front door, at right. Mops, brooms, dustpan, feather dusters lean against wall in one corner of room, and there is a box labeled "Cinders" near one wall. Cupboard and other kitchen furnishings complete set. Scenes 2 and 5 are set in throne room of royal palace. There is a throne up right. Scene 4 is the ballroom of the palace.

Lighting: No special effects.

Sound: Waltz music, roar of motorcycle, and, if desired, accompaniment for "Sunfish" song.

A Deputy for Broken Bow

Characters

TOM FEEBLE, *a deputy*
GRANNY FEEBLE, *his grandmother*
NELL BLATZ, *his girlfriend*
SHERIFF PHINEAS KINDLY (HUGHIE THE HOOD)
TWO COWBOYS
TWO GIRLS
WOMAN

BEFORE RISE: COWBOY *enters right in front of curtain, carrying easel and sign. He sets easel at right, and places sign on it:* BROKEN BOW, ARIZONA. TIME: A WHILE BACK, *then exits.*

SETTING: *Main street of Broken Bow, Arizona. There is a hitching post with hobbyhorse tied to it at left, and a café table and chairs are up center, with a barrel nearby.*

AT RISE: SHERIFF PHINEAS KINDLY *enters right, and edges across stage, glancing back over his shoulder from time to time. Suddenly loud noise is heard off right, and* KINDLY *stops in his tracks, throwing his hands in air. After a moment, he looks around, lowers hands, and sighs.*

KINDLY: Wonder who made that noise. (*Smiles dreamily*) Could it have been you, Nell? Fair Nell Blatz? (*He drops to one knee, with arms outstretched.*) Oh, Nell, have you finally abandoned your nitwit boyfriend, Tom Feeble? Nell, Nell, you need a man who's a hero (*Takes diamond bracelet from pocket and holds it up as if offering it to someone*), who can shower you with expensive gifts. (*Puts bracelet into pocket*) Nell, leave that hayseed, Tom Feeble. (GRANNY *and* TOM *enter left, unnoticed by* KINDLY. TOM *goes to pat head of hobbyhorse.* GRANNY *approaches* KINDLY.) Nell, you need a man like me!

GRANNY (*Loudly*): Howdy, Phineas Kindly (KINDLY *jumps up, frightened*), Sheriff of this one-horse town of Broken Bow, Arizona!

KINDLY (*With relief*): It's only you, dear, salty character, Granny Feeble.

GRANNY: Who were you expecting? Mary Poppins?

KINDLY: If Mary is coming to this town, she's headed for trouble.

GRANNY: Trouble in this peace-lovin', every-man-for-himself, frontier paradise? What is it this time?

KINDLY: Alas, Granny, I speak of that masked terror, Hughie the Hood. (*He trembles.*)

GRANNY: Hughie the Hood! But you sent him to jail months ago.

KINDLY (*Going to café table and sitting*): Alas, Granny.

GRANNY: You already said that.

KINDLY: Alack, then. (*Stands*) There has been a new outbreak of robberies that bear the unmistakable mark of that wily scoundrel, Hughie, who was so long the terror of our highway. Last night he held up the stage near Grubby Gulch and robbed a poor widow lady of the last diamond bracelet she had in the world.

GRANNY (*Musing*): Hm-m. That sounds like Hughie, all right.

KINDLY: And the description the widow lady gave me matches up: the muffled voice . . . the black hood and gloves . . . the agility of an acrobat.

GRANNY: Why do you suppose he's come back here to Broken Bow? (*She sits.*) Maybe he wants to bump you off, Sheriff.

KINDLY (*Sitting*): And you wonder why I shake and tremble.

GRANNY: Aw, come on, Sheriff. You nailed Hughie before. You can do it again. But it seems to me you need some kind of help—somebody to share the load, like a deputy.

KINDLY (*Proudly*): I've always been a loner, Granny.

GRANNY (*Snickering*): But that was before you started losing your grip.

KINDLY (*With flourish, as* GRANNY *rises and sneaks around in back of him*): I know my duty! In spite of the threat of danger, I, Phineas Kindly, will apprehend the scoundrel again—single-handed.

GRANNY: Boo! (KINDLY *jumps.*) Just as I thought. Your nerves are shot. You'd better get yourself a deputy before you crack up.

KINDLY (*Angrily*): I've never had a deputy, and I'm not going to have one now!

GRANNY (*Ignoring him*): And I have just the man for you. (*Walks about, gesturing dramatically*) Rough, tough, brave, true. (*She goes to* TOM.) A real defender of the defenseless. (*She pushes* TOM, *who looks bewildered, toward* KINDLY.) My grandson, Tom Feeble, is the man who'll catch that thief.

KINDLY: Tom Feeble? Catch a thief? He couldn't catch chicken pox!

GRANNY: You're just afraid Tom will take your job away from you.

KINDLY (*Amused*): All right, Granny. You know how much I aim to please. (TOM *looks confused.*)

GRANNY: You mean you'll let Tom help you? (KINDLY, *with affected gestures, takes off his badge and pins it on* TOM'S *shirt.*) Great! And you won't regret it, Sheriff Kindly.

KINDLY (*Chuckling*): I'm sure I won't, Granny. (*To audience*) I need a few good laughs.

GRANNY (*Happily, spinning* TOM *around*): Beware, Hughie the Hood. You're about to meet your match!

NELL (*Running in left*): Tom!

KINDLY (*Smiling, to audience*): The fair Nell Blatz. Devoted to Tom Feeble like a coyote to a full moon. Pretty thing, isn't she?

NELL: What a cute badge, Tom!

TOM: Sheriff Kindly has made me his deputy. (COWBOYS *and* GIRLS *stroll in right.*)

NELL: Imagine, my shy, bashful boyfriend is now a fearless law enforcement officer! I swear, Tom Feeble, there's not a thing you can't do once you put your mind to it.

1ST GIRL: You really made Tom a deputy, Sheriff Kindly? (KINDLY *nods.*)

NELL (*Dubiously*): You *are* fearless, aren't you, Tom?

GRANNY: Of course he is.

TOM (*Gulping*): If you say so, Granny.

2ND GIRL: Maybe you'll go down in history, Tom.

TOM (*Dreamily*): Gosh, that would be kinda nice.

GRANNY: But first you have a job to do!

TOM: I have?

GRANNY: You have to catch Hughie the Hood.

TOM (*Quaking, until* NELL *and* GRANNY *hold him up*): Hughie the Hood! (*He gasps.*) That might be pretty hard! (COWBOYS, GIRLS *and* KINDLY *laugh.*) How do you reckon I should go about it? What *do* deputies do?

1ST COWBOY: Well, out here on the frontier, one thing they always do is ride around a lot.

NELL (*To* TOM): You may have to learn to ride a horse.

TOM (*Glancing suspiciously at hobbyhorse*): Never did take much to riding horses. D'ya think I could learn?

2ND GIRL: Looks as if you'll have to!

TOM (*Reluctantly*): Well, O.K.

2ND COWBOY (*Pointing to hobbyhorse*): If you can ride *him,* your future's as bright as a new silver dollar. (*He laughs.*) Here. (*He pushes* TOM *onto hobbyhorse.*) Up you go!

TOM: Look, Granny. No hands! (*He pushes horse along at plodding pace.*)

1ST COWBOY: There he goes, riding like the wind. Flash Feeble!

TOM: Giddyap, horsie.

GRANNY: No question about it, Tom. You can ride a horse. (*She helps him dismount.*)

NELL: Tom, I'm so proud of you.

TOM: Aw, gee. It wasn't anything.

1ST COWBOY (*As* COWBOYS, GIRLS, *and* KINDLY *start to exit*): If you see Hughie the Hood, Tom, tell him there's a card party tonight down at the Golden Nugget Malt Shoppe. (*They exit.*)

TOM: I never knew ridin' horses was so much fun, Granny.

GRANNY: Now you're ready to ride out and catch Hughie the Hood.

TOM: But after I ride out, what do I do then?

GRANNY: You do what everybody else does when he's out to catch a varmint. You set a trap.

TOM (*Pulling mousetrap from his pocket*): You mean a trap like this?

GRANNY: Not that kind of trap!

TOM (*Putting trap back into his pocket*): I picked this trap up on the bargain counter at the five-and-dime store.

NELL: Tom, you're wonderful—always prepared for any emergency.

GRANNY: I know you're devoted to him, fair Nell, but don't be carried away. What you need, Tom, is a plan.

TOM (*Pulling map from his pocket*): I have one here.

NELL (*Taking map from* TOM *and smiling*): Tom! You did this yourself? (*Reading*) "Plan for Subway System for City of New York."

TOM: My pen pal back East sent it to me in trade for a genuine coonskin cap.

GRANNY (*Exasperated*): Enough of this mad banter, deputy. You have work to do. Come on. And don't forget your horse. (TOM *mounts hobbyhorse.*)

NELL (*Skipping, as she,* GRANNY, *and* TOM *move left*): Oh, this is going to be such fun! (*They exit left.* COWBOY *enters right and changes card on easel to read:* THAT AFTERNOON. HUGHIE, *wearing a black hood over his head and face, runs in left, with* TOM, *mounted on hobbyhorse, in hot pursuit.*)

TOM (*Yelling*): Stop, Hughie the Hood! Stop in the name of the law! (HUGHIE *stops, but* TOM *charges on and disappears off right. There is a loud crash.* HUGHIE *shakes his head, covers his eyes with his hands, then exits left.* COWBOY *changes sign to:* NEXT MORNING. GRANNY *enters right. She carries an umbrella and she wears some sparkling costume jewelry.*)

GRANNY: A decoy is what Tom needs. (*She walks to chair and sits down.*) I'll just sit down here and let these fake diamonds sparkle in the sun. (HUGHIE *enters and tiptoes up behind her.*) That should attract the thief, all right. (TOM *enters and tiptoes up directly behind* HUGHIE. *Just as* HUGHIE *starts to reach for jewelry,* TOM *reaches for* HUGHIE, *who sidesteps quickly so that* TOM *lunges at* GRANNY. HUGHIE *runs off right as she jumps to her feet and knocks* TOM *on the head with her umbrella.* TOM *staggers off right, and* GRANNY *follows.*) Tom? Tom? Don't fall down, Tom! (*Card is changed to read:* A SHORT WHILE LATER.)

WOMAN (*Running in left*): Help! Sheriff! My diamonds. Help!

TOM (*Entering right*): Did Hughie the Hood steal your diamonds, lady?

WOMAN (*Bewildered*): Hughie the Hood?

TOM (*With gesture*): He's a guy about this tall.

WOMAN: Hughie the Hood? How do you know it was Hughie the Hood?

TOM: I didn't say it was.

WOMAN: You said it was.

TOM: I just asked you. Can you describe him?

WOMAN: I don't know what he looked like. He was wearing a hood.

TOM (*Shaking his head*): That sure complicates things.

WOMAN (*Screaming again*): Help! Sheriff! My diamonds! (*She exits right.*)

TOM (*Strolling left*): If people only knew the importance of descriptions. A guy in a hood could be anybody. (*He exits, and the sign is changed to read:* THE PLOT THICKENS. NELL *and* KINDLY *enter together.* NELL *sits at table.*)

KINDLY (*Taking bracelet from his pocket and presenting it to* NELL *with a flourish*): Fair Nell, please accept this priceless diamond bracelet as a small token of my esteem.

NELL (*Examining bracelet*): It is truly beautiful, Mr. Sheriff Kindly, but I cannot accept a gift like this from you.

KINDLY: But why not, fair Nell?

NELL: Well, I like your esteem and all, but I am true to my one and only boyfriend, your deputy, Tom Feeble.

KINDLY: Deputy Tom is a mite too busy these days to squire a lovely maiden like you on the social whirl of Broken Bow.

NELL: Be that as it may be, I cannot accept gifts from strangers.

KINDLY: Me? Phineas Kindly? A stranger?

NELL: That's the way I like to think of you, Mr. Kindly.

KINDLY: My heart is rent asunder. Here. (*He pulls out more diamonds.*) Would these make a difference?

NELL (*Standing up*): Are you trying to bribe me or something? Where did these jewels come from?

KINDLY: One question at a time, fair Nell. (*He stands up.*) Yes, I am trying to bribe you, and where this jewelry came from is none of your business.

NELL (*Sitting down again and speaking lightly*): Oh. O.K.

KINDLY (*Sitting down*): But, in case anyone should ask, these are all family heirlooms left to me to adorn the maiden whom I would one day choose to be my bride.

NELL: When you find her, you can give them to her.

KINDLY: I'm afraid, Nell, that you don't get my message.

NELL: What message is that, Mr. Kindly?

KINDLY: Fair Nell, I am trying to win your hand.

NELL: Win my hand? How do you reckon you'll do a thing like that?

KINDLY (*As he holds up the jewelry*): By showing you the advantages of a better way of life. (*He piles jewelry on table.*)

NELL: Better way than what way? You don't make yourself very clear, Mr. Kindly. (TOM *backs onto stage slowly, looking off.*)

KINDLY (*To audience*): How could anything so pretty be so (*He taps his forehead*) vacant upstairs! (TOM *backs into* KINDLY, *who jumps to his feet.*) You oaf!

TOM (*Turning around*): Oh, howdy, Sheriff. (*Eyeing the jewelry*) Say! What pretty sparklers!

NELL: They're Mr. Kindly's heirlooms.

TOM: Gosh, Sheriff, you'd better hide those away somewhere before Hughie the Hood sees them.

KINDLY: I wanted fair Nell to guard them for me.

TOM: Say, there's a good idea.

NELL (*Standing up*): He wanted me to take them as gifts!

TOM: Well, that's right nice of you, Mr. Kindly.

NELL: But, Tom! Don't you know what that means?

TOM: Sure! Mr. Kindly likes you.

NELL: But, Tom! I belong to you!

TOM (*Aghast*): You do?

NELL (*Bursting into tears*): Oh, how could you? How could you? (*She starts to run off left, stops, runs back, takes the jewelry from table, and then pauses, crying again.*) I repeat, how could you, how could you? (*She exits left.*)

TOM: How could I what? Girls sure are funny, aren't they, Mr. Sheriff Kindly?

KINDLY: A million laughs, Flash. See you around. (*He darts off after* NELL.)

TOM (*Scratching behind his ear*): I shouldn't think any girl'd want to turn down those jewels.

GRANNY (*Entering right*): Tom, I think we'll have to work out some new tactics.

TOM: What are tactics?

GRANNY: Ploys. Ruses.

TOM: Can you buy them at the five-and-dime store?

GRANNY: Believe it or not, Tom Feeble, there are some things the five-and-dime store doesn't sell.

Tom: Well, I don't know, Granny. Their sign says they carry just about everything.

Granny: I swear, if you weren't my own grandson, I'd have to admit that you're just about the dumbest thing in the West.

Tom: I think that secret's out, Granny.

Granny: Oh, stop that! You weren't brought up to be the village idiot.

Tom (*Grinning*): I know. I guess I just grew into the job.

Granny: If you knew the strings I pulled to get you that badge! The least you can do now is make something of yourself. If you don't, you're going to lose fair Nell Blatz, I can promise you that. A girl can be loyal and true-blue for just so long!

Tom: Whatever you say, Granny.

Granny (*Pushing him*): Go out there and get that thief! Go on! And don't come back until you have Hughie the Hood in handcuffs.

Tom: I don't have any handcuffs, Granny.

Granny: Then pick some up at the five-and-dime store!

Tom: O.K., Granny. (*He exits right.* Granny *looks after him for a moment, shakes her head, and exits left. Card is changed to read:* THE CHASE GOES ON. Kindly, *as* Hughie the Hood, *enters stealthily and hides behind barrel.*)

Tom (*Entering right on his horse*): O.K., Hughie. I know you went someplace around here. Where'd you go? (Kindly *holds up a sign with an arrow:* THAT A-WAY) Oh, thanks. (Tom *gallops off left.* Kindly *emerges from behind barrel and stands looking right as* Tom *enters left on foot. He carries a lasso and, nearing* Kindly, *he throws the lasso around* Kindly's *shoulders.* Kindly *grabs the rope, turns and starts running around and around* Tom *so that* Tom *is quickly tied.* Kindly *then stuffs handkerchief into* TOM's *mouth, waves and calmly walks off right as* TOM *groans, and manages to hop off left. Card is changed to read:* NELL'S SORRY PLIGHT. TOM, *wearing a few bandages, limps in with* GRANNY *and sits at the café table.*)

NELL (*Running in left*): Tom! Please protect me!

TOM (*Casually*): Why, sure. What can I do?

NELL: It's Sheriff Kindly. He wants to marry me. And I know as soon as he asks my Pa about it, Pa will say yes. (*She collapses in a chair.*)

TOM: Then it's all taken care of.

NELL (*Pleading*): But I don't want to marry Sheriff Kindly!

TOM: Looks as if you may have to, if your Pa says so.

GRANNY (*Standing*): Tom Feeble, can't you see the girl is pining away for you?

TOM: Aw, that's too bad. You do look a little pale, Nell.

GRANNY (*Drawing* TOM *up by back of his collar*): Why don't you run to see Nell's Pa before the Sheriff does?

NELL: Please, Tom.

TOM: Well, that might be a good idea, all right, except what'll I do if her Pa says it's O.K.?

GRANNY: You'll marry her, of course!

NELL: Do your best, Tom. In the meantime, I'll just sit here and shed some tears. Wa-a! (*She cries bitterly.* TOM *and* GRANNY *move away from her.*)

GRANNY: So far you're batting zero, Tom, you know that.

TOM (*Pulling mousetrap out of his pocket*): That's because I still haven't set this trap here.

GRANNY: I told you before. You don't catch thieves with that kind of trap.

TOM (*Putting trap back*): I heard you say that, Granny. But it seems to me the thing I have to do is nitwit Hughie the Hood.

GRANNY: *Outwit,* not nitwit, you nitwit!

TOM: Well, I think I may've found a way to do some of that outwitting.

GRANNY (*Delighted*): You mean you've actually thought of a scheme? All on your own?

TOM: Yup. And I'm right proud of it, too. Want me to tell you about it?

GRANNY: You'd better. I'll be able to help you out just in case there's a flaw in the plan.

TOM: A flaw?

GRANNY: A flaw! You know! They sell them at the five-and-dime. Come on. Tell me what you're going to do. (*They exit right. The card is changed to read* THE TRAP. NELL *sits at table, crying.* KINDLY, *disguised as* HUGHIE, *tiptoes in and hides behind barrel.* TOM, *as "widow," enters, right. He wears a long black coat, and his face is hidden by a black veil. He wears mass of sparkling jewelry and carries a large black bag.*)

TOM (*Speaking in a high voice*): Good grief, child. What ails one so pretty as you?

NELL: My life's being ruined, that's what ails me. It looks as though I'm going to be married off to rich Sheriff Kindly whether I want to or not. And I *don't* want to marry him. I want to marry my stalwart sweetheart, Tom Feeble. (*Standing*) Say, who are you, anyway?

TOM: Just a poor widow lady passing through town.

NELL (*Sitting*): Oh. You'd better be careful. We have a mean thief here who goes for ladies with lots of jewelry.

TOM: You don't say. (*Sits*) Tell me more about this Sheriff —the rich one.

NELL: He has lots of heirlooms. Diamond bracelets and things.

TOM: Never heard of a sheriff out here who was rich.

NELL: Sheriff Kindly's been offering me rich presents and lots of jewelry.

TOM: Do you like lots of jewelry?

NELL: I only like Tom Feeble. But my Pa thinks Tom's hardly able . . . hardly able to do anything to support me. And he thinks the Sheriff has a good, solid future. (*She wails.*)

TOM: Where did the Sheriff get all his heirlooms?

NELL: Where everybody gets heirlooms, I guess.

TOM: Heirlooms are nice things to have. Here. (*Takes off a bracelet*) Why don't you take one of these bracelets and tell your Pa stalwart Tom Feeble gave it to you. That should shake things up a bit. (KINDLY, *disguised as* HUGHIE, *jumps out from behind barrel.*)

KINDLY: I'll take those rocks, sister!

NELL (*Jumping up on chair*): Eek! It's the mean old thief himself!

KINDLY: That's right—Hughie the Hood.

TOM: I suppose you want my jewels?

KINDLY: Every single one. Boy, what a haul!

NELL: I really think I ought to scream for help. (*She screams.*) Help!

TOM: Do you realize that these jewels represent all I have in the world?

KINDLY: You're breaking my heart.

TOM: You're pretty mean and selfish, aren't you?

NELL: Help! Sheriff! Tom! Come to our aid!

KINDLY: You don't get rich by being kindly, lady.

TOM: Kindly. Isn't that the name of your sheriff?

NELL: Sheriff Kindly! Where are you?

KINDLY (*After he has taken jewels*): And now, what about the pocketbook?

TOM (*With little protest*): No. Have mercy.

KINDLY: Give it to me.

NELL: Where *is* everybody?

TOM: You'll be sorry if you open that bag!

NELL: Whenever anybody calls for help against Hughie the Hood, Sheriff Kindly seems to be someplace else. (KINDLY *plunges his hand into bag and shouts*)

KINDLY: Ay! Yow! (*He jumps around, then pulls his hand out. His hand has been caught in* TOM's *trap*) Ow! Get this thing off me! (*He drops bag.*)

TOM (*Picking up bag and hitting* KINDLY *on the head*): Help me, fair Nell! (KINDLY *falls into chair,* TOM *reaches into bag and brings out handcuffs and rope.* NELL *helps, as they handcuff* KINDLY *and tie him well.*)

NELL (*To* TOM): How did you know my name?

TOM: Because (*Going to center and speaking in his normal voice*) I am in reality none other than your sweetheart, stalwart Tom Feeble.

NELL (*As* TOM *removes disguise*): Tom! My hero!

GRANNY (*Entering left*): What's all the noise about?

NELL (*As* COWBOYS, GIRLS *begin entering right*): Tom. He's captured Hughie the Hood.

GRANNY (*Astounded*): You mean that lame-brained scheme worked?

1ST COWBOY: You mean Tom did that? (*He walks around* KINDLY.)

1ST GIRL: Tom Feeble?

NELL: I saw it with my own eyes.

TOM (*With authority*): Here's your thief, citizens of Broken Bow, Arizona. Shall I unmask him?

2ND GIRL: Oh, yes, you great, big, brave and handsome thing, you.

NELL (*To* 2ND GIRL): You stop that. He's mine.

TOM (*As he pulls off hood, revealing* KINDLY): Oh! Well, howdy, Sheriff!

ALL (*Ad lib*): Sheriff Kindly! No! It couldn't be! (*Etc.*)

GRANNY: Seems as though it is. (KINDLY *hangs his head.*)

How'd you get into a racket like this, Sheriff? Robbing diamond bracelets from widows?

KINDLY: I wanted to be rich enough to win the hand of fair Nell Blatz.

ALL: Aw!

KINDLY: When Hughie the Hood was terrorizing our town a while back, I learned his every trick.

ALL: Tsk, tsk, tsk!

KINDLY: And so the idea came to me. I could do the same kind of thing, pretend I was hot on Hughie's trail and then, when my fortune was made, I could pretend I'd driven Hughie out of town again.

ALL (*In a singsong*): Sheriff Kindly, you are a terrible, terrible man.

KINDLY (*As* COWBOYS, GIRLS *and* GRANNY *start to drag him off right*): Curses on you all. Foiled by Feeble!

ALL: It's off to jail we go!

GRANNY: And we'd better get the sheriff's office spruced up for the new man.

ALL: Sheriff Tom Feeble! (*They exit.*)

NELL: Tom, I'm so proud of you.

TOM: Wasn't anything much.

NELL: Tom, would you have let my Pa give me away to Mr. Kindly?

TOM: Give you away? I thought you were going to marry him.

NELL: I wasn't. Pa wanted me to.

TOM: How could he have given you away, then?

NELL: Give me away. Give me away! Don't you know what that means?

TOM: Sure. Like presents on birthdays.

NELL (*Giving up*): Oh, come on, Tom.

TOM: O.K. Nell, do you think I'm dumb?

NELL: Tom, what a notion. You've just shown everybody you're the smartest man in town.

TOM: I guess I did.

NELL: Come on. Let's see what your new office looks like.

TOM (*Picking up jewelry, handing it to* NELL): Would you like some of these heirlooms? Best stuff the five-and-dime has to offer.

NELL: Why, thanks. (*They stroll off right, hand in hand, and* TOM *turns the card on the easel to show* THE END. *Curtain*)

THE END

Production Notes

A DEPUTY FOR BROKEN BOW

Characters: 4 male; 5 female; as many extras as desired for other Cowboys and Girls.

Playing Time: 35 minutes.

Costumes: Traditional Western costumes. At the beginning, the Sheriff wears a badge, and as Hughie, he wears a black hood over his head and face. At end of play, Tom disguises himself as a widow, in a long black coat and black veil. He carries a large black handbag and wears a mass of sparkling jewelry.

Properties: Easel, signs, as indicated in text; "diamond" bracelet, other costume jewelry (bracelets, rings, necklaces, etc.), mousetrap, badge, map, umbrella, lasso, handcuffs, rope, handkerchief, hobbyhorse.

Setting: The main street of Broken Bow, Arizona. A hitching post with a hobbyhorse tied to it is at left, and a café table and chairs are up center. Nearby is a barrel. Exits are at right and left.

Lighting: No special effects.

Sound: Offstage crash, as indicated in text.

The Fairest Pitcher of Them All

Characters

QUEEN, *ruler of the Duchy of Poco-Holstein*
BLANCHE, *her stepdaughter*
PAGE
SEER
MIRROR
GOVERNESS
HUNTSMAN
LION
BARKER
THE SEVEN DWARFS
EIGHT LADIES-IN-WAITING

SCENE 1

SETTING: *Throne room of the palace in Poco-Holstein. If desired, the curtain may part only a few feet to reveal the throne backed by a screen.*
AT RISE: QUEEN *is seated on the throne.*

QUEEN (*Clapping her hands and calling*): Page! Oh, Page! (PAGE *enters right and bows several times.*) Oh. I wondered where you were.

PAGE (*Walking to throne*): I'm right here. (*Pointing off-stage*) I was out there, of course, but you know I'm always around somewhere.

QUEEN (*Knowingly*): At the jousts, usually.

PAGE: Where else is there to go around here? And, after all, jousting is the national sport.

QUEEN: Well, I wish someone would think of another one. Jousting is (*Yawning*) such a bore.

PAGE: I can't say that I care for it myself very much. But (*Bowing with a flourish*) pray tell, Your Highness, why have you summoned me?

QUEEN (*Rising*): I would like you to fetch my magic mirror.

PAGE (*Folding his arms in disgust*): Not that again!

QUEEN (*Begging*): Please?

PAGE (*Shrugging his shoulders*): Oh, all right. But every day it's the same old thing. And you think *jousting* is a bore.

QUEEN: But every day I must find out whether everything is still the same.

PAGE: Sure, everything's the same. (SEER *enters left, as* PAGE *starts to exit right.*)

SEER: It's the same. (*He sighs.*) It's always the same.

QUEEN (*To* SEER): Oh, poof. (*She sits down suddenly.*) What do you know?

PAGE: A lot more than he's telling, I'll bet. (*He exits right.*)

QUEEN (*Calling after* PAGE): You and your bets and wagers. (*To* SEER) Well? How are you today, Court Prophet?

SEER (*Leaning on the throne*): Tired. I think it's eyestrain from gazing into my crystal ball. There's a limit to everything, you know. (PAGE *re-enters, followed by* MIRROR. NOTE: MIRROR *is a girl with a "mirror" hung sandwich-board fashion from her shoulders.*)

PAGE: There's certainly a limit to this kind of nonsense. (*Stopping abruptly at center*) All right. (*Indicating* MIRROR) Here it is. You might as well go ahead.

QUEEN (*Standing majestically*): Mirror, mirror, on the wall. . . .

PAGE: It isn't on the wall. Not at all.

MIRROR: A mere detail.

QUEEN (*Anxiously to* MIRROR): You don't mind being called a mirror on the wall when you're nothing of the kind, do you?

MIRROR: Of course not. But do go on.

QUEEN (*Resuming commanding tone*): Mirror, mirror, on the wall, who's the fairest one of all?

PAGE (*To the audience*): I can hardly wait to hear the answer.

SEER (*To* PAGE): Don't be such a pain.

MIRROR: Well, if you really want to know, Your Majesty—

QUEEN: And I do.

MIRROR: The fairest one in this old land is you.

QUEEN (*Sitting down and pounding her fists on the arms of the throne*): Curses!

PAGE (*Mocking*): I told you so.

QUEEN: It's not that I mind being fair, you understand.

SEER (*Yawning*): We understand, Your Majesty.

QUEEN: I'd much rather be fair than ugly, that's for sure. (*To* MIRROR) But what about my beautiful stepdaughter, the lovely Blanche?

MIRROR: Are you kidding?

QUEEN (*Rushing to* MIRROR *and shaking it*): Isn't she ever going to make the grade?

MIRROR (*Pulling free from the* QUEEN'S *grasp*): You shouldn't answer a question with a question. But I'll ignore that. I can't look into the future, you know. For that sort of thing you should ask the Seer.

QUEEN (*Turning to* SEER): Well, what about it, Herman? Is Blanche a lost cause?

SEER (*Pacing the floor and speaking pretentiously*): I remember well the day Blanche's mother looked out at the snows of our fair land and asked that she be given a daughter with skin as fair as white crystal, with lips as ruby red as the blood that trickled from her finger when she stabbed herself with a sewing needle.

QUEEN: I don't think "stabbed" is the right word.

SEER (*Continuing*): With hair as black as the frame of the window from which she was gazing.

QUEEN: I never heard that part of it.

SEER (*Halting in front of* QUEEN, *at center*): There's one thing you might as well face, Your Majesty.

QUEEN (*Lightly*): What's that, Herman?

SEER (*Facing audience*): Blanche (*Pause*) is a bomb.

PAGE (*Retreating several steps from* QUEEN *and pointing to* SEER): He said it. I didn't.

QUEEN (*Pointing accusingly at* PAGE): But you think so, too.

PAGE: It's hard for me to say. I'm in your loyal service, for one thing.

QUEEN: But aside from that. . . .

PAGE (*Loudly*): Aside from that, I've seen Blanche in a suit of armor riding to the jousts and knocking two-hundred-pound knights from their charging steeds as if they were tin toys on hobbyhorses. (QUEEN *begins to pace back and forth, hands behind her back.*)

QUEEN: All right. She has grit and determination.

SEER (*Pleading slightly*): Let's face reality, Your Majesty. Nobody looks for that kind of thing in a young woman —any young woman—let alone the Princess of the Duchy of Poco-Holstein. She's a terror, Blanche is, and something must be done about her.

QUEEN (*Facing others*): Don't think I haven't tried.

MIRROR: We know you've tried, Your Majesty. Can you imagine how it hurts me to have to tell you every day that Blanche is *not* the fairest in the land?

QUEEN (*To* MIRROR, *hopefully*): Is she the second fairest?

MIRROR: You're answering a question with a question again.

QUEEN (*Wringing her hands*): Sorry. I'm so distraught.

MIRROR: No, she is not the second fairest. She is so far down the list that it would turn me purple with embarrassment to tell you about it.

QUEEN (*Pushing* SEER *aside and sitting on her throne*): Oh, dear.

MIRROR (*Parading across stage*): If you want someone to fight off the invading hoards, call on Blanche. If you need to storm a castle or put down thieves or capture a wild boar, call on Blanche. But if you're looking for the fairest maiden in the land— (GOVERNESS *rushes in left, wringing her hands.*)

GOVERNESS: She's at it again, Madame. (*Loud crash is heard from offstage.*) Tackling the ancestral suits of armor in the main hall. You must stop her!

QUEEN (*Pointing at* GOVERNESS): You're her governess!

GOVERNESS (*Protesting*): But I have no control over her, Madame. Do you know what she did this morning? She insisted on showing her fencing master a new wrestling hold, and the Court Physician has sent him to bed for a week.

QUEEN (*Relieved*): Is that all?

GOVERNESS (*Dumfounded*): All?

QUEEN (*Slumping further down*): There have been worse mornings, Mademoiselle.

GOVERNESS (*Pleading*): Madame, I have tried. I have tried to teach her French and deportment and the art of

gentle conversation. But it isn't any use. You will forgive my saying it, Your Majesty. . . .

QUEEN (*Impatiently*): Oh, go ahead.

GOVERNESS: Blanche is tougher than (*Loudly*) Richard the
Lion-Hearted.

QUEEN (*Standing*): Now, Mademoiselle.

GOVERNESS: I knew I would offend you. But I've had it
(*Drawing her finger across her throat*) to here.

SEER (*Shrugging*): So have we all. (*Moving to center*) It is
clear that Blanche is growing worse by the day. She's
not going to blossom into a fair maiden by staying
around here.

GOVERNESS: Are you looking for a land of miracles?

SEER (*Taking command*): Let's put our heads together.
You, too, Mirror. We're all fed up with Blanche, right?

ALL (*With enthusiasm*): Right!

SEER: We all want her to have a dose of her own medicine.
(*Turning apologetically to* QUEEN) I mean, we want her
to become the fairest maiden in the land and marry a
prince charming.

GOVERNESS (*Sadly*): Ah, what a dreamer you are, Herman.

QUEEN (*Desperately*): There must be some prince who'd
marry her. (*All are deep in thought for a moment.*
QUEEN *sits forward suddenly and gestures triumphantly.*) A thought has occurred to me. (*All take a step
toward her.*)

ALL (*Eagerly*): Yes?

QUEEN (*Calling*): Huntsman! (HUNTSMAN *enters right.*)

HUNTSMAN: Right on call, Your Majesty.

QUEEN: Come here, will you? I have a job for you to do.

SEER (*Anxiously*): Your Majesty, please! Don't be hasty!
We can go too far.

GOVERNESS (*Smiling and rubbing her hands together*):
How far *can* we go?

HUNTSMAN: Your faithful huntsman, Your Majesty (*Pretending to take aim with bow*), at your service.

PAGE (*Shaking his head*): There must be neater ways. (*Looking delighted*) Poisoned apples, for instance!

QUEEN (*Placing her hand on* HUNTSMAN's *head*): Huntsman, I want you to take Blanche out to the deepest part of the darkest forest of the Duchy of Poco-Holstein. Tell her you're going to practice archery.

HUNTSMAN (*Jumping to his feet and trembling*): Oh, no! Not that. She always wants to hunt bears and shoot things off the top of my head for practice.

QUEEN: Not this trip. She will be unarmed. But *you* will be equipped with an ample supply of bows and arrows.

HUNTSMAN (*Stammering*): Your Majesty! I—I admit I can't stand the sight of the girl, but—but . . .

QUEEN: No buts, Huntsman. You shall take her into the forest, and when you've found a suitable place, you'll draw your bow and . . .

HUNTSMAN: She'll beat me to a pulp!

QUEEN: And you'll run off in pursuit of imaginary game and leave Blanche all alone.

SEER: What kind of plan is that?

PAGE (*Hopefully*): You mean we're going to lose her forever?

QUEEN (*Impatiently*): Of course not!

ALL (*Taking a step in retreat*): Oh.

QUEEN: After one night alone in the forest, Blanche will be back here as meek as you please and ready to behave herself. (*To* SEER) Herman? (SEER *stands at attention.*) Whatever became of your old friends, the Seven Dwarfs?

SEER: Oh, they're still doing some diamond mining in the thickest part of the thickest forest in the kingdom.

QUEEN: A grim little group, as I recall. Do you think they'd have time for administering some discipline?

(SEER *smiles broadly and makes a sweeping bow, as others nod approval to one another.*)

SEER: Your Majesty, your plan has genius. (*Turning to PAGE and snapping his fingers*) Bring me a telephone, will you, Page?

PAGE (*Astonished*): Nobody's invented that yet.

SEER: Then it's about time somebody did. (*Waving his arms impatiently*) Bring me a telephone! (PAGE *reaches behind curtain and brings out a phone.*)

PAGE: You're so demanding. (SEER *takes phone and lifts receiver.*)

SEER (*To* QUEEN): I wonder how the old boys are.

GOVERNESS (*To* MIRROR): I don't understand any of this. (MIRROR *shrugs.*)

SEER (*Speaking into phone*): Operator? I want the cottage of the Seven Dwarfs. (*Pause*) That's right. No, I don't know the number. I don't know the area code, either. (*Gesturing off right*) It's off in the woods somewhere. (*Impatiently*) Well, how many cottages with seven dwarfs can there *be* in this country?

MIRROR (*To* GOVERNESS): I haven't heard of any dwarfs around here in ages.

PAGE (*To* MIRROR): You don't know everything, after all.

SEER (*Looking pleased*): Ah. There. (*Into phone*) Hello, Doc? Well, how are you, old buddy? (*Pause*) This is Herman! Herman the Seer! (*Sitting down on an arm of the throne*) That's right. Listen, Doc, I have a bit of a job for you fellows. By this afternoon there should be a girl by the name of Blanche wandering around your neck of the woods. I want you to give her a job.

QUEEN (*Tapping* SEER *on shoulder*): Be specific, Herman.

SEER (*Into phone*): Blanche is a funny kid, Doc. (*Knowing glances are exchanged among others.*) Thinks she's the greatest little gal in the land. (*Others restrain laughter.*)

Rough. Tough. Spoiled. You know the type. (*Others nod repeatedly.*)

PAGE: What a salesman!

SEER (*Into phone*): That's right—Blanche. (*Pause*) It means "white." Call her anything you want. Make her work in the mine. (QUEEN *nods in approval.*) You bet she can. Make her clean your place and mend your clothes. Make her work like a dog. She'll get tired of it. (*To* QUEEN) I don't think he understands.

QUEEN (*Grabbing phone*): Hello, Dwarf? This is the Queen. (PAGE *bows,* GOVERNESS *and* MIRROR *curtsy.*) Blanche is my stepdaughter. You've heard of us? (*All seem a little surprised.*) Good. The girl needs a little discipline. It also wouldn't hurt her to learn to keep house. She's not likely to end up in a palace. (GOVERNESS *shakes her head emphatically.*) You do the best you can. All right. We'll be in touch. Bye-bye. (*She stands up, hands the phone to* PAGE, *who returns it behind the curtain.*) I think it's going to work out splendidly.

GOVERNESS (*Incredulously*): You don't think Blanche will really learn to do housework!

QUEEN: She might. She might just be scared out of her wits. We're sure to accomplish something or other.

HUNTSMAN (*Bowing and speaking weakly*): I suppose I should be off.

QUEEN: Yes. You may leave now. And good luck.

HUNTSMAN: I hope I return alive.

QUEEN: We hope so, too. We're counting on you. (HUNTS-MAN *moves toward right exit.*)

HUNTSMAN (*Calling sweetly*): Blanche! Blanche, dear. I have a surprise for you. (BLANCHE *bursts in right.*)

BLANCHE: Oh, yeah? What is it this time?

HUNTSMAN (*Trembling*): Why not come along and see?

MIRROR: I'm leaving. (*Exits quickly left*)

PAGE (*Starting to exit left*): Call me if you have any news, Your Majesty.

GOVERNESS (*Following* PAGE): That Huntsman certainly is brave.

SEER (*Following* GOVERNESS): I'll keep an eye on the whole project through my crystal ball. (*They exit.*)

QUEEN (*Calling to* SEER): And keep your fingers crossed while you're at it, Herman.

BLANCHE: Well?

HUNTSMAN: We're going hunting in the woods. (*He clears his throat.*)

BLANCHE: Hunting in the woods *again?* (*She starts after* HUNTSMAN. *He turns and runs in a circle, with* BLANCHE *following.*) Yaaa! I'll chase you all the way. Yaaaa!

HUNTSMAN: Help! Help! She's after me! Help! (*He exits right with* BLANCHE *chasing him. His cries grow fainter offstage.*) Help! Help! Help! (*Curtain.*)

*   *   *

SCENE 2

SETTING: *A clearing in the woods. Up left is a high fence with a sign:* HOME OF THE SEVEN DWARFS, *and nearby are a ticket booth and a cage.*

AT RISE: LION *is asleep in cage.* HUNTSMAN, *clutching his bow, leads* BLANCHE *on right.* BLANCHE *kicks at an imaginary stone.*

HUNTSMAN (*Looking about*): Well, here we are. (*He pats his supply of arrows.*)

BLANCHE (*Sarcastically*): Where are we?

HUNTSMAN (*Reaching for an arrow*): In the deepest part of the darkest forest in the kingdom. A good place to practice archery, don't you think? (HUNTSMAN *fits arrow into bow.*)

BLANCHE: Gross. If this is your idea of an outing, Step-mommy should have you shipped off with the rest of the nincompoops.

HUNTSMAN: There are lots of things around here for us to hunt.

BLANCHE (*Sarcastically*): Like chipmunks and sparrows?

HUNTSMAN (*Haughtily*): I'm a huntsman, you know.

BLANCHE: What else is new?

HUNTSMAN (*Prowling about*): There might be a wild boar hiding here somewhere. (BLANCHE *sneaks up behind* HUNTSMAN.)

BLANCHE (*Shouting*): Yaaa! (HUNTSMAN *jumps, and trembling, turns to face her.*) See, 'fraidy cat? How you ever landed the title of "Huntsman" will remain the mystery of the age. I'm bored with this game. Let me practice my karate on you, and I'll flip you from here to the Roman Colosseum. (HUNTSMAN *backs away slowly as* BLANCHE *starts to close in.*) Oh, yes, I will. Here I come, ready or not.

HUNTSMAN (*Desperately*): Remember, I'm armed. I'll give you a chance to run away and save yourself.

BLANCHE: You'll give *me* a chance? Tell me another. For the likes of you I won't even have to roll up my sleeves!

HUNTSMAN (*Shakily trying to fit an arrow in bow*): Run, Blanche. Run!

BLANCHE: Gee, I'm frightened. Frightened as can *beee!* (*She lunges at* HUNTSMAN, *who drops his bow and arrows and sidesteps her.*)

HUNTSMAN: Oh, there must be an easier way to make a living. (BLANCHE *lunges at him again.*) There *must* be an easier way. (*Running left*) Save me, somebody! (*He exits.*)

BLANCHE (*Laughing*): Look at him go. I haven't seen anything so funny since a unicorn chased Cousin Guinevere into the moat. Ha ha! (*She sits on a log and surveys the scene.*) This isn't a bad spot. Why don't I camp out here and have a real vacation? No governess. No lessons in deportment. I have enough arrows to keep me in food for a while. And when I get back to town, I'll write about my experiences and sell the story to the *Reader's Digest*—"I Survived Alone in the Black Forest!"

LION (*Stretching in cage*): Brother!

BLANCHE (*Jumping to her feet*): No remarks from you.

LION: In the first place, how do you know you'll survive? You're only a girl.

BLANCHE (*Flexing her arm*): I'm rough and I'm tough. And I've won every marksmanship medal the Girl Scouts have to offer.

LION: I didn't know the Girl Scouts gave medals for marksmanship.

BLANCHE: They do in Poco-Holstein.

LION: And in the second place, this isn't the Black Forest. Did you ever see a lion in the Black Forest? Indeed you never did, no matter what you may say.

BLANCHE: I didn't say I did. (LION *comes out of cage.*)

LION: Well, you were going to. I know your type. As a matter of fact, there aren't any lions in this forest, cither, but don't tell anybody. I'm just a fake.

BLANCHE (*Haughtily*): That's nothing to brag about.

LION (*Leaning on cage*): At least I'm not unemployed.

BLANCHE (*Approaching* LION): Are you part of a circus?

LION (*Examining his claws*): That's the word for it, although I've never known a circus to lack customers. No, sweet thing, if this were a circus I'd sign you up right now as part of the sideshow.

BLANCHE (*Picking up bow and arrows*): For that I'll spend my first arrow on you, you flea-bitten bath mat.

LION: Why don't you go off and hunt real game? I told

you. I'm a fake. (*Takes off false head.*) See? A low-grade bit of tomfoolery, I'll admit, but every team needs a mascot.

BLANCHE (*Exasperated*): You have an awful nerve. (*She turns to exit right.*) I'm going to find myself a real lion.

LION: Good luck to you. (*She turns to face* LION *again.*)

BLANCHE: And you put your head on again. As a lion you're a lot better looking.

LION (*Stroking the mane of his false head*): Alas, you're right. But aren't you curious to find out what I'm doing here in this rig?

BLANCHE (*Throwing up her arms*): Oh, what a bore! Everything in my stepmother's kingdom is a bore.

LION (*Approaching* BLANCHE *slowly*): Your stepmother's kingdom! You don't want me to believe that you're the Princess Blanche!

BLANCHE (*Proudly*): The very same.

LION (*Pointing a paw at her*): You?

BLANCHE: And what's so incredible about that?

LION (*Shaking head in disbelief*): I've seen some desperate cases in my time, but you top them all.

BLANCHE: For that I'll bring back a live lion and sic him on you. (*She storms off right.*)

LION: And I call myself a fake. (*With resignation*) Oh, well, it's almost game time. (BARKER *enters from behind fence, carrying a megaphone.*)

BARKER (*Through megaphone*): It's almost game time.

LION: You'd better start selling some tickets, then.

BARKER (*Through megaphone*): Step right up, knights and ladies, serfs and lords. See the newest game on the continent!

LION (*Surveying audience*): I don't see anybody coming to buy tickets.

BARKER: You're telling me. Look, Your Highness, I think

we should give this up as a bad job. Just because the King told you to go out and make something of yourself before he'd give you your share of the kingdom. . . .

LION: Which is something I never understood. After all, if I make something of myself, I'm not going to need my share of the kingdom.

BARKER (*Brightly*): But remember, he promised you the hand of the fair Princess Blanche of Poco-Holstein. (LION *leans on* BARKER'S *shoulder*.)

LION (*Dejectedly*): Oh, I've just had a terrible shock, Otto. A creature wandered past here a while ago and said she was the Princess Blanche.

BARKER: Ridiculous. Probably only a passing gypsy.

LION (*Uncertainly*): Probably. Either that or the Queen of Poco-Holstein has one of the best press agents going.

BARKER: Shall I tell the boys to pack their uniforms and head back to the manor? (*He starts to go behind fence.*)

LION: I hate to give it up as a failure. I still think it's a good idea.

BARKER (*Rejoining* LION): Your Highness, look. When everybody can go to see the jousts for nothing, who wants to pay good gold sovereigns to see a bunch of grown men run around in a square?

LION (*Slightly insulted*): It isn't a square. It's a diamond. I think that gives the game more status, don't you?

BARKER (*With emphasis*): But it isn't paying off, Your Highness. (LION *paces back and forth*.)

LION: Our location is against us, Otto. Even wandering minstrels don't wander this far.

BARKER (*With still more emphasis*): But you can't take the team into town until we've smoothed the rough edges.

LION (*Patiently*): Which is why we're here. I still feel there are one or two points that I haven't perfected as yet. For instance, it's difficult for the batter to toss the ball in the air and hit it at the same time. (*He pantomimes tossing a ball up and swinging at it.*)

BARKER: One of the Dwarfs nearly smashed his thumb doing that yesterday.

LION (*Continuing his pacing*): And the game lacks some sort of sparkle. I thought that having a lion as a mascot might add something, but that's only a beginning.

BARKER: Let's find the ending soon, eh, Your Highness? The boys are getting tired of playing to an empty grandstand. They're talking about taking off on a few crusades.

LION (*Raising a pacifying paw*): I'll think of something. In the meantime, though, you might as well proceed. Are you ready?

BARKER: I'm ready. (*Calling through megaphone*) Ready, Dwarfs?

DWARFS (*In unison, from behind fence*): Ready! (BLANCHE *enters right, dragging a large, furry "animal."*)

BLANCHE: Here. I brought this back as a sample of what I can do. (*She drops "animal" and kicks it toward* LION.) And I didn't even use one arrow. So don't think I can't survive around this forest, whether it's black or not.

LION (*Examining animal*): O.K., you've proved your point.

BLANCHE (*Wandering near fence*): I really came back to ask you about that sign.

LION (*Poking animal with his foot*): The sign? It's clear enough, isn't it?

BLANCHE (*In disbelief*): You mean there are seven *dwarfs* living behind that fence?

LION (*Proudly*): *The* Seven Dwarfs! That's right. (1ST DWARF, *captain, wearing baseball uniform marked "Dwarfs," enters from behind fence.*)

1ST DWARF (*Annoyed*): We said we were ready.

BLANCHE: He's not a dwarf!

LION (*Casually*): That's the name of our baseball team.

BLANCHE (*Groaning*): Of all the dumb ideas!

LION (*Suddenly*): But there's one thing I want to know. If you didn't kill that creature with an arrow, how did you do it?

BLANCHE (*Picking up an imaginary rock*): I took a rock like this, see? Then (*Winding up for pitch*), carefully aiming right between the eyes, I wound up and let 'er go!

LION (*To* BARKER): Did you see that? (*To* 1ST DWARF) Did you see that? Get the team out here.

1ST DWARF (*Calling*): O.K., men! We're ready now, all right. (*To* BLANCHE, *as six more* DWARFS *in baseball uniforms and carrying gloves, bats, etc., run in from behind fence*) Try that again!

LION: Show us how you did it. Show us again.

BLANCHE: Oh, are you dense! I aimed right between the eyes, see? And I wound up and let 'er go! (*She pantomimes another windup and pitch.* DWARFS *cheer.*)

LION (*Putting on his false head*): O.K., Dwarfs! Play ball! Blanche, you pitch. (DWARFS *take up positions about the stage as* BLANCHE *prepares to pitch to* 1ST DWARF. *Curtain.*)

*   *   *

SCENE 3

SETTING: *The same as Scene 1.*

AT RISE: QUEEN *enters left.*

QUEEN (*Calling*): Page! Oh, Page! (PAGE *and* MIRROR *enter right.*)

PAGE: I know, Your Majesty.

MIRROR: All right. Let's get it over with.

QUEEN (*Standing before her throne*): Mirror, mirror, on the wall. . . .

MIRROR: You're the fairest in the land, Your Majesty, and I wish you'd accept your fate and be done with it.

QUEEN (*Eagerly*): But what news of Blanche?

MIRROR: She's in the forest with the Seven Dwarfs.

QUEEN: Oh, good. We're getting somewhere, then. (SEER *enters right, carrying a crystal ball.*)

SEER: Of course we're getting somewhere. The Huntsman returned, mission accomplished. He's resting quietly on the couch of the court psychiatrist.

QUEEN: And what do you see in your crystal ball?

SEER: The crystal ball speaks only in symbols. I see a sign: HOME OF THE SEVEN DWARFS. And I see a large diamond. That represents the mine. (*He deposits the crystal ball at the foot of the throne.*) But just to be sure everything's going according to plan (*To* PAGE)—telephone, please (PAGE *reaches behind curtain and produces phone.*)—I shall call the Dwarfs to see how they're doing.

QUEEN (*Sitting*): I hope the Huntsman will be all right.

SEER (*Into phone*): How are you this afternoon, operator? I want the same place. Area code seven, number seven. Yes! I wrote it down. Aren't you tickled? (*Pause*) Ah! Hello, Doc? Herman the Seer here. I'll bet you're a frazzled lot of fellows this afternoon.

QUEEN (*Grabbing phone*): How's my baby, Doc? You're not working her too hard, are you? (*Slight pause*) She isn't there? You haven't seen her?

SEER (*Grabbing phone*): But Doc, old pal, I saw her there in my crystal ball. Oh, yes I did, and don't you go calling me a phony! I always thought you boys walked around on your knees! (*He slams down receiver and hands phone to* PAGE, *who puts it behind curtain.*)

QUEEN (*Standing and shouting*): This is the way empires

fall! A court filled with incompetents. One disaster on top of another!

GOVERNESS (*Scurrying in left*): And another disaster on top of that. Blanche is back, Your Majesty, and she's rousing the ladies-in-waiting to some sort of revolt. I'm resigning. I'm taking the night coach to Paris.

QUEEN: I tell you, it's hardly worth the trouble of giving a command around this duchy for all the good it does.

GOVERNESS (*Timidly*): You will give me a reference, won't you, Your Majesty?

QUEEN: Incompetents! All of you! Just bring Blanche to me, and be quick about it!

GOVERNESS (*Backing offstage*): I've already left, Your Majesty. (*She exits.* HUNTSMAN *enters, right.*)

QUEEN: Well! What do you have to say for yourself?

HUNTSMAN (*Holding up a large apple*): This time I'll *really* lose her. So help me, I've had it.

PAGE: Robbing the orchard again, eh?

HUNTSMAN: Persecuted, humiliated by a teen-age tomboy!

GOVERNESS (*Rushing back onstage*): Your Majesty, I tremble to tell you this, but she's gone again. This time she's taken all her ladies-in-waiting with her. I saw them running for the forest and waving clubs. They were wearing pants, Your Majesty. (*She puts her hand to her head and starts to fall into the* MIRROR's *arms.*) I think I'm going to faint.

QUEEN: Don't you dare! (GOVERNESS *snaps to attention*). After them, all of you. (*She points left dramatically.*) After them! (HUNTSMAN, PAGE, MIRROR *and* GOVERNESS *run off left.*) And just to be sure you don't fail another time— (*She descends from throne.*) I'm coming with you. Wait for me! (*She follows the others off left. Curtain.*)

*   *   *

Scene 4

SETTING: *The same as Scene 2.*

AT RISE: LION, *wearing his false head and looking disheveled and perplexed, is draped over a log, fanning himself.* BARKER *is sitting next to him.*

LION: I'm exhausted. What a workout!

BARKER (*In disbelief*): Not one hit! Every single one of the Dwarfs struck out.

LION (*In disgust*): Dwarfs! A good name for them. And to think I almost called them the Giants! Well, there's no use sulking. We'll just have to practice some more.

BARKER: Maybe it was only beginner's luck, Your Highness.

LION: She probably throws javelins and who knows what all else.

BARKER (*Standing*): You'll have to admit, though, that she's added something to the game. Instead of the batter throwing the ball in the air himself, we now shall have someone to pitch the ball to him.

LION (*Fanning harder*): It's getting too complicated. This means another player.

BARKER (*Walking back and forth, pausing to emphasize his ideas*): Another whole team, Your Highness. I envision the pitcher as a member of a team that tries to defeat the batter's team. And then there should be another man to stand in back of the batter to catch the pitches that the batter misses, if you follow me.

LION (*Suddenly interested*): I follow you. That means still another man on the team. Nine Dwarfs instead of seven. I'll have to have the sign repainted—that is, if I can find two more players.

BARKER (*With enthusiasm*): The important thing is to find

a good pitcher who can force the other team's batters to strike out.

LION: And now we have the added problem of finding another team. (*Sinking into dejection again*) I don't know, Otto. I think I'm about ready to throw in the sponge.

BARKER (*Rushing to* LION's *side*): But two teams, Your Highness! We could have the Dwarfs play teams from every duchy in Europe. Think of the traveling we could do!

LION (*Standing*): But where should we start? First of all we have to find *one* team to play against. (BLANCHE *enters right with* EIGHT LADIES-IN-WAITING. *All are dressed in dungarees and sweat shirts, and carry baseball bats, gloves, etc.*)

BLANCHE: And here we are! I've briefed the girls on the essentials of the game, and . . .

LION (*Climbing on log and raising his paw*): But it's my game! I thought of it first!

BLANCHE: Then you can be the arbitrator and pass on the rules. (*To* LADIES) All right, girls. Start warming up. (LADIES *begin tossing whiffle balls to each other, taking practice swings with bats, etc.*)

LION: Ha! I'd hate to argue with the likes of you!

BLANCHE: And why not? Nobody wants to argue with me. I always get my own way. It's a terrible bore.

LION (*Waving a conciliatory paw*): O.K., O.K. We'll see how it goes.

1ST LADY: Oh, keen. (*She swats the air with her bat.*)

2ND LADY (*Walking to* LION): I don't know who you are, but anybody who could think of something to do other than jousting is sure a friend of mine.

3RD LADY (*Tossing a whiffle ball in the air*): It's been pretty boring year in and year out.

4TH LADY (*Clapping her hands together to receive a catch*):

Watching one suit of armor get poked off a horse by another suit of armor.

5TH LADY: Always the same old thing.

6TH LADY (*Jumping into air for catch*): Your game has real possibilities.

LION (*Moaning*): But I never dreamed of playing against a team of girls.

6TH LADY: What other team do you have to play against?

BARKER (*Through megaphone*): Good question.

7TH LADY: Besides, once the game catches on, we'll retire, cheer from the grandstand and throw roses.

8TH LADY: You'll have lots of teams to play against once the game catches on.

LION (*Stepping down from log*): All right. Let's play ball. (LADIES *squeal with delight, and* LION *calls.*) Dwarfs? (DWARFS *run in. They are all in uniform.*) We're going to try something different today.

1ST DWARF (*Moving forward*): What's that?

2ND DWARF (*Pointing at* BLANCHE): It's that girl again.

3RD DWARF: Oh, no!

4TH DWARF: Aw, come on. It's better than jousting.

5TH DWARF: Safer, too.

6TH DWARF: But a team of *girls?*

7TH DWARF: I suggest we try to win.

1ST DWARF: They can have first turn at bat to show we're knights and gentlemen. (BARKER *goes to ticket booth, and* DWARFS *take positions at right, as* LADIES *gather at fence, left, near home plate.* LION *goes to center, and with back to audience, studies the field for a moment, then addresses* DWARFS.)

LION: Now, there are still a few details to be worked out. We need a catcher to stand in back of home plate, and we need someone to pitch the ball to the first batter.

(BLANCHE *steps up to home plate and takes a few practice swings with her bat.*)

HUNTSMAN (*Entering left*): I'll pitch something to her.

BLANCHE (*Calling*): Go ahead and try. You couldn't hit a castle wall from five feet away, not even with a good tail wind.

HUNTSMAN: Here's the pitch! (*He pretends to pitch apple.*)

BLANCHE (*Preparing to swing*): And it's an easy home run.

LION (*Waving his arms*): Wait! Wait a minute! Wild pitch! He didn't throw a baseball; he threw an apple, and that's not fair.

BLANCHE (*Leading with her chin*): Who says?

LION: I say.

BLANCHE: So what?

LION: So plenty. You don't play baseball with apples. (*He picks up an apple from behind log as if retrieving* HUNTSMAN'*s throw.*) Apples are for eating. (*He raises apple to his mouth.*)

HUNTSMAN (*Running to* LION): No! Stop! (LION *pauses, looks at him.*) That's not for you. It's for Blanche. (LION *tosses apple to* BLANCHE *and shrugs.*) It's a charmed apple. (QUEEN *enters right, followed by* GOVERNESS, PAGE, MIRROR, *and* SEER, *as* BLANCHE *prepares to bite into apple.*)

QUEEN: That apple has been treated with a low-calorie magic potion that will put you to sleep for years. And don't take a bite just to prove it, Blanche.

BLANCHE: Oh, yeah?

MIRROR: You'll be sorry. (QUEEN *joins* BLANCHE *at center.*)

QUEEN: One bite of that apple, and you'd remain sleeping until a prince charming came along and kissed you.

1ST LADY: A prince charming! What's that?

QUEEN: A prince. Any kind of prince. (*To* BLANCHE) What

young man would want to kiss a girl with a disposition like yours?

BLANCHE: Big deal. (*She bites into apple.*)

MIRROR: Don't say nobody warned you.

PAGE: How's she going to say anything if she's asleep?

QUEEN: Will you never do anything you're told?

BLANCHE (*Chewing*): No stupid potion would ever work on me. (*She stiffens, drops the apple and then slumps to the floor.*)

SEER (*Moving to QUEEN's side*): I was almost afraid she wouldn't try it on a dare.

GOVERNESS: Ah, how peaceful it's going to be around the palace now. I don't think I'll go to Paris after all!

PAGE: No more punches in the nose. No more kicks around the floor!

QUEEN: No one to worry about. (*She sniffles and brings out an enormous handkerchief.*)

GOVERNESS (*Comforting QUEEN*): There, now, Madame.

HUNTSMAN: Now there won't be anyone to use me for target practice. I might even miss that.

MIRROR: Without Blanche around, I'm going to be out of a job.

SEER: No reason for me to gaze into my crystal ball.

QUEEN: But you'll have to search for a prince charming to awaken her, Herman.

GOVERNESS: There must be some prince somewhere. With Blanche gone—(*Pauses*) nothing's going to happen anymore!

SEER: Things certainly will be calm.

PAGE: Dull, you mean.

HUNTSMAN: I'm sorry, everybody. I just wanted to show off my pitching arm.

LION (*Moving forward*): And what's going to happen to

my game? I was hoping that it would become the national sport.

QUEEN (*Interested*): A game to take the place of jousting?

BARKER (*Calling through megaphone*): Well, is it game time or isn't it?

LION: No game, Otto. The other team has just lost its captain and star pitcher.

QUEEN (*Calling to* BARKER): And we're desperately trying to find a prince who can kiss the Princess Blanche and rouse her from her slumber.

BARKER (*Joining others at center*): If it's a prince you're looking for, we have one of those. That lion—take off that crazy mask, will you?—is the Prince of Upper Holstein.

LION (*Removing lion head*): Your Majesty.

QUEEN: Well? Kiss her.

LION: Kiss that?

SEER: There are worse-looking girls in the world.

1ST DWARF: That man's been around.

3RD LADY: We'd like to have her back, Your Highness. She may not be a beauty contest winner, but she certainly made life interesting.

LADIES: Hear, hear!

1ST DWARF: And you do need her for the game, Your Highness.

QUEEN (*To* LION): If you've invented a game that can take the place of jousting and can take the boredom out of our feudal existence, young man, you've made a great contribution to civilization.

BARKER (*Through megaphone*): There you are, old lion. You've made something of yourself.

QUEEN: I'd even consider giving you the hand of the Princess Blanche in marriage.

LION: Now wait a minute!

LADIES (*Singing*): "Here comes the bride . . ."

4TH LADY: We haven't had a wedding at the palace in a long time.

QUEEN: On the other hand, I could have a talk with your father and see to it that you are banished to a salt mine or thrown into a dungeon.

LION: Why, that's positively medieval!

QUEEN: Of course it is. What do you think *we* are?

LION (*Feigning enthusiasm*): Yes, sir. Blanche is the best little pitcher the game of baseball will ever see.

ALL (*Ad lib, shouting*): Yea! That's the way! Now you're talking! (*Etc.*)

LION: I guess I do need her after all. And she does like a good argument. (*He kisses* BLANCHE.)

QUEEN: Oh, that she does.

BLANCHE (*Scrambling to her feet*): The next time you knock me down—

QUEEN: It was the apple, dear.

BLANCHE (*Brushing off her clothes*): I told you that potion wouldn't work on me. I heard every word you said.

QUEEN: Before we have any more of that, I'd like to see this famous game.

BLANCHE (*Sweetly*): Root for my team, will you, Mom?

QUEEN: It's only a game, dear.

LION (*Clapping his paws and organizing everyone*): O.K. Let's go. Huntsman, you can pitch for our team. (HUNTSMAN *goes to center.*) Page? You're the catcher. (PAGE *takes position behind home plate.*)

QUEEN: What can I do?

BARKER (*Through megaphone*): Wait till the game catches on, Your Majesty. You can run the hot dog stand.

QUEEN: Really? What fun! Come on, Blanche. Slam it out there! (QUEEN, SEER, MIRROR, *and* GOVERNESS *sit on log, and shout and cheer as* BLANCHE *steps up to home plate and takes a few practice swings.*)

BARKER (*Through megaphone*): Step right up, lords and ladies, serfs, knights, princes and kings. See the greatest game of the modern age!

LION (*Shouting*): O.K., everybody! Play ball! (*Teams simulate the opening of the game, as shouts and cheers increase, and the curtain falls.*)

THE END

Production Notes

THE FAIREST PITCHER OF THEM ALL

Characters: 12 male; 12 female.

Playing Time: 35 minutes.

Costumes: Appropriate court dress for Queen, Page, and Governess. Queen has a large handkerchief in one pocket. The Seer wears flowing robes and a pointed hat, and the Huntsman wears rough jacket and trousers. The Mirror has a board painted silver or covered with foil hung from her shoulders, sandwich-board fashion. Blanche and the Ladies wear sweat shirts, dungarees and sneakers, and the Dwarfs have on baseball uniforms with "Dwarfs" written across the shirts. The Barker wears a gaudy sports jacket and a straw hat, and carries a megaphone. The Lion's costume should have a head or mask which can be removed easily.

Properties: Telephone, crystal ball, large furry "animal," apple, bow and arrows, baseball bats, gloves, whiffle balls, megaphone.

Setting: Scenes 1 and 3: The throne room of the palace in Poco-Holstein. The curtain parts only a few feet to reveal the throne, backed by a screen, and the action takes place in front of the curtain. Scenes 2 and 4: A clearing in the woods. There is a high fence up left with a sign: HOME OF THE SEVEN DWARFS. Nearby are a ticket booth and a cage large enough to hold the Lion. There is a log up center. Exits for all scenes are at right and left.

Lighting: No special effects.

Sound: Offstage crash, as indicated in text.

Peace, Pilgrim

Characters

GUIDE
EMERSON T. WEATHERBY VI
MRS. WEATHERBY
MISS SMITH } *tourists*
MISS ALDEN
JOE STANDISH

SMILEY
FOXEY
THUNDER } *Indians*
MOONBEAM
RAINBOW

PILGRIM PEACEMAKER
JANE
PRISCILLA } *Pilgrims*
STANDISH
DINERS

TIME: *Thanksgiving Day.*

SETTING: *A clearing in a forest.*

AT RISE: GUIDE, *holding a map, enters right, pushing his way through underbrush with difficulty.* MR. *and* MRS. WEATHERBY, MISS SMITH, MISS ALDEN, *and* JOE STANDISH, *all quite distraught, follow* GUIDE, *pushing aside bushes to reach clearing.* GUIDE *stops at center, looks*

69

about uneasily, while tourists brush off clothes, straighten hats, etc.

GUIDE (*To himself*): It must be here someplace!

MRS. WEATHERBY (*Angrily, to* GUIDE): My stockings are being ripped to shreds, tramping through the woods like this!

MR. WEATHERBY (*Gruffly*): Serves you right for wearing stockings on a safari. (MRS. WEATHERBY *turns and faces her husband.*)

MRS. WEATHERBY: A safari is the last thing this guided tour is supposed to be.

MISS SMITH (*Adjusting her hat*): You're absolutely right, Mrs. Weatherby. This is the poorest excuse for a guided tour I ever did see.

GUIDE (*Impatiently*): I'm your guide. You're having a tour. Stop complaining.

MRS. WEATHERBY: Wait till the home office in Boston hears about this!

MISS ALDEN (*Whining slightly*): At the rate we're going, we may never see Boston again.

JOE STANDISH (*To* GUIDE): Look, we only wanted to see the site of the first Thanksgiving. That's all. Then we can all go home.

MISS ALDEN (*Stepping forward and speaking proudly*): We're not just curiosity seekers, you know. All of us here had ancestors at that first great Thanksgiving feast—Mr. Standish (*She gestures toward* JOE, *who nods*), Miss Smith (*Indicates* MISS SMITH), and I am an Alden. (*She faces audience and places her hand over her heart.*) We are making a pilgrimage. (*She gazes off into space, as if in a trance.*)

MR. WEATHERBY (*Indicating his wife*): Mrs. Weatherby

and I trace both our families to a little-known ship which landed the year before the *Mayflower*. Mrs. Weatherby, of course, was a Pettigrew before I married her.

JOE: You've been telling us about the Weatherbys and the Pettigrews all day. Go ahead and name that little-known ship, why don't you?

MR. WEATHERBY (*Turning and walking left*): I'm not giving away any family secrets.

MISS SMITH (*To* JOE): You may be a Standish, young man, but you certainly act like an upstart.

MRS. WEATHERBY (*To* JOE): I wouldn't be surprised if your branch of the family didn't arrive here until long after the Louisiana Purchase.

GUIDE (*Throwing up his hands*): Oh, what difference does it make?

MISS ALDEN (*Coming out of her trance*): It makes all the difference in the world! Either you're authentic or you're not!

GUIDE (*Trying to understand*): Authentic *what*, Miss Alden?

MISS ALDEN (*Emphatically*): Authentic American, of course!

MISS SMITH: Anybody understands that.

GUIDE (*Shrugging*): If you say so, Miss Smith. (*Raising voice to get attention of others*) Look here, everyone, I want to get out of here as badly as you do. I have a family at home waiting for me to carve the turkey.

MISS SMITH (*To* MISS ALDEN): Personally, I favor something more elegant than turkey for Thanksgiving. Pheasant, for instance.

GUIDE (*Ignoring her*): I guess we ought to admit it. We're lost.

MRS. WEATHERBY (*Somewhat hysterically*): I knew it! I

knew it! (*She dabs at her eyes with a lacy handkerchief.*)

MISS ALDEN: That's ridiculous. How can anybody be lost in Massachusetts?

JOE (*Sarcastically*): Have you ever tried taking the scenic route to Cape Cod?

MR. WEATHERBY (*To* JOE): Now see here, Miles Standish!

JOE: *Joe* Standish. We stopped naming children "Miles" in our family years ago.

MR. WEATHERBY: A family of cowards, you Standishes were, in any case. (*Turning to* MISS ALDEN *for confirmation*) Isn't that right, Miss Alden?

MISS ALDEN: Absolutely. The Standishes were the laughingstock of the colony for years.

GUIDE (*Interrupting and raising his voice*): I guess the only thing to do is to stay right here until somebody comes looking for us.

MISS SMITH (*Nastily*): And how long will that take, do you suppose?

MR. WEATHERBY (*Standing on his toes and looking off right*): Look! I think—yes—I see a path over there!

MRS. WEATHERBY: Good! Let's follow it. (*She stuffs her handkerchief into her sleeve and starts to move right.*)

MISS ALDEN (*Sitting down on a rock*): I'm too weary to walk another step.

MISS SMITH (*Proudly*): That's not the way our ancestors would have talked.

MISS ALDEN (*Massaging her feet*): They didn't wear high heels.

GUIDE (*Trying to organize the group*): All right, Pilgrims. I'd suggest we all stick together. There's no point in getting lost one by one.

MRS. WEATHERBY (*Sarcastically*): Dear me, no. Let's stay lost as a group. It's so much chummier that way.

JOE (*Moving to path*): Stop talking and let's go. It's getting late.

MR. WEATHERBY: Right. We don't want to be stuck out here after dark. (*Goes toward path.*)

MISS ALDEN (*Pulling herself to her feet*): I hope this path leads somewhere.

MISS SMITH (*Knowingly*): All paths lead somewhere.

MISS ALDEN: But not necessarily where one wants to go. (MISS SMITH *and* MISS ALDEN *follow the others, and one by one they all exit right. As the last person exits,* FOXEY, *an Indian, peers out from behind bushes at left. Then he stands and motions off left.*)

FOXEY (*Calling over his shoulder*): O.K., kids. You can come out now! (SMILEY, MOONBEAM, THUNDER, *and* RAINBOW, *other Indians, enter left, one by one.*)

SMILEY (*Looking off right and shaking his head*): Every year it's the same old thing. Wouldn't you think they'd have something better to do?

THUNDER: I don't know why we don't put on a good show for them. Do a few tribal dances, wave some tomahawks around. (*He demonstrates dance.*)

RAINBOW (*Shrugging and moving to center*): That kind of thing never pays off. They end up by taking your land away from you so that they can give it back to you with a lot of split-level tepees on it.

MOONBEAM: That's what they did to my aunt in New Mexico, so she started selling them surplus Army blankets colored with leftover hair dye. (*She starts looking behind bushes.*) Has anybody seen my transistor radio? I want to hear the Top Ten show. (*Finds radio behind a bush*) Here it is. (*She turns it on and holds it close to her ear.*)

RAINBOW (*Rubbing her hands together*): I'm hungry. Who's going to start dinner?

FOXEY: We'll all pitch in. Take a look in the freezer, will you, Thunder? We may be a little short.

SMILEY (*Jokingly*): We wouldn't be if you'd go out and spear a fish once in a while.

MOONBEAM: Or tend the corn.

FOXEY: Corn, corn, corn. Year in and year out it's the same old thing.

SMILEY: The settlers still think it's great. I don't know why you should sneer.

FOXEY: I don't like corn, that's all. Do you mind?

THUNDER (*Moving forward*): Wait a minute. (*They all look at him.*) Today's the fourth Thursday in November. You know what that means.

SMILEY: We know. Why else were the tourists prowling around?

MOONBEAM (*Sighing*): I don't know why they get so worked up about a turkey once a year.

SMILEY (*Seriously*): It's not the turkey itself. It's the significance of the day. Everybody's supposed to be thankful for what he has.

RAINBOW (*Indicating the path*): That group didn't seem very thankful to me. They complain even more than Foxey.

FOXEY (*Smiling*): I don't complain. I just like to liven things up once in a while.

MOONBEAM: Go liven up some corn, then. Is there a turkey in the freezer, Smiley?

SMILEY: We're fresh out. We have some caviar left over from Thunder's peacepipe party, though.

MOONBEAM (*Doing a few dance steps*): That was a swinging little get-together.

RAINBOW (*Firmly*): We must have a turkey. It's the thing to do.

SMILEY (*Jesting*): O.K.—who's going to go out and shoot a turkey?

THUNDER (*Shaking his head*): Not me. I never took to a musket.

FOXEY (*Shivering*): And I can't stand the sight of blood.

RAINBOW: Go call a Pilgrim, then. They usually end up with the same job every year.

MOONBEAM: Sure! Gives them something to do.

SMILEY (*With resignation*): That means we have to invite them to dinner again.

RAINBOW: Oh, the Pilgrims aren't such a bad lot.

MOONBEAM: I can take any one of them but that Priscilla woman. She's so prim and proper.

SMILEY: None of them is much fun.

FOXEY: Standish is the one who gripes me. He's so grumpy. And how many years can you court a girl?

MOONBEAM: They're just a little behind the times, Foxey. But you'll have to admit they're quaint.

RAINBOW (*Gossiping gleefully*): Did you hear that the Alden fellow was sent over here from England because his family there couldn't *stand* him for another minute?

SMILEY: It doesn't surprise me. All they ever do is talk about their ancestors.

RAINBOW: Some of them act as if they were direct descendants of Attila the Hun.

SMILEY: Now, Rainbow. Try to be hospitable. I'll beat out an invitation. (*He goes behind bush and brings out a bongo drum.*)

THUNDER: Ask Jane to bring along some of her pickle relish. (SMILEY *sits down and begins to beat drum.*)

MOONBEAM: Say, Smiley, that's a pretty good beat. (*She does a few dance steps.*) Maybe Hepzibah could bring along her zither and we could have a hootenanny after dinner. (*Others dance a few steps.*)

RAINBOW (*Shaking her head*): No. That would be too noisy. (PILGRIM PEACEMAKER *enters left, carrying a turkey in his arms.*)

PILGRIM (*Shifting turkey to left arm and raising right hand timidly*): Peace! (SMILEY *stops beating drum, and all turn and stare at* PILGRIM.)

FOXEY: Well, peace to you, too, Pilgrim.

SMILEY: These drum messages are getting through awfully fast these days.

PILGRIM (*Awkwardly*): I bring offering. Show Pilgrim heart in right place.

THUNDER (*Laughing*): We were going to ask you to bring the bird anyway.

PILGRIM (*Solemnly*): Me bring-um peace offering.

SMILEY (*Standing*): Yes. You already made that clear.

PILGRIM: Ugh!

MOONBEAM (*Going to* PILGRIM): Do you have a cold, Pilgrim?

RAINBOW (*Joining* MOONBEAM *as* PILGRIM *steps back slightly*): We'll admit it's chilly here, but then England isn't very balmy, either.

FOXEY (*To* PILGRIM): You fellows come on over for dinner in a little while. It'll take some time to roast the turkey.

MOONBEAM (*Taking turkey from* PILGRIM): Let's see. How many minutes of cooking time to a pound? (*She hefts turkey to test weight.*)

RAINBOW: You really can't figure it out, Moonbeam. The thermostat in the oven hasn't been working. I wish we could get it fixed.

PILGRIM (*Saluting again*): How!

RAINBOW (*Surprised*): How? Well, if I knew *how*, I'd fix it.

SMILEY: Maybe he means how do you prepare the turkey?

MOONBEAM: Heap big Indian secret, Pilgrim. We'll give you the recipe for a Christmas present.

PILGRIM (*Dropping to his knees*): Also teach Pilgrim how you plant corn? Please?

SMILEY (*Throwing up his hands in disgust*): Oh, for crying out loud. Haven't you learned that yet?

FOXEY (*Kneeling beside* PILGRIM *and making exaggerated gestures*): You take the little seed, see? (PILGRIM *nods.*) And you stick it in the ground, see? (PILGRIM *nods.*) And before you know it the seeds grow. (PILGRIM *and* FOXEY *rise slowly, looking up as if watching growth of corn stalk.*) Provided they have the proper amount of rain, sunshine, drainage and fertilizer, of course. (PILGRIM *is silent.*)

MOONBEAM: You're confusing the Pilgrim, Foxey. I don't think he understands.

FOXEY (*Pointing to himself and* PILGRIM): Me show-um you-um in springtime. And this year you'd better write everything down.

PILGRIM (*Solemnly*): Settlers try survive another cold New England winter.

SMILEY (*Kindly*): You'll make it.

PILGRIM (*Coughing*): Pilgrim not so sure.

SMILEY: Just pretend you're in England with no central heating.

RAINBOW (*As* PILGRIM *sniffs*): That's not funny. Look. The poor man's upset.

THUNDER (*Putting his arm around* PILGRIM's *shoulder*): Hey, now. Don't cry. You all come over for a nice dinner, and we'll knit you some sweaters and show you how to light a fire without matches.

PILGRIM (*Moving forward, raising his hand again and speaking loudly*): Peace!

SMILEY (*Turning to others*): You know, I don't think we're going to get anywhere with these Pilgrims until they learn the language.

FOXEY (*Nodding in agreement*): I often have the feeling that we're not communicating at all.

MOONBEAM (*Sighing*): That takes care of my winter project. I'll have to open a school for the Pilgrims.

PILGRIM: Indian no fight Pilgrim.

SMILEY: They seem to have a fixation about fighting all the time.

PILGRIM (*Loudly*): No want-um war!

SMILEY (*Impatiently, to* PILGRIM): Indian no want-um war any more than you do. I wish you'd get that through your ten-gallon hat!

RAINBOW: You'll have to admit we gave them a hard time in the beginning.

SMILEY: Oh, that. That was nothing but a welcome to the new neighborhood. It was a long time ago.

THUNDER (*Ominously*): They say a Pilgrim never forgets.

FOXEY: They also say the Pilgrims are bringing European civilization to the New World.

PILGRIM (*Threateningly*): Pilgrim civilize Indians yet!

INDIANS: How!

MOONBEAM (*Going to* PILGRIM *and taking his arm*): And we'll teach you to read. That's fair, isn't it? (THUNDER *takes his other arm, and he and* MOONBEAM *start left, guiding* PILGRIM, *who walks backward between them.*)

THUNDER: You Pilgrims all come over later, and we'll have a nice, civilized dinner, all of us together. (*They let go of* PILGRIM, *who backs off left.*)

PILGRIM (*As he exits*): Ugh!

INDIANS (*Waving*): Ugh, ugh!

RAINBOW (*Calling after him*): And bring the kids, too, if you can't find a babysitter. (THUNDER *goes behind bushes and brings out several card tables and folding chairs which Indians set up at center.*)

THUNDER: If there's anything I detest, it's a banquet where the guests have nothing to say to each other.

MOONBEAM (*Surveying tables thoughtfully*): We'll have to be very careful about the seating arrangements. One Indian on the right side of every Pilgrim.

SMILEY (*Laughing*): They'll think we're preparing an attack.

THUNDER (*Momentarily stopping his work*): Then what do you propose—all the Pilgrims at one end of the table and all the Indians at the other?

FOXEY: That wouldn't look very good.

SMILEY: Perhaps we should serve dinner buffet-style. Then there wouldn't be any question about it.

MOONBEAM (*Dismissing idea*): That's too sloppy.

THUNDER: It's our party. We'll do it our way. (*They finish setting up tables.*) I'll get out the Venetian lace tablecloth, and you polish the silver, Moonbeam. (*She nods.*) Foxey? Bring out the candlesticks and crystal glasses. We'll make the Pilgrims as welcome as we know how.

RAINBOW (*Straightening tables*): It's terribly depressing, really. You somehow get the feeling that they don't trust us one bit. (*Stands back and surveys tables*)

MOONBEAM: I think I'll try something new—pumpkin pie.

FOXEY (*Horrified*): Eat a *pumpkin?* I thought they were just for Halloween.

MOONBEAM: Pumpkin pie is great with ice cream on it. You'll see. Now let's get to work! (*Indians exit left. Stage is empty for a moment, and then* MR. WEATHERBY *appears on path up right, followed by* GUIDE. *As they come down center,* MRS. WEATHERBY, MISS ALDEN, JOE, *and* MISS SMITH *enter up right and join them.*)

GUIDE: You're just backtracking, Mr. Weatherby.

MR. WEATHERBY: No I'm not. I wasn't a Boy Scout for
nothing.

MRS. WEATHERBY: I think the guide is right, dear. This
certainly looks like the same clearing we were in before.

JOE (*To* GUIDE): Is this place on your map?

GUIDE (*Spreading map on a rock*): I don't think it is. (*He
looks closely at map.*)

MISS SMITH (*Pointing to tables*): Mr. Weatherby is right!
This *is* a different place. Look—tables!

JOE: A picnic area. (*Looking over* GUIDE'*s shoulder*) Now
that must be on your map.

GUIDE: Not in this vicinity.

MRS. WEATHERBY (*Walking about*): It looks just like
Settlers' Wood, doesn't it, Miss Alden?

MISS ALDEN (*With enthusiasm*): Maybe we're in the right
place at last!

MISS SMITH: The site of the first Thanksgiving! You
weren't so far off after all, were you, Guide?

GUIDE (*Folding his map*): Look, I hate to tell you this, but
according to my calculations. . . .

MRS. WEATHERBY (*To her husband*): I didn't know you
were such a trailblazer, dear.

MR. WEATHERBY: O.K. We've seen the place and we can
tell our friends we've been here. Let's go home.

MRS. WEATHERBY (*Walking about and speaking dramatically*): Imagine! The first Thanksgiving took place on
this very spot. Don't your hearts fill with pride? Aren't
you all but overcome with the beauty of the occasion?

JOE (*Looking at his watch*): I'm hungry.

MISS ALDEN (*Echoing* MRS. WEATHERBY'*s tone*): Think of
how our Pilgrim Fathers prepared that feast (*She gestures toward tables*) to show the Indians they had come
to the New World bringing the friendship and civilization of the Old World!

Miss Smith (*Joining in*): Think of the patience it must have taken our ancestors to teach the Indians the proper way of doing things.

Mrs. Weatherby: Think of how difficult it must have been just to speak to them! (*Pausing center and looking up*) I think we should have a moment of silence in memory of our noble ancestors. (*With pride*) I'm so glad I'm not descended from the common herd!

Joe (*Not unkindly*): Our ancestors were rather simple folk, Mrs. Weatherby.

Mrs. Weatherby (*Insulted*): Simple? How do you mean that?

Joe (*In matter-of-fact tone*): Simple. That's how I mean it. They didn't come over here First Class on the *Queen Elizabeth II.*

Mrs. Weatherby: Really, Mr. Standish! Perhaps *your* background is a bit spotty, but you needn't cast aspersions on anyone else's lineage.

Joe: You misunderstand me, Mrs. Weatherby. I merely think that some of us are inclined to go a bit overboard on this ancestor business.

Mrs. Weatherby (*Offended*): Speak for yourself, Mr. Standish.

Guide (*With his right hand raised; wearily*): Peace, Pilgrims. It's been a rough day. (*Indians enter left, carrying tablecloths, dishes, silver, candles, glasses, etc., and start to set tables. They pay no attention to tourists.*)

Miss Alden (*Excitedly, pointing to Indians*): Look! It's a pageant. A Thanksgiving Pageant!

Miss Smith: The tour company didn't tell us about this!

Mrs. Weatherby: You splendid guide! You kept it as a surprise. (Guide *looks dumfounded.*) Now quiet, everybody. (Joe *shrugs.*) Let's sit down on these rocks and enjoy every minute of this heartwarming experience. I

feel giddy with anticipation. I can feel myself trans-
ported back over three hundred years! (*Tourists settle
themselves on rocks, and watch Indians intently.*)

MOONBEAM (*To* THUNDER): Do you think we'll have
enough room without adding more tables? (*She spreads
tablecloth to cover card tables.*)

THUNDER: I think so.

SMILEY (*Straightening tablecloth*): One problem—who's
going to carve the turkey?

FOXEY (*Putting stack of dishes on table*): A Pilgrim.
There's no use in fighting for the knife.

MRS. WEATHERBY (*Knowingly, to tourists*): You see? The
civilizing influence of the Pilgrims.

THUNDER: You're right about the knife, Foxey. (*He and
MOONBEAM begin to arrange plates.*) Last year Standish
thought I was going to scalp him and he knocked the
carving set right into the dirt.

MOONBEAM: And broke the bone handles, may I add. You
know (*Looks about*), we ought to have this area screened
in. (*She swats at air.*) There are still a few flies left over
from last August.

THUNDER: Get out the bug spray.

JOE (*As Indians continue setting table*): What a miserable
bunch of actors.

MISS ALDEN (*Loudly*): Shh!

MISS SMITH (*Curiously*): Are they ad-libbing?

MISS ALDEN: Really!

RAINBOW (*Placing bowl of fruit on table*): There we are.
The silver is polished, and the crystal is shining. We
have apples and pears and an assortment of preserves.

THUNDER: Let's dig into the caviar before the Pilgrims arrive, eh?

SMILEY: That's not the proper spirit.

THUNDER: There isn't enough to go around. Besides, anybody who eats nothing but boiled cabbage certainly isn't going to miss a spoonful of caviar.

MOONBEAM (*Repelled*): Boiled cabbage!

THUNDER: It's their dietary staple.

RAINBOW: No wonder they think corn is so exotic.

MOONBEAM: I left the oysters out of the stuffing this time. I noticed that last year the Pilgrims picked out all the oysters and left them on their butter plates.

RAINBOW (*To* MOONBEAM): How's the turkey doing, Moonbeam?

MOONBEAM: Almost done—and it smells just marvelous. I tried roasting it in aluminum foil this time. It's supposed to keep the bird moist.

SMILEY: Will we have enough for turkey sandwiches later?

FOXEY (*Rubbing his stomach*): Or turkey salad? I love turkey salad.

MOONBEAM: We will if you don't eat too much today. (*Standing back from table*) I guess we're ready. Everyone get into his finery. We might as well play this to the hilt.

MR. WEATHERBY (*Standing and addressing Indians*): Don't you think you're overdoing it as it is?

SMILEY (*Facing* MR. WEATHERBY): Indeed! And who, may I ask, are you?

MR. WEATHERBY (*With authority*): I am Emerson T. Weatherby VI, husband of a Daughter of the Colonial Revolution. And I insist that you be a little more faithful to the original events of this historic day.

FOXEY (*Stepping forward*): Mr. Weatherby, we don't know what you're talking about.

MRS. WEATHERBY (*To tourists*): Actors! What do they know about anything?

RAINBOW (*Rather annoyed*): Actors! There hasn't been an actor around here since a Shakespearean touring company was shipwrecked on its way to Virginia.

JOE (*Standing*): I can believe it! You have a nerve to put on a pageant like this and take any liberties you choose.

SMILEY (*With a sigh*): Do be quiet and let us get on with our feast.

THUNDER: It's hard enough to entertain a lot of foreigners without so many interruptions. We're doing the best we can.

MOONBEAM: You have no idea of the odds we're up against.

RAINBOW (*Approaching tourists*): Have you ever tried to make people feel at home when they won't let you?

SMILEY (*Trying to settle matters*): You're perfectly welcome to stay if you wish, but we'd like a little consideration.

MR. WEATHERBY: All right. But stay with the script and save the nonsense for the comedians. (*Indians start to exit left and* MR. WEATHERBY *sits down.*)

FOXEY (*To Indians*): Ignore them. They may go away. (*Indians exit.*)

JOE: Now what's this? An intermission?

MRS. WEATHERBY (*To* GUIDE): I really think the tour company could have come up with a better show than this.

MISS SMITH: They couldn't bring in a company from Broadway just to play for us.

MISS ALDEN (*Kindly*): They're probably only local amateurs, and I think it's sweet of them to take time out on Thanksgiving Day to put on a playlet for us.

JOE: I'm hungry. (*He sits.*)

GUIDE (*Meekly*): It *is* getting awfully late.

MRS. WEATHERBY (*Indignantly*): You don't think we're going to leave before the pageant is over, do you? We paid good American dollars for this, and I want my money's worth.

GUIDE (*Standing*): But you don't seem to understand, Mrs. Weatherby!

MRS. WEATHERBY: Besides, it's rude to leave the theater before the final curtain. Anybody who is well-bred knows that much.

JOE: Oh, I don't know. If the actors are as bad as these, I don't see much point in sticking around.

MRS. WEATHERBY: But we've already discussed how questionable your background is, Mr. Standish.

JOE: Now look! (*He stands.*) I've had just about enough out of you. My credentials will match yours any day.

MRS. WEATHERBY: We'll see about that.

JOE: Just because I don't go around waving them at everybody. . . .

MISS ALDEN: Sh-h. I think they're coming back.

JOE: Don't "sh-h" me. I have just as much right to be here as (*Pointing to* MRS. WEATHERBY) she has.

MRS. WEATHERBY (*To* MISS ALDEN): Pay no attention to the boy, dear. (*Indians enter left, carrying platters of food.* MOONBEAM *has a tray of crackers. They now wear elaborate seventeenth century costumes instead of Indian dress. They set platters on table.*) Look at those costumes! How perfectly elegant! Is that what the Indians in Massachusetts wore at the time of the Pilgrims?

JOE (*Turning his back*): You're the authority. You tell us.

MISS ALDEN: They look awfully stylish to me. I thought they wore buckskin and feathers all the time.

MISS SMITH: Let's not be so critical. Those costumes are probably the only thing the players could find.

MOONBEAM: Now, a last minute check. Is the silver properly placed?

RAINBOW (*Looking at tables*): It's perfect, I'd say.

MOONBEAM: The turkey's in the warming oven, and all
we need to do is wait for our guests. I suppose we might
as well have some of the caviar in the meantime. (*She
passes around tray of crackers.*)

THUNDER: Good. (*Each Indian takes cracker.*) Let's have
our caviar and give thanks for all the fine things in life
that are ours.

INDIANS (*Raising their crackers in a toast*): Cheers!

FOXEY: We do have a great deal to be thankful for.

THUNDER (*Greedily*): For caviar, for instance.

SMILEY: For caviar and for corn and for each other.

THUNDER: I'll take caviar to any one of you.

SMILEY (*Handing him tray*): Then, here. Help yourself.

THUNDER (*Taking tray and helping himself*): Thanks.
(*Eats crackers*) Mm-m. This is great. (*Indians continue
to eat, talking quietly among themselves.*)

JOE: I'm hungry.

MR. WEATHERBY: They're doing a lot better now.

MRS. WEATHERBY: It's still not authentic.

MISS ALDEN: But it is convincing. They really look as
though they're eating something delicious. (PILGRIM
PEACEMAKER *enters left, carrying a musket.*)

PILGRIM: Peace! (*Indians stop eating and look up.*)

SMILEY: Oh, put that musket down, will you? As a matter
of fact, I'm going to insist that all muskets be checked
at the door. (PILGRIM *places musket carefully beside a
bush.* JANE, PRISCILLA, STANDISH, *and other Pilgrim*
DINERS *enter left. Men leave muskets beside bush. Pilgrims do not notice tourists.*)

MOONBEAM (*Cordially, to* PILGRIM): We were just enjoy-
ing some caviar. Would you care for some, Pilgrim? (*She
offers him tray of crackers.*)

PILGRIM (*Holding up his hands to refuse*): No like-um. Me
meat-and-potatoes man.

MOONBEAM: I expected as much. (*She smiles and crosses to* JANE.) Ah, Jane, did you bring some of your marvelous pickle relish?

JANE (*Raising her hand*): Peace!

MOONBEAM (*Patting* JANE's *hand*): Well, that's all right. We have plenty, you know, and you're welcome to stay as long as you wish. (*Turning to* PRISCILLA) Priscilla, dear, how are you?

PRISCILLA (*Raising her hand*): How!

RAINBOW (*To* PRISCILLA): She said how are you? Your health, you know? No cough, sinus, migraine?

PRISCILLA: Ugh.

MOONBEAM: Oh—you have a cold. I'm sorry.

RAINBOW (*To* STANDISH): Mr. Standish. How sweet of you to come. I know what an effort it is for you to meet people socially.

JOE (*Standing*): That does it.

SMILEY (*To Pilgrims*): Where are the children? We had some amusing games planned for them. Bows and arrows. (*Pilgrims dive for their muskets.*) Just toys! (*Shouting*) T-O-Y-S! Oh, put down those muskets, will you? (*Pilgrims put down muskets, but remain standing near them, warily watching Indians.*)

FOXEY: Don't lose your patience, Smiley. I have a feeling this is going to take years.

MR. WEATHERBY (*Standing*): Well, I'm losing *my* patience. (*At sound of* MR. WEATHERBY's *voice, Pilgrims, startled, turn and stare at tourists, seeing them for first time.*)

SMILEY (*To* MR. WEATHERBY; *annoyed*): You again?

MOONBEAM (*To* MR. WEATHERBY): I wish you'd stop being so irritable. You're ruining our dinner party.

THUNDER: It's taken us a long time to push diplomatic relations to this point, and we have no intention of letting you spoil them.

MR. WEATHERBY (*Moving a few steps toward Indians*): I
don't care whether you're amateur actors or what you
are—this has gone far enough.

MISS ALDEN (*Standing*): What a shame. I was just beginning to enjoy myself.

SMILEY (*To* MISS ALDEN): Then you can stay for the party
and send that old grump back to wherever he came
from. (*Points to* MR. WEATHERBY)

MRS. WEATHERBY (*Standing*): He is not a grump. A little
touchy, perhaps, but . . .

MR. WEATHERBY: I just want to know where our guide
dug up this crew.

GUIDE (*Standing*): I didn't dig them up anywhere. They
were just here!

MISS SMITH: Local amateurs. We decided that already.

SMILEY: We're local, all right. We've always been here.
So far as we're concerned, you're intruding and you're
not very well-mannered.

THUNDER: We've invited you to join us. We're being as
hospitable as we know how, and if that isn't good
enough for you, you're perfectly free to leave.

MR. WEATHERBY: I'm leaving, all right, but not until I
find out who you actors are.

SMILEY: Mr. Weatherby, I told you before. We are not
actors. There haven't been any actors around here in
years.

MR. WEATHERBY (*Protesting*): I know, I know! You told
me!

SMILEY (*Coolly*): Well, then, what's the problem?

MR. WEATHERBY: Who *are* you?

SMILEY: We're natives. Locals, as that lady said.

MR. WEATHERBY: The State of Massachusetts should be
ashamed of you.

FOXEY (*Going to center*): To be more specific about it,

Mr. Weatherby, we're native Indians. You know. I'm Little Fox. (*Introducing other Indians, who extend their hands to tourists.*) This is Smile of the Sun Spirit, and this is Great Thunder. (*Pointing to Pilgrims*) Ask them if you don't believe me.

MR. WEATHERBY (*Walking to Pilgrims*): Well?

PILGRIMS (*In unison*): Peace!

MR. WEATHERBY (*Turning to join tourists*): This is the most preposterous thing I've ever heard.

SMILEY: Oh? I've heard of moon flights and atom bombs and cold wars. I don't see what's so preposterous about us.

JOE (*Flustered*): But . . . but you were wiped out a long time ago.

MOONBEAM (*Sweetly*): Please join our party and have a good time. (*She gestures to table.*) The turkey should be excellent this year.

RAINBOW: Yes. Please sit down. You may have something in common with our Pilgrim friends. We haven't been able to communicate very well with them.

MR. WEATHERBY (*Blustering*): That's because you're Indians, and Pilgrims at least speak English!

SMILEY: Now you've lost me.

MR. WEATHERBY: Speak-um English! Like, ugh! Ugh!

FOXEY (*Putting his hand to his head*): I feel a tremendous cultural backslide is taking place.

JOE (*Moving toward Pilgrims*): You there—Standish. You're no Indian.

STANDISH (*Stepping forward*): Me no Indian.

JOE: Then what are you? Speak up, man!

MOONBEAM: Mr. Standish just doesn't speak up. That's one of his problems. (*She exits left.*)

JOE (*Turning and going back to other tourists*): I give up.

SMILEY: But you shouldn't, you know. *We're* still trying.

MISS ALDEN (*Whimpering*): You're all playing a mean joke on us.

MOONBEAM (*Re-entering, carrying turkey on platter*): Here's the turkey! It's just right.

THUNDER: Let me help you with that. (*They place turkey on table.*)

MRS. WEATHERBY: Which actors are playing the parts of my ancestors, the Pettigrews?

MR. WEATHERBY: And where's the Weatherby family? (*Pilgrims look at one another, puzzled.*)

THUNDER: Never heard of anybody by the name of Weatherby in this colony, or Pettigrew either.

MRS. WEATHERBY: Guide, I've had enough. Take us back to Boston.

GUIDE: I'll try, but I've been trying to tell you that we're lost.

MRS. WEATHERBY (*Angrily*): Lost? We can't be lost! (*Tourists circle around GUIDE, arguing, waving fists, in pantomime.*)

MOONBEAM (*In exasperation*): Oh, honestly! Let's take our party somewhere else and enjoy ourselves. (*Turning to Pilgrims*) Are you coming with us?

PILGRIMS (*Together*): Ugh! (*Pilgrims and Indians pick up dishes, silver and glasses on table, leaving tablecloth and turkey. Pilgrims exit left.*)

RAINBOW (*Looking at tourists, who still argue with GUIDE*): No wonder the world is in such a mess.

SMILEY (*Shrugging*): It will straighten out in time. Meanwhile, we're going to have our Thanksgiving dinner as planned. (*Indians start to exit left.*)

MOONBEAM: Look! The Pilgrims have gone off and left their muskets!

FOXEY: So they have. I guess we may be getting somewhere with them after all. (*Indians exit.*)

MR. WEATHERBY: Never have I been subjected to anything like this. Never!

MRS. WEATHERBY (*To* GUIDE): The Daughters of the Colonial Revolution are certainly going to strike your travel agency off their list.

MISS ALDEN (*Sitting down and rubbing her feet*): This is the last time I wear high heels for a walking trip.

MISS SMITH (*Pointedly, to* MR. WEATHERBY): And this is the last time I'll take anybody's word about the age of his family tree.

MR. WEATHERBY (*Waving his arm in direction of departed Pilgrims*): Just because there was no Weatherby family among those fakes?

MRS. WEATHERBY (*Whimpering*): I don't feel very well. I want to go home!

GUIDE: O.K., O.K. We'll try to retrace our steps.

JOE: I'm starving.

MR. WEATHERBY: Why don't you try eating some of the pasteboard turkey those stupid actors left on the table. (JOE *looks at turkey as* GUIDE *leads others off right.*)

JOE: I *could* eat a pasteboard turkey I'm so hungry. (*He goes to turkey, pulls off a leg and takes a bite.*) Say. It's not bad. (*He takes another bite.*) Not bad at all! It's . . . it's the best turkey I've ever tasted! It's great! (*Calling after tourists*) Wait a minute, everybody! (*He runs after them.*) Wait a minute! (*He exits right. After a short pause,* RAINBOW *and* MOONBEAM *come back in at left.*)

MOONBEAM: They're gone. (*Pointing to turkey*) You were right. We did leave the turkey here. Imagine forgetting the most important part of Thanksgiving dinner!

RAINBOW: I'll take the tablecloth. (MOONBEAM *picks up turkey platter, and* RAINBOW *folds tablecloth.*)

MOONBEAM: Oh! Don't forget my transistor radio! (RAINBOW *looks under bush, holds up radio.*)

RAINBOW: Here it is. (*Shaking her head*) I hope those people find their way back to Boston.

MOONBEAM: We'll have a good dinner in spite of it all. Let's go. (*Singing, as she proudly carries turkey off left*) "Over the river and through the woods. . . ."

RAINBOW (*Joining in*): "To Grandmother's house we go." (*They exit, singing, as curtain falls.*)

THE END

Production Notes

PEACE, PILGRIM

Characters: 8 male; 7 female. As many extras for male and female Pilgrim Diners as desired.

Playing Time: 40 minutes.

Costumes: Guide wears uniform and an official-looking cap, and carries a map. Tourists wear modern, everyday street dress (suits for men, suits or dresses, hats and heels for women). Indians wear appropriate costumes of buckskin, etc., and change into elaborate seventeenth century costumes for dinner. Pilgrims wear appropriate costumes, and the men carry cardboard muskets.

Properties: Map, transistor radio, bongo drum, turkey for Pilgrim, card tables and folding chairs, tablecloth, dishes, silverware, candlesticks, glasses, bowl of fruit, platters of food, tray of crackers, large turkey on a platter.

Setting: A clearing in a forest. At back and left and right are bushes, representing the forest. Those at left should be big enough to conceal card tables, chairs, bongo drum, and radio. A few rocks or logs are down right. There are exits at right and left.

Lighting: No special effects.

Last Stop

Characters

IRENE STEWART, *a spoiled girl of 17*
MARTHA STEWART, *her sister*
SANDY BEECH, *an ambitious girl*
ETHEL, *a waitress*
BESSIE, *the hotel's proprietress*
REEVES DONOVAN
CHUCK YANKOVICH
PAUL
RADIO ANNOUNCER'S VOICE

SETTING: *The porch and street in front of a dilapidated hotel in a Western ghost town.*
AT RISE: *The lights are dimmed, and from offstage, the sound of a distant windstorm can be heard.* PAUL *enters followed by* REEVES, IRENE, *and* MARTHA.

PAUL (*To* IRENE): You're not being much help.
IRENE: I don't intend to be much help. I'm exhausted, hot, bored. And I'm quite fed up. I just want to sit down in the shade.

94

MARTHA (*Looking around*): Why couldn't we have come here for our picnic? This place has atmosphere! (*Sits on steps*)

IRENE: It depends on what kind of atmosphere you want. (*Sits down on porch steps, then sighs deeply*) When I think of that beautiful car just one big *wreck!*

REEVES (*In a bored tone*): It was insured.

IRENE: But Daddy will never buy me a car like that again!

REEVES: He'll just give you a lecture and tell you not to go out with me any more.

MARTHA: He's already tried that routine.

IRENE (*To* MARTHA, *sarcastically*): Oh, thank you, sister dear. I don't know why I dragged you along on this trip, anyway.

PAUL (*Moving to center*): The point is that Reeves had our lives in his hands.

REEVES (*Casually*): I was just having fun.

IRENE (*Standing*): You didn't have to drive at one hundred miles an hour!

PAUL: One hundred and ten. I was watching over his shoulder.

IRENE (*To* REEVES): All because you wanted to race sweet little Sandy Beech and that miserable Chuck Yankovich in his hot rod.

REEVES: We were winning, weren't we?

IRENE: And who's going to give you a silver loving cup for that?

MARTHA: Don't blame Reeves. Nobody could have seen anything, with all that sand blowing around us.

IRENE (*Bowing with a flourish*): Well! Bow to the Reeves Donovan Fan Club. I didn't know there was anything between you two, Martha dear.

MARTHA (*Challenging* IRENE): Could *you* have seen?

IRENE (*Haughtily*): Reeves always drives at one hundred and ten miles an hour, sis. In fog, in tornadoes, in sandstorms.

REEVES (*Annoyed*): Come off it, Irene. You were cheering me on.

IRENE (*Strolling back and forth on porch*): Poor Sandy! What a pity! Imagine a sweet little belle named Sandy Beech being blasted in a sandstorm. Too bad she isn't famous. It would make a good headline. "Desert Sands Cover Sandy Beech."

PAUL (*Concerned*): What *did* happen to Sandy and Chuck, anyway?

REEVES: It's hard to notice anything when you're crawling through the desert on your hands and knees.

IRENE: Don't worry about them. Sandy's indestructible. (*In a lighter tone*) Oh, Reeves! You should have seen yourself! You looked so funny crawling along.

REEVES (*Angrily*): I can out-crawl, out-swim, out-anything-you-want-to-name any fellow in school, and you know it!

IRENE: What about Chuck Yankovich? Now, there's a man!

REEVES: Why is it that whenever a new guy comes to town he's automatically better than anybody else?

IRENE (*Snapping at* REEVES): What about new girls—like Sandy?

REEVES (*Eagerly*): What *about* Sandy!

IRENE (*Mocking*): "I do declare, Reeves, honey, you're just about the handsomest thing." It would be more like her to say, "I just love your money, sugar."

REEVES: So what if I can show her a good time? The poor kid hasn't had very much.

IRENE: And what does she care if she steps on anybody, so long as she gets to the right side of the tracks.

MARTHA: Cut it out, will you?

IRENE: Why, Martha! You're absolutely agitated. (IRENE *settles herself in a porch chair.*) Why don't you poke your nose inside this place and see whether there's a bath.

MARTHA (*Sarcastically*): I'm sure there's a bath and air-conditioning, too.

PAUL: We'll have to call home and tell them where we are.

REEVES: I'll bet the lobby is lined with phone booths.

IRENE: Send a wire, then. Just get us out of here.

MARTHA (*Feigning inspiration*): We'll go down to the railroad station, that's where we'll go! The little man who sells the tickets also sends the telegrams. It's just like the old western movies.

PAUL (*Taking his cue from* MARTHA): Hark! I can hear the distant whistle of the 12:02 right now. Folks around these parts kinda wait for that 12:02. Makes 'em know there's a great, big world out there somewhere. And makes 'em glad they're livin' quiet-like here in friendly old Silvergulch.

IRENE: Very funny, Paul.

REEVES: I saw that one at the drive-in last month. (*To* IRENE) I took Sandy—to answer the question you were just going to ask, Irene.

IRENE: My, my! Aren't you the mind reader!

MARTHA: How could we tell anybody to come get us if we don't even know where we are?

IRENE: Your quaint little telegraph man should know where he's sending telegrams from, Martha dear.

MARTHA (*Laughing*): Maybe he's lost, too.

IRENE (*Jumping to her feet*): Oh, what's the use. As usual, I suppose I'll have to do everything myself.

PAUL: That's not quite fair, Irene. Look. (*He holds up radio and the camera.*) I carried your transistor radio and Polaroid camera through the desert. Now, how's that for devotion?

IRENE (*Grabbing radio and turning dials*): Thanks a lot. You're a real hero! (*She bangs radio, then shakes it.*) What's the matter with this thing? (*Radio emits scratchy sounds.* IRENE *turns off the radio and moves toward hotel entrance.*)

PAUL: If you can't find a telephone in there, try to come up with a ghost or two.

IRENE (*Turning briefly*): It would be a pretty hard-up spook that would bother haunting this place. (*As she reaches door,* BESSIE *bustles out, carrying a large register.*)

BESSIE: O.K., kids, sign the register. (*She holds out register and pencil.*)

IRENE (*Startled*): Good grief!

MARTHA: Where did you come from?

BESSIE: Wait a minute! I'm the one who asks the questions around here. This is my place, you're the strangers, and it should be obvious that I came from in there. Now (*She holds out the register*), sign the register, and don't be fresh.

IRENE: We have no intention of staying here.

BESSIE: That makes no difference. You're here now, and I have to keep a record of these things.

REEVES: You mean this place is really a hotel?

BESSIE (*Pointing to sign*): Can't you read signs?

PAUL (*Moving forward*): If you'll show me to the telephone, we'll make arrangements to be on our way as soon as possible.

BESSIE: Sorry, kids. No phone.

MARTHA: Then we'll send a wire.

BESSIE: No telegraph, either.

IRENE: Look, whoever you are . . .

BESSIE: I'm called Bessie by most people, even by some raggedy kids in off the street.

IRENE (*Brushing at her clothes*): We're not exactly used to spending our afternoons in a sandstorm.

BESSIE: Smart folks stay indoors.

REEVES: We were on a picnic, Bessie—an all-day outing. The sandstorm blew up out of nowhere and wrecked our car.

MARTHA: We dragged ourselves through the sand and ended up here quite by accident.

IRENE: Now you see, don't you?

BESSIE: Sure! You'll be stayin' here 'til you leave. How about some iced tea while you're waitin'?

MARTHA (*Pleased*): Oh, I'd love some.

PAUL: What we'd really like to know is how we're going to get out of here.

BESSIE: Most folks don't stay too long.

REEVES (*In an affected manner*): What a shame, Bessie. Such an interesting hotel, and run by such a charming woman. We'd spend weeks here if we could, but we have to get back to school.

PAUL (*To* REEVES): She understands.

BESSIE: Sure I understand. I don't mind bein' flattered, not even by a wild kid.

REEVES: I'm no kid!

IRENE: And he's not very wild. He just likes to make girls think a date with him is a great adventure.

BESSIE (*To* IRENE): You're kinda spoiled and nasty, aren't you, girl?

IRENE (*Imperiously*): Do you know who my father is?

REEVES (*Echoing* IRENE's *tone*): Irene's father is a very important person.

BESSIE (*Unimpressed*): We've had a few important people stop here from time to time. Even had a movie star once.

IRENE (*Sneering*): Old mining towns are so picturesque.

BESSIE: You look at it any way you like, dearie. I'll send out the tea. (*She moves to the hotel door.*)

PAUL: But we still haven't made arrangements for leaving here.

BESSIE (*Stopping and turning*): There's a bus that comes through now and again.

PAUL: Do you have a schedule? A bus schedule?

BESSIE: It doesn't run on any schedule as far as I know.

IRENE (*Sarcastically*): I suppose it's easy to lose track of time in a garden paradise like this.

BESSIE: Why don't you relax? You can't get out of here before the next bus comes.

REEVES (*With a bow*): You're so comforting, Bessie. (*She exits.*)

IRENE: She's straight out of a horror movie.

PAUL: I don't think I'd go out of my way to annoy her, if I were you.

REEVES: We were being as polite as can be!

IRENE: Well? Are we trapped in this hole? There must be some way to contact the civilized world.

MARTHA (*Sitting on the steps*): She told you to relax.

PAUL: I suppose we're lucky the place is on a bus route.

IRENE (*Pacing*): Nobody's going to make me believe she runs this place without a telephone or delivery service or something. She must have electricity. How else would she make ice for the tea? And where there's electricity, there's a little man who comes around to read the meter.

MARTHA: I didn't know you knew about such things.

PAUL: We might just as well relax and wait for the bus. (*Lights begin to come up.* SANDY *enters at right.*)

SANDY (*Calling back over her shoulder*): Here they are,

Chuckie! Right here on that porch. (*To others*) Hi, y'all!

IRENE (*Disgusted*): The voice of the minx.

REEVES (*Delighted*): It's Sandy!

IRENE: Sandy, honey! I was taking it for granted you were buried in a sand dune. (SANDY *walks to center.* CHUCK *enters right, and follows her.*)

SANDY: That cute li'l ol' sports car turned over four times. It's amazin' we got out alive, but here we are without one itty-bitty scratch.

CHUCK: Man! Wait'll you see me win next year at Indianapolis.

SANDY: What can you win there, sugar?

IRENE (*With exaggerated friendliness*): Sit down, Sandy honey.

SANDY: Thank you kindly, Irene. My, but all that sand and dust on your face makes you look dried up!

IRENE (*Sweetly*): I do declare! A carnivorous magnolia!

SANDY (*Sweetly, to* CHUCK, *as she continues to look at* IRENE): Chuckie, why do you want to go for anythin' that looks like that?

IRENE (*Furiously*): Now you look here!

SANDY (*Patting* IRENE'*s hand*): But I couldn't blame you for going after him. He's just been tellin' me his daddy's struck somethin' or other in Tulsa. What do they strike in Tulsa, Chuckie?

IRENE: Ambitious little girls who talk too much, I hope. (IRENE *and* SANDY *glare at one another.*)

PAUL (*Moving left*): I'm going to walk up the street and see whether there's anything else alive around here.

REEVES (*Following* PAUL): I'll go along, if you don't mind.

PAUL: Anyone else? Chuck?

CHUCK (*Joining them*): Sure. I'm not tired. What kind of town is this, anyway?

REEVES: A ghost town. Obviously.

CHUCK: Terrific, man. Maybe we could all come back some-time and throw a swingin' party.

PAUL: Right now, I think we're more concerned with get-ting *out* of here.

CHUCK: Why, man? What do you have to go home to, any-way? (CHUCK, PAUL *and* REEVES *exit*.)

MARTHA: And as the sun sinks slowly in the west . . .

SANDY (*Annoyed*): You keep your eyes off Chuck, hear?

MARTHA: I wouldn't dream of looking at a boy who couldn't pass third grade.

IRENE (*To* SANDY): And while we're on the subject, why don't you keep away from Reeves' bank account?

SANDY (*Moving away from* IRENE): You know, I met a beauty contest judge one time. He thought I was the prettiest li'l thing he'd ever seen, and he said, "Sandra," he said, "there's one thing to remember if you want to get to the top in life. It don't matter . . ."

IRENE: It doesn't matter.

SANDY: That's the way he spoke: "It don't matter how you get to the top. You can walk there or ride in a limousine. The only thing you want to do is get there." (*Harshly*) I'd sooner ride in a limousine myself.

IRENE: And how long did he think the trip would take you?

MARTHA: That's enough out of both of you. (*She stands up.*) I've had to listen to that sort of thing all day long, and I'm not about to listen to it any more.

IRENE: Go ahead and leave. I don't care.

MARTHA (*To* SANDY): Your dark roots are showing, Sandy.

SANDY (*Nervously patting her hair*): They are? Where? I touched it up yesterday.

IRENE (*Laughing uproariously as* MARTHA *snickers*): Ha! Look at her panic! Good work, Martha. You're back in the family.

SANDY: Humiliatin', that's what it is. And from a dumpy ol' bookworm.

IRENE: One of the first rules of the game you're playing is to keep up your guard on all sides.

MARTHA: It's not an easy thing to do. (ETHEL, *a waitress, enters from hotel, carrying a tray on which are glasses and a pitcher. She has a white tablecloth over her arm.*)

ETHEL: I hope you don't mind iced tea without any ice in it. We don't have electricity here, and deliveries aren't what they once were.

SANDY: Don't you have anything but iced tea?

IRENE: A malted for Miss Beech with a pinch of strychnine on the side.

ETHEL (*Spreading the cloth on the table*): I thought there were four of you. (*She pours three glasses of tea.*)

MARTHA: There are six now. The boys went for a walk. (*Taking a glass from* ETHEL) Thank you.

ETHEL: You're welcome. We don't have any lemon or sugar, either.

SANDY: What kind of place is this?

ETHEL: I hope you'll be comfortable. It may be some time before the bus arrives.

IRENE: Bessie said it doesn't run on any particular schedule.

ETHEL: Bessie may look like a character, but she knows what she's talking about. She's been here since long before I came.

IRENE: And when was that?

ETHEL: In June—1940.

SANDY (*Laughing*): Oh, come on, now, honey. You're hardly any older than I am.

ETHEL (*Ignoring* SANDY *and moving to hotel entrance*): Ring if you want anything more.

SANDY (*To* ETHEL): Consider I've rung. (ETHEL *stops at door and looks back at* SANDY.)

ETHEL: Yes?

SANDY: What's this about waitin' for a bus? I want to get out of here.

ETHEL: You'll have to be patient.

SANDY: Patient! Who could be patient hangin' 'round this fallen-down cracker crate? (ETHEL *exits*.)

MARTHA (*Tasting the tea*): It's bitter.

IRENE: At least it's liquid.

SANDY: I want to see some bright lights. I want to go dancin' tonight and have some fun!

MARTHA: Oh, stop whining. We've all had it with the desert today, and some of us have had it with you, too.

IRENE: Maybe the boys will be getting some help.

SANDY: Chuckie will get help. He'll get me out of here if he has to go to the ends of the earth.

IRENE: Oh, let's hope so. You deserve each other. (*Standing*) Come on, Martha. The boys may have found an abandoned gold mine.

SANDY: I'm sittin' right here 'til that bus comes.

IRENE: That's a relief. I thought you might want to follow us.

SANDY: I'm followin' nobody, sugar. Not now, not ever.

IRENE: Good. You just sit there and flounce your crinoline. (IRENE *and* MARTHA *start to exit left*.)

SANDY (*Shouting after them*): Just 'cause you're a spoiled li'l rich girl, don't go takin' a high-handed tone with me!

IRENE (*To* MARTHA): Funny. I can't imagine why a girl like that could be so popular.

MARTHA: It is funny. I used to wonder the same thing about you. (IRENE *looks quickly at* MARTHA, *and they exit left. There is a pause, as* SANDY *looks after them, pouting.* BESSIE *enters from hotel and walks up behind* SANDY.)

BESSIE: Did you sign the register?

SANDY (*Jumping to her feet, startled*): You ol' crone! What do you mean sneakin' up an' scarin' people like that?

BESSIE: Where are the others? I just wondered if everything was all right.

SANDY: No, ma'am, everything is not all right!

BESSIE: Too bad. But I guess we're used to taking things as they come around here.

SANDY: Look here, my name is Sandy Beech, and I demand a li'l attention.

BESSIE (*Looking up and down the street*): I hope they didn't wander too far off. Might miss their bus.

SANDY: Well, I'm not missin' it, not me!

BESSIE: My name's Bessie. I run this place.

SANDY: Well, goody for you, sugar.

BESSIE: Why don't you amuse yourself while you're waitin'?

SANDY (*Defiantly*): Doin' what?

BESSIE: Girl, if you don't know, don't ask me. Might be a good idea for you to hold your tongue a little, though.

SANDY: If you aren't the limit!

BESSIE (*Going back into the hotel*): Maybe it's just too late. (*She exits.* CHUCK *enters left.*)

SANDY (*Calling after her*): Too late for what?

CHUCK: It's always too late for something, baby.

SANDY: When you're as old as that hag, maybe, but not for me! (*Hurrying to* CHUCK'S *side*) Come on, Chuckie. Let's get out o' here. This place is givin' me the creeps.

CHUCK: Just calm yourself and sit down. What do you want to do, walk home? How many days do you think that would take?

SANDY: At least we might get there.

CHUCK: I'll take the bus, thanks.

SANDY: What's the matter with you? I'd expect a man to carry me across the desert, if he had to.

CHUCK: But I don't have to. I'm just not that desperate.

SANDY: Are you making a play for Irene Stewart? Are you? 'Cause if you are, I have some other fish to fry.

CHUCK (*With enthusiasm*): You look so pretty today, honey. (SANDY *relaxes*.) You know we were goin' over a hundred miles an hour? With the wire wheels flashin' in the sun, and you with your hair blowin' pretty in the wind, and your scarf flyin', you really looked pretty as a picture.

SANDY: Jus' like that movie! Remember? The one with all the surf-ridin'? Maybe I'll be in the movies some day. I think I'd like that.

CHUCK: Sure. You'd be great.

SANDY: I've been takin' singin' lessons. An' you know I can dance pretty well. (*She moves forward and begins dancing by herself as* CHUCK *notices table.*)

CHUCK: I'm hungry.

SANDY: Ever see me do this step, Chuckie? (*She continues to dance in rapt concentration.* CHUCK *pours a little tea into a glass and tastes it.*)

CHUCK: Is this iced tea?

SANDY: That's what the waitress called it.

CHUCK: Waitress? You mean there's food in this place?

SANDY: How should I know? There's an ol' witch spookin' around inside. Go ask her. (*Dancing*) One, two, one and two. (CHUCK *goes into hotel.*) One, two. One, two, one and two. (REEVES *saunters in slowly, leans on the porch rail, and watches* SANDY *dance.*)

REEVES: There's my girl.

SANDY (*Gradually slowing down her dancing and smiling*): Why, Reeves Donovan! I thought you'd forgotten all about me.

REEVES: Wait'll we get back home.

SANDY (*Breathlessly*): Oh, Reeves! Can we go to a real fancy

place where I can wear an outfit that'll knock 'em all
dead?

REEVES (*Laughing*): You name it! There ought to be a few
good parties this weekend, too.

SANDY: Come on, honey. Try this step with me. Will there
be dancin' at the parties?

REEVES (*Beginning to imitate* SANDY's *dancing motions*):
There will be if you're there.

SANDY: You know what I was jus' thinkin'? I was jus'
thinkin' that I ought to be in the movies. Now how's
that for an idea? Then I could be rich an' famous an'
have everyone fallin' at my feet.

REEVES: You're doing well enough as you are.

SANDY: Why, thank you, sir. (*Continuing to dance*) One,
two. That's the way.

CHUCK (*Entering from hotel*): There's nothing to eat in
this crummy joint. (*Seeing* SANDY *and* REEVES) Hey!
What're you two doin'?

SANDY: Dancin', of course. You can see that.

CHUCK (*Annoyed*): Well, cut it out.

SANDY: Don't you get snippy with me, Chuck Yankovich.
When a lady wants to dance, she wants to dance, and if
one fella's more interested in eatin' than obligin' a
lady's wishes, then another fella's goin' to come along,
sure as anythin'.

CHUCK (*Angrily*): Cut it out, I said. (REEVES *stops dancing
as* CHUCK *approaches him with his fists clenched*.) You've
never felt these knuckles on that nice, snobby nose of
yours.

PAUL (*Entering behind* CHUCK, *from left*): Take it easy,
Yankovich. We've got knuckles, too.

CHUCK (*Turning on* PAUL): Gangin' up on me? All right.
I can lick you both.

SANDY (*Delighted*): You goin' to have a fight over me?

PAUL: We're not going to have a fight over anybody. We have other things to worry about. This town looks as though there hasn't been a human being around for a hundred years. Except Bessie, I guess.

SANDY: That sure is stretchin' the meanin' of humanity, honey.

PAUL: Where's Irene?

SANDY: Why, she went lookin' for you. Doesn't that just fill you with thrills? Why, look at him! He's blushin' to the ears!

PAUL: Cut it out, Sandy. (*To the others*) Any word of the bus? I hope Bessie wasn't making that up.

REEVES: If there isn't any bus, we'll have to walk, that's all.

SANDY: You'll carry me across the desert, won't you, Reeves?

CHUCK: Look. Bessie's livin' here. She has to get food and stuff from someplace. She didn't make that tea from sagebrush.

SANDY: You didn't taste it.

CHUCK (*To* SANDY): Go find Bessie, honey.

SANDY (*Sitting*): Uh-uh. Not me. You brought me here, and you're gettin' me back home. I want a man who can take care o' me.

REEVES (*Going to hotel door*): I'll find her.

SANDY: There. That's better than knockin' somebody in the jaw to win a lady's favor, I'd say. (*To* REEVES *as he exits*) Come back soon. (*She giggles.*)

PAUL (*Visibly annoyed*): Can't you think of something sensible to say for once?

SANDY: I didn't know I could make you lose your temper.

CHUCK (*To* PAUL): Listen, you runt, you just don't go talkin' that way to a lady.

PAUL: You're right. The deadly species is immune to its own poison.

SANDY (*Standing quickly*): Paul, just what do you mean by that? You hit him, Chuckie, hit him right now!

CHUCK: It'll be a pleasure. (*He lunges at* PAUL, *who ducks and steps aside.* CHUCK *goes sprawling to the ground, as* IRENE *and* MARTHA *enter, stop and stare.* SANDY *laughs, and* CHUCK *looks up to see* MARTHA *and* IRENE.) It wasn't fair. I tripped!

SANDY: Pick yourself up, Chuckie honey. What's Irene to think with you flat on your face in the dirt like that? (CHUCK *gets to his feet.*)

PAUL (*To* MARTHA): Did you find anything?

MARTHA: A lot of broken-down buildings, all of them empty.

IRENE: It's very strange. Everything is abandoned, as if nothing were alive or real here but us. (BESSIE *enters from hotel with* REEVES.)

SANDY: Don't get the idea everybody aroun' here's for real, either, sugar.

BESSIE: Now, what's the trouble?

PAUL: We were wondering about the bus.

BESSIE (*Impatiently*): Land sakes' alive, I told you about that. What's the matter with you kids? Are you deaf, or don't you believe what people tell you?

PAUL: We only want to be sure.

IRENE: There is a bus, isn't there?

BESSIE: Well, I'm not one to give you a wild story, and I'm not one to go repeatin' myself all the time, either.

CHUCK: But what if the bus doesn't come this time?

REEVES: You said it didn't run on any schedule.

BESSIE: I know what I said.

MARTHA: How often does the bus usually come?

BESSIE: Can't say. It depends on how often people are waitin' for it, I guess.

SANDY: That doesn't make any sense at all! How could the

bus driver know how many people are waitin' for him here, if you can't call him or anythin'?

CHUCK: I know! Pony express!

BESSIE: Well, if you kids want to joke about it, go right ahead, but don't go expectin' me to sit around here tryin' to give you straight answers to a lot of stupid questions. I have work to do.

PAUL: What work do you do?

BESSIE: Oh, I see. You think my place looks as if nobody tends to it much, eh?

MARTHA: He didn't say that.

SANDY: There she goes, hoppin' to lover boy's defense.

BESSIE: So the place doesn't look like the Ritz. Can't say that there's much inspiration around here to do any fussin' or fixin'.

REEVES (*Affectedly*): The place looks lovely, Mrs. Bessie— just the way a desert inn ought to look.

BESSIE: The place looks awful. It always *has* looked awful, even when the town was boomin'.

IRENE: How long ago was that?

BESSIE: Eighty years. Ninety years.

SANDY: Back when she was a teen-ager.

BESSIE (*To* SANDY): You're not a very nice little girl, are you?

SANDY (*Innocently*): Why, I pride myself on my sweet, lovin' an' gentle ways!

CHUCK: Well, how about it, Bessie? How do you manage to live here?

REEVES: We've walked around town. Nobody lives here but you and Ethel.

BESSIE: I know that!

MARTHA: What do you do for companionship?

PAUL: And the practical things, Bessie, like food. Where do you get your food?

BESSIE: I grow it—shoot it when I have the chance.

CHUCK: Bullets, then. Where do you get those?

IRENE: Or tea?

BESSIE: If you aren't the nosiest kids! I'll show you the storeroom sometime. People lived around here long before supermarkets came along, you know.

SANDY: Not all alone, they didn't.

BESSIE (*To* SANDY): I reckon I know a lot more 'bout that than you do. Besides, there's more than one way to be alone. (*Meaningfully, to* SANDY) I'd say a girl like you is about as alone as they come.

SANDY (*To* CHUCK): Are you goin' to let her get away with that?

BESSIE: Not much he can do about it.

SANDY (*Furious*): I haven't gone without a date one single night since I was fifteen years old.

BESSIE: That has nothin' to do with it.

IRENE: Bessie, I'm sure you mean well.

BESSIE: Sometimes I do, sometimes I don't, but you shouldn't go around patronizing old ladies.

MARTHA: Irene means that we're not looking for lectures.

BESSIE: I know, I know. It's not up to me. Somebody else'll take care of that end of it. But you deserve a lot more than a lecture, let me tell you.

SANDY: An' what for?

BESSIE: What for? For drivin' over the speed limit.

IRENE: You were eavesdropping!

BESSIE: Takin' other people's lives into your own hands, wreckin' private property, not to mention bein' as nasty as they come.

CHUCK: Anybody can have an accident.

REEVES: We were just having fun.

MARTHA: Bessie's right, and you know it.

PAUL: There's no use arguing now.

SANDY: Well, she sure wouldn't have to lecture (*To* PAUL *and* MARTHA) you two.

BESSIE: Oh, yes, I would. They went along for the ride, didn't they?

IRENE: You should have heard them screaming in the back seat. "Slow down! Stop! We'll all be killed!"

CHUCK: The world's prize party poops.

BESSIE: They should've stayed home. They knew what the rest of you were up to.

CHUCK: And just what are *you* up to, old lady?

REEVES: That's no way to . . .

BESSIE: I don't mind. I like bein' called a lady, and I don't fool myself about bein' old. But I'm not up to anythin'.

SANDY: Then quit flappin' your gums.

BESSIE (*To* SANDY): But if it were up to me, I'd start with you.

SANDY: All you have to do is find our bus, an' we'll go away an' bother you no more, ma'am.

BESSIE: Don't worry. I'll be glad to see you out of here, all right. If it was up to me, I'd have had that bus here hours ago.

REEVES: Why, Mrs. Bessie! I'll bet you'll shed more than one tear of sorrow when we leave.

BESSIE: You go bettin' like that and you'll lose an awful lot of gold, sonny. (*Going to the table*) Just amuse yourselves for a while. I'll clear these things away.

MARTHA: Why don't we take pictures with Irene's Polaroid camera?

REEVES: Good idea. Bessie, we'll want several pictures of you to show the folks back home.

SANDY: You know what? I have an inspiration.

IRENE: You're kidding.

SANDY: Why don't we take pictures of Bessie and that waitress and this whole town, and do a story on it for the paper?

MARTHA: I hate to admit it, but she's got something there.

SANDY: Sure I have, and I get most of the profit 'cause I thought of it first. An' I want a good, big picture of me in case the paper goes to Hollywood.

CHUCK: I'll send the paper to Hollywood myself, baby.

REEVES: Call the waitress, Bessie.

BESSIE: I can't see any harm in it. (*Calling*) Ethel?

IRENE (*Arranging the others in a stereotyped pose*): Let's see. You stand over there, Sandy, and, Bessie, you lean on the railing next to her. There. (*Backing up and looking into camera*) Like that. O.K. Got it!

BESSIE: I feel like a tintype. (ETHEL *enters.*) Come on, Ethel, get your picture taken.

SANDY: We'll make you famous.

REEVES: We might even drum up some business for your hotel, Bessie.

CHUCK: Make the town a tourist trap. What did you say was the name of this place?

BESSIE: I didn't say . . . but it's called Last Stop.

PAUL: Couldn't be better. You'll have to mark it on the map. (IRENE *removes picture from camera and waves it in the air.*)

IRENE (*Looking at picture*): Too bad. It didn't turn out. Well, we'll try another. Bessie and Ethel this time.

ETHEL: What shall I do?

IRENE: Stand there and smile at Bessie. (ETHEL *moves next to* BESSIE.) The rest of you get in back of them. (*All take places.*) There. Around to the left, Sandy.

SANDY: I don't want to be in the background.

IRENE (*Surveying group*): Good, that's fine. Then I'll take one of you alone, Sandy. There, now. Hold it. (*She takes picture.*)

BESSIE: Say, this is fun. Do you think that one came out?

IRENE: It should have.

ETHEL: I'll take the glasses back to the kitchen.

BESSIE: Good girl. (ETHEL *picks up tray of glasses.*)

SANDY: Say, how about the radio? We could have some music an' some dancin' while we're waitin'.

BESSIE: At least you won't be destroying anything.

CHUCK (*Laughing*): You've never seen her dance!

PAUL: We already tried the radio. There's too much static.

SANDY (*Fiddling with the radio*): Well, we'll just try it again. I know this radio's yours, Irene, but you won't mind, will you, honey?

IRENE (*Looking at second picture and speaking slowly*): No, I won't mind at all. (*Radio plays a popular song. There is no static.*)

SANDY: Hm-m-m. That was easy.

PAUL (*To* IRENE): How'd the picture turn out?

IRENE: It didn't. (ETHEL *goes into hotel.*) It's like the other one. You see? (*Shows it to* PAUL)

PAUL: Sure it turned out. There's the porch and the hotel. (MARTHA *and* REEVES *examine picture.*)

MARTHA: Yes. But where are we? Irene, you must have moved.

IRENE (*Flustered*): I didn't move! I had you focused perfectly.

SANDY (*Holding radio*): Listen to that swingin' sound! Civilization!

CHUCK: Come on, everybody. Let's dance! (*He and* SANDY *begin dancing while* PAUL, MARTHA, IRENE *and* REEVES *continue to examine pictures.*)

ANNOUNCER (*From radio*): And now the news. The state's

death toll from automobile accidents appears to have risen by six today.

SANDY: Darn the news.

ANNOUNCER: The burning wreckage of two cars that was spotted earlier by a weather bureau plane on a scouting run. . . .

SANDY: What's he talkin' about?

CHUCK: Quiet!

ANNOUNCER: . . . without any evidence of drivers or passengers. Helicopters have been sent to comb the vast desert area in search of possible survivors. Names of the six teen-agers believed to be involved in the accident will be withheld until . . . (*The static resumes.*)

SANDY: There it goes again. (*To* IRENE) I should've known it would be a no-good radio if it was yours.

CHUCK: Isn't this a stroke of luck, though! We're in the news! On the radio! Man, will that paper buy our story when we get back!

PAUL: It may not have been us he was talking about. (*The sound of distant engines is heard.*)

SANDY (*Running forward and looking up*): He's jus' got to be talkin' about us, 'cause look! See it? A helicopter! (*Others join* SANDY *and look up.* BESSIE *returns to hotel unnoticed.*)

REEVES (*Pointing*): There it is! Hey! We'll be out of here sooner than we thought! Back from the dead! I'll bet we go on TV.

IRENE: Come on. Let's signal them. Grab the tablecloth. Come on! (*While* CHUCK, SANDY, IRENE *and* REEVES *begin writing on tablecloth,* MARTHA *and* PAUL *return to chairs and sit quietly re-examining pictures.*)

CHUCK: Here. Give me your lipstick, Sandy.

SANDY: Mine's too pale, sugar.

IRENE: Here. Use mine.

SANDY: Mm-m. Love that shade, honey. (*As they write* HELP *on tablecloth, helicopter engines grow louder.*)

REEVES: That's it. They'd have to be blind to miss that. Now. Stand at one end, everybody, and wave. There. (*Calling*) Hey! Help!

CHUCK, IRENE *and* SANDY (*Ad lib*): Help! We're right down here! Hey! Here we are! (*Etc.*)

CHUCK: Look at him, man. He's dippin' down so low he's almost on top of us!

SANDY: I will go dancin' tonight! I will!

REEVES (*Screaming as the engine roar reaches its peak*): Lower the ladder! (*They all continue shouting until the engine noise begins to subside.*) Hey! What's he doing?

CHUCK: He's goin' off again!

REEVES: Help! Get us out of here!

SANDY: He looked right at us. I saw him!

IRENE: Come back! We're here! We're alive!

SANDY (*Hysterically*): You miserable . . . (*She collapses on steps, buries her head in her arms, and others stand silently as noise of helicopter fades.*)

MARTHA: I think . . . I think Sandy's the only person in the world I never thought I could feel sorry for, but I do.

IRENE (*Furiously*): How could they! How could they go off and leave us in this place!

CHUCK: Wait'll I get my hands on that guy.

PAUL (*In a controlled voice*): We'll wait. We may wait a long time.

CHUCK: Now where'd that Bessie go?

PAUL: She went back inside.

CHUCK: Stupid woman! (*He goes to hotel door.*) It's up to her to get us out of here now. (*He goes into the hotel.*)

REEVES (*Sitting next to* SANDY *and putting his arm around her*): It's O.K., honey. We'll get out of here one way or another.

IRENE (*Watching* REEVES): I always thought so, but I guess it doesn't matter.

MARTHA: Sit down. We'll just have to wait.

IRENE: I'll never forget the way that pilot looked at us—through us, almost. As if we weren't even there.

PAUL: Like these pictures. We weren't there, either.

MARTHA: I wonder who Bessie really is.

PAUL: And that girl—Ethel. Do you remember how long she said she'd been here? And Sandy was right. She didn't look any older than any of us. I thought she was kidding.

MARTHA: And Bessie. I thought she was kidding, too.

IRENE: It did happen the way the announcer said, didn't it? (*Pause*) And not a scratch on any of us. Sandy said that, too.

PAUL: I don't remember that the car burned. (CHUCK *returns, carrying register.*)

CHUCK: Well, where is she?

PAUL: I imagine that she's gone.

CHUCK: The only thing I found was this. (*He shows the register.*) And this note: "Show this to the bus driver, then leave it on the porch. Have a good trip. Love, Bessie." And look inside. You see? She has our names. Our full names written in this old-fashioned handwriting.

IRENE (*After a pause, quietly, with a glance toward* SANDY): Do you think Sandy knows?

PAUL: She may.

CHUCK (*Sitting down*): Funny old girl, that Bessie. (*Pauses*) I wonder what they're going to say about us back home.

MARTHA: I wonder, too.

CHUCK: I guess they'll call us all kinds of things, but we'll straighten it all out when we get back. They'll be so glad to see us, they'll forget about everything. (*Lights begin to dim.*)

IRENE: That would be nice, Chuck.

MARTHA (*After a pause*): It's almost time for dinner.

CHUCK: I don't feel hungry or thirsty or anything, any more.

PAUL: That's good. I wonder how long we'll have to wait.

CHUCK (*Jumping up*): Say! How about some music? (*He turns on radio. Music is heard.*) Well? Doesn't anybody want to dance? (*They shake their heads slowly.*) Huh. Anybody'd think you were half dead. (*He stops, turns slowly to look at his friends, who remain seated and immobile as the lights grow dimmer. Music continues playing, as curtain falls.*)

THE END

Production Notes

LAST STOP

Characters: 3 male; 5 female; 1 male voice (radio announcer).

Playing Time: 35–40 minutes.

Costumes: Everyday modern dress for teen-agers. Bessie wears very old clothes, and Ethel has on a waitress's uniform.

Properties: Portable radio, camera, white tablecloth, tray with glasses and pitcher, lipstick, register, pencil, note.

Setting: The porch and street in front of a dilapidated hotel in a Western ghost town. The set should be imaginative rather than realistic, with the doorway into the hotel, broken windows, hotel's sign, porch steps and railing silhouetted against a light backdrop. On the porch are a table and some wooden chairs.

Lighting: Lights come up and are dimmed, as indicated in text.

Sound: Windstorm, static and music from the radio, engines of helicopter.

Another Man's Family

Characters

HARRY SMITH
MILDRED SMITH, *his wife*
JUNIOR
STEPHANIE } *his teen-age children*
ALFIE, *Stephanie's date*
MR. PHILLIPS-BIRT, *Alfie's father*
ACE McSHANE, *Junior's friend*
YOUNG HARRY, *Harry Smith as a teen-ager*
DAD
MOM } *his parents*
GWEN, *his sister*
ROBBIE, *her date*
CHARLIE HART, *Young Harry's friend*
TELEVISION ANNOUNCER'S VOICE
TWO LADIES
SINGERS } *voices in television commercials*
RADIO ANNOUNCER'S VOICE
LADY
SINGERS } *voices in radio commercials*

Scene 1

Time: *The present.*

Setting: *The Smiths' typical American living room.*

At Rise: Mr. Smith *is reading a newspaper,* Mrs. Smith *is sewing a dress, and* Junior *is sprawled on the floor, eating popcorn and watching a television set which faces upstage so the picture is out of view of the audience.*

Announcer (*From television set*): There we have it, folks, another heart-warming session with the Jones family in "Leave It to Pop," the story of kind, generous, hilarious Pop Jones, his understanding wife and their happy brood of typical teens. Tune in next week, when Pop thinks he's signing Junior's report card but is actually signing a loan to buy Junior a new Jaguar XKE. (Mr. Smith *puts down his paper,* Mrs. Smith *chuckles,* Junior *laughs heartily.*) Remember . . . this show has been brought to you by Buffo, the new floor wax by Peterson's. Shall we drop in on a typical American kitchen?

1st Lady (*From television set*): Lucille, what are you using to wax your floor?

2nd Lady (*From television set*): Something new. Look.

1st Lady (*From television set*): That's not new. That's old Buffo.

2nd Lady (*From television set*): This is the *new* Buffo! With a new *secret* ingredient. My floor is so shiny, it's the envy of the neighborhood. And new Buffo is so easy to use, even my husband can wax the floors. (Mr. Smith *leans forward to listen, and* Mrs. Smith *smiles.*)

1st Lady (*From television set*): I'm going to buy my husband a can of Buffo for his birthday! (*Background music for commercial is heard as* Mr. Smith *goes to set and turns it off.*)

MR. SMITH: Junior, do you have to watch that silly junk?

JUNIOR: What else is there to watch until "Monster Man" comes on? Besides, I like Pop Jones.

MR. SMITH: You could do something else. Read a book. Improve your mind.

JUNIOR: I finished my homework when "Killer From Kansas" was on!

MR. SMITH: You might read something on your own. Isn't there anything you'd like to know more about?

JUNIOR: Sure! Girls!

MRS. SMITH: You asked for that one, Harry.

MR. SMITH (*Pacing about*): What drivel to do homework by! How can you concentrate?

JUNIOR: It isn't easy. Tonight I got so involved with algebra I almost missed a massacre. (*He goes to set and turns it on.*)

ANNOUNCER (*From television set*): And now, the continuing story of "Monster Man," a typical dentist from a small New England town in the year 3000.

MR. SMITH (*Collapsing onto chair*): Oh, no!

SINGERS (*From television set; singing to the tune of "Pop Goes the Weasel"*):

> Put Snappies in your breakfast bowl,
> Watch them dance and smile,
> As they explode in milk or cream
> You'll know your life's worthwhile!

MR. SMITH (*Standing suddenly*): Turn that off!

JUNIOR (*Meekly*): O.K., O.K. (*He turns off set, shakes his head.*) You're frothing at the mouth just like Pop Jones.

MR. SMITH (*Shouting*): Any similarity between Pop Jones and me is purely a figment of your imagination!

MRS. SMITH (*Looking up from sewing*): Pop Jones isn't so

bad, Harry. I don't see why you object to Junior's watching his show.

MR. SMITH: It's disgusting, that's why.

MRS. SMITH (*Standing, walking to him*): Why are you in such a foul mood, Harry? (*Patting him on the head*) Did you have a hard day at the office?

MR. SMITH: I always have a hard day at the office, but what does anybody around here care about how tough it is to make a living . . . to buy food . . . to buy TV sets! (MR. SMITH *slumps in his chair.* MRS. SMITH *returns to her sewing, and* JUNIOR *drapes himself on the arm of* MR. SMITH's *chair.*)

MRS. SMITH (*Chuckling*): I can hardly wait to see what happens to Pop Jones next week.

JUNIOR: Yeah—when he buys his son a Jaguar XKE. Can I have one of those, Dad?

MR. SMITH: Are you stark raving mad?

JUNIOR: I just thought I'd ask.

MRS. SMITH: You might have said yes, Harry. You know how preoccupied you are at times.

MR. SMITH (*Standing, pacing*): Well, that does it. I am sick and tired of these TV shows that picture the average American father as a buffoon, a clown who polishes floors and buys sports cars by mistake—and froths at the mouth to get laughs.

MRS. SMITH (*Standing, holding up dress*): Here, Harry. Try this on, will you?

MR. SMITH (*Indignantly*): I will not.

MRS. SMITH (*Sweetly*): I have to pin the hem.

MR. SMITH: Can't Stephanie try it on for you?

MRS. SMITH: She's getting ready for a date.

MR. SMITH: But she's always going out!

MRS. SMITH (*Placing a footstool at center*): She's popular,

Harry. I should think you'd be glad. You wouldn't want a daughter whose knees knocked and whose eyebrows grew together, would you?

MR. SMITH (*Protesting*): Let Junior try the dress on.

MRS. SMITH: I would, Harry, but some of his friends might walk by and see him through our typical American picture window, and what would they think?

MR. SMITH: But if any of *my* friends walked by our typical American picture window and saw me having my hem fixed, nobody would care!

MRS. SMITH: They'd understand, Harry. You're a father.

MR. SMITH: Like Pop Jones?

JUNIOR: Sure! He's the most typical father of all.

MRS. SMITH: The makers of Buffo say he is. (MR. SMITH *puts on dress.*)

JUNIOR (*Slyly*): And if you can't believe what the makers of Buffo say, what can you believe?

MR. SMITH: You'll swallow anything you hear on a commercial, won't you?

MRS. SMITH: Buffo is a good product, Harry. (MR. SMITH *steps up on stool.* MRS. SMITH *smiles slyly at* JUNIOR) And if the Buffo people say Pop Jones is the typical American father, then it just might be so. After all, doesn't Mrs. Jones seem like the typical American mother?

MR. SMITH: She does not. Always playing her husband for some kind of idiot. (MRS. SMITH *begins pinning hem.*) Always calling neighbors to talk about some new laundry product.

MRS. SMITH (*In a matter-of-fact tone*): You don't think the typical American woman is like that, Harry?

MR. SMITH: Always saying the right thing at the right time, smiling, in her neat gingham apron, and ruling the roost with an iron hand! No! There's nothing typical about that at all. And furthermore, if the teen-agers on the show were *my* children, I'd give them a good old-fashioned spanking and send them to bed without supper.

JUNIOR: Gee, Dad. Why?

MR. SMITH: Why not? Take the young boy on the show— the way he dresses in those shrunken pants and baggy shirts. (JUNIOR *looks at his own clothes.*) He hasn't had a haircut in months. (JUNIOR *shrugs.*)

MRS. SMITH: That's the style, Harry.

MR. SMITH: When I was a boy, I'd have been hooted off the streets if I ever let my hair grow like that. And the daughter on the show—

JUNIOR: Candy! She's cute.

MR. SMITH: One date after the other. She couldn't possibly have time to do her homework, yet we're supposed to believe she's a straight-A student.

MRS. SMITH: That reminds me, Harry. Stephanie brought home her exam reports today. She had straight A's. (MR. SMITH *smiles.*)

JUNIOR: Wonder how she managed that!

MR. SMITH (*Protesting*): She's brilliant.

JUNIOR: Maybe Candy Jones is brilliant, too. She talks as if she might be.

MR. SMITH: That's another thing. The language the kids use on that show. Nobody can understand them.

JUNIOR: But that's one of the funniest parts!

MR. SMITH: And their dancing and their shouting and wailing.

JUNIOR: That's music, Dad! (STEPHANIE *enters right, dressed according to the latest casual fad.*)

STEPHANIE: I'm ready. Where's Alfie? Gee, Dad, you look pretty silly in that getup. (*Approaching him*) I mean, if Alfie came in now, what would he think?

MR. SMITH: I gather he'd think I'm a typical American father!

STEPHANIE: Well, you look silly to me. Alfie's father would never dress up like that.

MR. SMITH: I am not "dressed up"! (*He starts to take dress off.*)

MRS. SMITH: I'll only be another minute, Harry. (*Continues to pin hem*)

MR. SMITH: Who is "Alfie," anyway?

JUNIOR (*Flopping into chair*): A creep.

STEPHANIE (*Haughtily*): He's Alfred Plompton Phillips-Birt III. They're in the social register.

JUNIOR: A real creep. But his old man's loaded.

STEPHANIE (*Whirling about to face* JUNIOR): Are you insinuating that I'd go out with a boy just because he has money?

JUNIOR: Sure. You're not stupid. You're ugly, but you're not stupid.

STEPHANIE: That's more than I can say for you.

MR. SMITH: Stop the bickering!

STEPHANIE: Alfie is the most distinguished, the most sophisticated gentleman in town. His father is English.

JUNIOR: I don't care if his father is the whole British Empire. Alfie is the missing link.

STEPHANIE: You should talk. The kids in school don't call you "Monk" for nothing.

JUNIOR (*Standing, facing his sister*): They call me "Monk" 'cause I have an ape for a sister.

STEPHANIE (*Shrieking*): Ape!

ALFIE (*Entering suddenly up center*): Here I am!

STEPHANIE (*Turning quickly*): Alfie! (MRS. SMITH *stands,* JUNIOR *slumps onto chair again, and* MR. SMITH *struggles to take off dress, then stops and extends his hand sheepishly to* ALFIE.)

MR. SMITH: Good evening, young man. I am Stephanie's father.

ALFIE (*Amused*): Well, hi, man! (*To* MRS. SMITH, *who nods and smiles*) Hi, Mrs. Smith. (*To* STEPHANIE) Ready, Steph?

STEPHANIE: I sure am, Heathcliff.

MR. SMITH (*Authoritatively*): You'll have Stephanie home by eleven!

ALFIE: Sure, Dad! The discothèque shuts up about five or six.

MR. SMITH: I mean eleven tonight!

STEPHANIE (*Indicating* ALFIE): He understands, Poppy. Nightie-night.

MRS. SMITH: Have a marvelous time, kids. (STEPHANIE *and* ALFIE *wave and exit*.)

MR. SMITH (*Finally shedding dress, giving it to* MRS. SMITH): What's a discothèque?

JUNIOR: Man, where've you been?

MRS. SMITH: A discothèque is a place where they play records so that people can dance—wave their arms in the air—you know.

MR. SMITH: A juke-joint, you mean.

JUNIOR: A what?

MRS. SMITH: Harry, really! (*Sitting*) Don't you think Alfie is a nice boy, Harry?

MR. SMITH (*Mumbling*): A nice boy! (*Loudly*) He's ill-mannered and sloppy, and I can't imagine why any self-respecting young lady would want to be seen in public with him. "Hi, man!" There's a greeting for you! No respect at all! And Stephanie—going out in that—that "outfit."

MRS. SMITH: What would you expect her to wear to a discothèque?

MR. SMITH (*Pacing about*): Just like the Pop Jones family.

I can see it! We're all headed straight downhill. Mildred, the average American family is being re-molded (*He waves his arm at TV.*) by that box. It's warping our minds! The average American home is nothing but a place to keep shiny so your neighbors will envy you while you spend all your time at a disco-place. The average American father is turned into a lunkhead who isn't worth any more consideration than, "Hi, man!" (*Dramatically*) It wasn't that way when I was a boy!

JUNIOR (*Standing, and starting to sneak out*): Uh-oh. Here it comes.

MR. SMITH: My father was a man we respected. When he spoke, everybody listened.

MRS. SMITH (*Smiling*): Your father was a dear man I could wrap around my finger.

MR. SMITH: He was crazy about you, Mildred, that's why. But with his family! Ah, *there* was the typical American father as he *should* be! No nonsense! Discipline! Values!

JUNIOR (*Softly*): Think I'll walk over to see Ace McShane.

MR. SMITH (*Carried away; shaking fist at television set*): Let me tell you, Mr. Television, you're not turning this man's castle into the kind of cage Pop Jones lives in! Things are going to change around here right now. (*He starts toward set, but stops when he sees* JUNIOR *leaving.*) And where are you going, young man?

JUNIOR (*Impatiently*): To see Ace McShane!

MR. SMITH: And how do you know Ace McShane wants to see you at this hour? (*He waves at clock.*)

JUNIOR: Ace likes to see me at any hour 'cause he's dumber than I am, and I help him with his homework.

MR. SMITH: Aha! Doing Ace's homework for him!

JUNIOR: *Help* him, I said! Gee, if this is the way your Dad treated you, it's no wonder you don't like Pop Jones. He's keen to his kids.

MR. SMITH: It is not the place of a father to be "keen to his kids" as if he were Santa Claus and the Easter Bunny rolled into one lovable package. It is the place of a father to be master in his own home and see that his children are brought up properly! I am your father, not your jolly buddy.

JUNIOR (*Weakly*): O.K.

MR. SMITH: I shall expect you home by ten o'clock.

JUNIOR: But, Dad!

MR. SMITH (*Booming*): Ten o'clock! And that is final! Your father has spoken, not Pop Jones!

JUNIOR (*Sadly*): Yeah.

MR. SMITH: Yes, sir! My father used to make us say, "Yes, Pater!"

JUNIOR (*Mumbling*): Yes, sir, Pater, sir. 'Bye, Mom.

MRS. SMITH (*Cheerfully*): 'Bye, dear. Say hello to Ace's mother for me.

JUNIOR: Sure, Mom. (*He exits.*)

MR. SMITH (*Proudly folding his arms*): Now. How's that, Mildred?

MRS. SMITH (*Putting away her sewing, not impressed*): Very masterful, Harry. I think I'll go over to see Vivian. (*She stands and removes her apron.*) She says she's found a new biodegradable detergent that cleans whiter than white.

MR. SMITH: Mildred! That is enough of that! There will be no more television talk in this house!

MRS. SMITH (*In same tone*): Vivian also found a new headache remedy that works faster than the other leading remedies and combines not one, not two, but five of the fatest-acting ingredients. See you later.

MR. SMITH (*Indignantly*): Why don't you give Vivian your leftover Buffo so that she can give it to her husband for his birthday?

MRS. SMITH: No use. He said he wouldn't wax a kitchen floor if the linoleum tile curled up and blew away. (*She exits.*)

MR. SMITH: Good for him! (*He goes to table, removes cloth.*) Yes, sir, Harry Smith, from now on, this house will be the way my home was when I was a boy. Good old Dad! A tower of strength, he was, a man we could look up to. (*He covers TV set with cloth*) Rest in peace, Pop Jones and "Monster Man." (*Facing audience*) Harry Smith is on the march! (*Curtain*)

*   *   *

SCENE 2

BEFORE RISE: JUNIOR *and* ACE McSHANE *enter in front of curtain from right.*

JUNIOR: Thanks for the soda, Ace.

ACE: You know me. Last of the big-time spenders. Anyway, I thought a walk and a soda might help. You're in for a rough time. I remember once my father got tough with us. He set us all on a work schedule, the kind he had when he was a kid, he said.

JUNIOR: What set your father off?

ACE (*Stopping*): Who knows? One day he just decided things were better when he was a kid. Can you imagine?

JUNIOR: How long did it last?

ACE: Two weeks. Mom got so fed up she invited my grandparents for a visit—my father's mother and father. They straightened things out. From what they said, my father's room was ten times worse than mine when he was my age, and the only chore he ever had to do was to take out the garbage, which he always forgot.

JUNIOR (*As they walk left*): You mean your grandfather wasn't as tough as your father remembered?

ACE: 'Course not. But my grandfather's father, wow! To hear Grandpop tell it, he really must've cracked the whip. (*Clapping* JUNIOR *on the shoulder*) Come on, Junior. Don't let it get you. Where's the happy-go-lucky, typical American teen-age boy we all know and love? Your father will snap out of it.

JUNIOR: Someday, maybe. But what happens in the meantime?

ACE: In the meantime you suffer.

JUNIOR: I wonder what things were really like when my father was a kid.

ACE: Terrible. No electricity, out to the pump every morning for water, walking five miles to school every morning after milking all the cows. Terrible! (*They exit left.*)

*   *   *

TIME: *1939.*

SETTING: *Living room of Harry Smith's parents. There are some old-fashioned, overstuffed chairs right and left; a table right, with an old-style radio on it; and a 1939 calendar on the wall.*

AT RISE: DAD (HARRY's *father*) *is reading paper*, MOM (HARRY's *mother*) *is knitting a dress.* YOUNG HARRY *is sitting in front of the radio, listening intently.*

ANNOUNCER (*From radio*): And there we have it, folks, another heartwarming session with Dad Young in "Another Man's Family." Until next week, when Dad Young thinks he's signing Junior's report card but is actually signing a loan to buy Junior a new Packard roadster (DAD *puts down the paper.* MOM *and* HARRY *laugh.*), remember . . . this lovable radio program has been brought to you by Peterson's, makers of the new floor wax, Buffo. (*Electric organ music*)

LADY (*From radio*): What's new about Buffo?

ANNOUNCER (*From radio*): Here. Read the label. It says N-E-W! That spells new! Old, reliable Buffo with a new *secret* ingredient.

LADY (*From radio*): Is this the wax that makes your floor the envy of the neighborhood?

ANNOUNCER (*From radio*): Right you are!

LADY (*From radio*): Is this the wax that's so easy to apply even husbands can do it? (*Giggles*)

ANNOUNCER (*From radio*): Right again. But how did you know?

LADY (*From radio*): My husband's been waxing our floor with Buffo for months! And is *he* the envy of the neighborhood!

DAD: Harry Smith, do you have to listen to that silly junk?

HARRY: What else is there to listen to until "Chicago Riot Act" comes on?

DAD: You could read a book. Improve your mind.

HARRY: But I finished my homework when I was listening to "The Lone Ranger."

DAD: How can you concentrate on your homework and listen to such drivel at the same time?

HARRY: I work at it.

ANNOUNCER (*From radio*): And now, "Chicago Riot Act," the show that brings big-time crime right into your living room!

SINGERS (*From radio; singing to the tune of "Twinkle, Twinkle, Little Star"*):

    Be a champion, be a winner,

    Make Mom give you hash for dinner!

    Not just any hash, that's certain,

    Just hash made by Sweet Ma Perkin!

DAD (*Standing*): Harry Smith, turn that off!

HARRY: But, Dad! I'll miss "Jack Armstrong, the All-American Boy!"

DAD: Turn it off!

HARRY (*Turning off radio*): When you get mad you sputter just like Dad Young.

DAD (*To* MOM): You see, Margaret? Radio makes the kids imagine all kinds of things.

MOM: But you do sputter when you're angry, dear. Not much. Just a little. (*Going to* DAD *and patting him on the head*) Did you have a hard day at the office, dear?

DAD: I always have a hard day at the office, but what does anybody around here care about how tough it is to make a living, to buy food . . . and radios.

HARRY: Can I have a Packard roadster, Dad?

DAD: Are you working at becoming a lunatic, Harry?

HARRY: Just thought I'd ask. You might have said yes.

MOM: You know how preoccupied you always are, dear.

DAD: That does it. I'm tired of these idiotic radio shows that make the average American husband and father sound like a baggy-pants comedian from a vaudeville act, a sputtering codger who is duped into buying his son a brand-new automobile—and gets laughs for doing it.

MOM (*Holding up dress*): Here, dear. Try this on, will you? I'm making it for your mother, and she's almost your size.

DAD: One indignity on top of another! (*Suddenly stares at* HARRY) Harry! What did you do to your hair?

HARRY (*Smiling*): I had it cut.

DAD: Cut? Shaved, you mean.

HARRY (*Proudly*): It's a crew cut.

MOM (*To* DAD): It's the style, dear.

DAD: When I was a boy, I'd have been hooted off the streets if I ever scalped myself like that.

HARRY: Sure, but there aren't any more Indians around now, so nobody cares.

DAD: Hear that, Margaret? Talking back to his father!

HARRY: I didn't think you'd mind a little joke. I always thought I could kid around with you . . . like kidding around with a good pal.

DAD (*As* MOM *gets out footstool*): I am not your pal. I am your father! I am lord and master of this typical American home! And I will not have my home ruined by a lot of crazy notions that are dispensed from that blasted little box. (DAD *puts on dress and* MOM *starts to pin hem.*)

MOM: But, dear, radio is here to stay.

DAD: Not in this house it isn't.

MOM: But I enjoy it, too. There are wonderful stories on all day about women doctors and career girls and backstage wives . . . and all kinds of helpful household hints. There's music, too.

DAD: Music? All I hear these days is a lot of notes up and down the scale—and pounding drums. No melody anymore.

MOM: Some of it is rather interesting. Take Benny Goodman, for instance.

DAD: Who?

HARRY: Mom's talking about swing.

MOM: Yes, dear. And some of the songs now are very engaging. I heard one this morning about a flat-foot something or other. (Gwen *enters.*)

HARRY: "A flat-foot floodgie with a floy-floy."

DAD (*Irate*): A what?

GWEN: A flat-foot floodgie, Pater.

HARRY (*To* GWEN): Speaking of flat feet, lover-boy hasn't arrived yet.

GWEN: I thought I'd be ready early for once. And Robbie doesn't have flat feet.

HARRY: Flat head, flat nose, flat chin. He looks as if somebody stepped on him all ways at the same time.

GWEN: If you aren't a miserable little drip.

DAD: Stop the bickering!

GWEN: We're not bickering, Pater. And I wish you'd take off that knit number before Robbie arrives.

DAD: If Robbie doesn't like my knit number, it's just too bad.

GWEN: I'm sure he's not used to seeing *his* father dressed up like a refugee from a Bette Davis movie.

DAD: Who is this "Robbie" anyway?

GWEN: Robertson Gilbertson Harrington II.

HARRY: A jerk.

GWEN: Why, you little creep.

HARRY: A rich jerk.

GWEN: Robbie's pater owns radio stock.

DAD: I hope you don't think that's commendable.

GWEN: And he's going to make more money in something called television.

ROBBIE (*Bursting in*): Greetings.

DAD: Who, may I ask, are you?

GWEN (*Nervously*): Pater, this is Robbie. (ROBBIE *extends his hand to* DAD, *who struggles out of dress with* MOM's *help*.)

ROBBIE: In the groove, Jackson! (MOM *nods and smiles.* ROBBIE *turns to* GWEN) Ready, Gwen?

GWEN: But definitely.

DAD: You'll have Gwendolyn home by ten?

ROBBIE: Sure. The juke-joint closes at two or three.

DAD: I mean ten tonight!

GWEN: Natch, Pater. Nightie-night!

MOM: Enjoy yourselves! Do a Charleston for me.

GWEN: Oh, Mother. Nobody does that anymore. Now it's swing. (*Waving, she and* ROBBIE *exit.*)

DAD: What's a juke-joint?

MOM: A place where they play records and dance. (*Sitting*) Don't you think Robbie is a nice boy?

DAD (*Muttering*): No respect. Sloppy. And Gwendolyn going out in that outfit. It wasn't like this when I was a boy.

MOM: Of course it wasn't.

HARRY: I think I'll go over to see Charlie Hart.

DAD: Things are going to be different around here. The radio is not going to turn this house into Dad Young's kind of bedlam.

HARRY: See you.

DAD: Where are you going, young man?

HARRY (*Impatiently*): To Charlie Hart's.

DAD: At this hour? To do what?

HARRY: To trade the tops from paper ice cream cups. (*Quickly*) I mean, I want to borrow a book.

DAD: See to it that you're back here by nine.

HARRY: Yes, Pater. 'Bye, Mom.

MOM: 'Bye, dear. (*Dropping dress, jumping up and following* HARRY) No. Wait, dear! I want to see Charlie's mother. She has a new vacuum cleaner I want to try.

HARRY: Charlie said she bought a whole new album of Tommy Dorsey records.

MOM (*Innocently*): Really, Harry? I didn't know that. Are they jivey? (*They exit.*)

DAD (*Taking cloth from table and putting it over radio*): Yes, things around here are going to change before this contraption does any more damage. I got along without a radio when I was a boy, and so will Harry. Time *can* march backward. The Smith house will be the way it was when my father was around. There was a tower of strength! Severe? Yes, but I thank him for it now. And Harry will thank me one day, too. You wait and see! (*Curtain*)

*   *   *

SCENE 3

BEFORE RISE: YOUNG HARRY *and* CHARLIE HART *enter in front of curtain from right.*

HARRY: Sure, I like my Dad, Charlie. But I never saw this side of him before. I never knew he was so old-fashioned.

CHARLIE: They all are at heart. I think it's just 'cause sometimes they wish they were kids again. My father always tells me this is the best time of my life. And then he sends me out to mow the lawn. Come on, Harry. Don't let it get you. Your father will pull out of it.

HARRY (*Doubtfully*): I hope so.

CHARLIE: What paper cup tops do you have to trade?

HARRY (*Dully*): One Clark Gable, two Loretta Youngs. Don't you think this is kinda kid stuff for us?

CHARLIE: Sure! But this is the best time of our lives. Let's enjoy it. (*Thumbing through ice cream tops*) Look. Here's one of a little kid—Elizabeth Taylor.

HARRY: Never heard of her.

CHARLIE: Me neither. Must be a replacement for Shirley Temple. (*They exit left.*)

*   *   *

TIME: *The present.*

SETTING: *The same as Scene 1.*

AT RISE: MR. SMITH *is tacking a bulletin board on the wall. The clock shows it is now 9:45. Current calendar hangs on wall.*

MR. SMITH: There we are! A schedule of chores for Junior and Stephanie. A place for gold stars for extra work. That should be an incentive to work. All kids like gold stars. (*A knock on the door is heard. He opens door and* MR. PHILLIPS-BIRT *enters.*)

MR. PHILLIPS-BIRT (*Speaking with an English accent*):

Good evening. I say, is this the residence of Mr. Harry Smith? (MR. SMITH *nods.*) I thought so. Just as Alfred described it. The cozy, comfy, typical American home. Oh, forgive me. I'm Alfred Plompton Phillips-Birt— father of a young man commonly known amongst the younger set, I understand, as (*Distastefully*) "Alfie."

MR. SMITH: Oh, yes—Alfie.

MR. PHILLIPS-BIRT: I can tell—you don't like him, either.

MR. SMITH (*Embarrassed*): I—well, I only met him this evening. But please do sit down, Mr. Phillips-Birt. (*Indicating board*) I have to put in one more tack. (*He goes to board.*)

MR. PHILLIPS-BIRT (*Following him*): What is this?

MR. SMITH: A schedule of chores for my son and daughter. And some projects for their spare time.

MR. PHILLIPS-BIRT (*Examining board closely*): They must run around like little dynamos from dawn till dusk. "Five A.M.: rise, calisthenics, milk cows." Do you keep cows here?

MR. SMITH: We're going to.

MR. PHILLIPS-BIRT: How quaint. Do your children mind having all their time scheduled like this? They don't even have time to watch television.

MR. SMITH: The schedule, Mr. Phillips-Birt, is something new. And as for watching television, that is forbidden.

MR. PHILLIPS-BIRT: How very strange. (*He sits.*)

MR. SMITH: Pretty unusual, eh? An American home where there's discipline, more work than play, no TV?

MR. PHILLIPS-BIRT: I suppose so. But that's not what strikes me as strange. It's the result, the final product— your children.

MR. SMITH (*Rushing to* MR. PHILLIPS-BIRT): What have they done? I knew it! All that bloodshed and violence on television!

Mr. Phillips-Birt (*Amused*): They haven't done anything! Anything wrong, that is. Quite the contrary. Ever
since your son has been delivering the newspapers, I've
been most impressed with him.

Mr. Smith (*Startled*): Delivering newspapers? (*He sits.*)

Mr. Phillips-Birt: And your daughter is charming, Mr.
Smith. I came over to tell you so myself—tonight, while
she and Alfred are out together.

Mrs. Smith (*Entering*): I'm back, Harry.

Mr. Smith (*As he and* Mr. Phillips-Birt *stand*): Mr.
Phillips-Birt, dear. Alfie's father.

Mrs. Smith (*Pleased*): I'm delighted to know you. I'm
quite taken with Alfie. (*They shake hands.*)

Mr. Phillips-Birt (*Incredulously*): Really? I was just
about to tell your husband that Alfie's always been a
complete mystery to me.

Mrs. Smith: Oh, he's just acting like a typical American
boy.

Mr. Phillips-Birt: Well, if he has any redeeming qualities at all, I have your daughter to thank. (*They all sit.*)
I've always had a terrible time with Alfred. We brought
him up in the old-fashioned way, you see . . . strict
discipline, basic values, no television, plenty of chores,
exactly the way a boy should be brought up. But in
spite of it all, Alfred turned out to be a complete disaster.

Mrs. Smith (*Laughing*): Alfie?

Mr. Phillips-Birt: It's true, Mrs. Smith. I despaired completely until your daughter came along, but since then,
Alfred's beginning to make an effort to be almost human. He's stopped revolting against his mother and me,
and can hold a near-civilized conversation at the dinner
table. (Mrs. Smith *looks smugly at* Mr. Smith, *who appears baffled.*) Really, we're most pleased, and I did want

to thank you. Your daughter has such beautiful manners, and her English is flawless. I was sure that, somehow or other, your system of bringing up your children—your home life in general—would be completely different from ours, but Mr. Smith seems to be even more of a taskmaster than I.

MRS. SMITH: He just has a tough exterior, Mr. Phillips-Birt.

MR. PHILLIPS-BIRT: It was the last thing I expected, too. He has something of a reputation. (MR. SMITH *starts*.) Oh, a very good one, Mr. Smith. To hear Alfie talk, you're something of the ideal father . . . easy to talk to, understanding, close to your children. (*Chuckling*) I thought surely you'd be a combination of Santa Claus and the Easter Bunny. (*He stands*.) But children get strange notions, don't they? I suppose the difference between your household and mine is simply that you've been luckier.

MR. SMITH (*Weakly*): Yes. I suppose you're right.

MR. PHILLIPS-BIRT: At any rate, I hope you don't object to your daughter's going out with Alfie. . . . I'm calling him that now, too, aren't I? He isn't a bad boy, you know.

MRS. SMITH (*Standing*): He's a very nice boy. We were just saying that earlier, weren't we, Harry? (MR. SMITH *looks dumfounded, then stands and looks preoccupied.*)

MR. PHILLIPS-BIRT: Sometimes I think he only seems to be frightfully repulsive because of the hair and the clothes and the language—you know, the usual teen-age business.

MRS. SMITH (*Following* MR. PHILLIPS-BIRT *as he moves to door*): I'm sure that's all it is.

MR. PHILLIPS-BIRT: Well, good night. A pleasure to have met you. And, Mr. Smith, good luck with the cows.

MR. SMITH: Cows? Oh. Yes! Thanks. (MR. PHILLIPS-BIRT *exits, and* MR. SMITH *turns to* MRS. SMITH *after a pause.*) Well, how's the new biodegradable detergent?

MRS. SMITH: What?

MR. SMITH: Didn't you go to Vivian's to test some new biodegradable detergent?

MRS. SMITH: Honestly, Harry, what's happened to your sense of humor? Sometimes I think you believe that everybody really does act like the characters on television. (*Noticing board*) What's that thing on the wall?

MR. SMITH (*Going to board*): An experiment. (*He takes it down.*) An abandoned experiment. (*Puts it behind chair*)

MRS. SMITH (*Sitting*): And what did Mr. Phillips-Birt mean about cows?

MR. SMITH: We were talking about life on the farm when we were kids.

MRS. SMITH: Harry Smith, you've lived in a suburban neighborhood all your life, and you know it. Did you throw the tablecloth on the television? (*He nods.*) Why?

MR. SMITH: Keeps the dust off the screen. (*He sits down.*)

MRS. SMITH: It's nice to hear a compliment or two about the children, isn't it?

MR. SMITH (*Smiling*): They're good kids.

MRS. SMITH: But it's nice to hear somebody else say so. We certainly are fortunate, Harry. Not that the children just happened to turn out the way they did. You've had a lot to do with it.

MR. SMITH: Do you really think Alfie's a nice boy?

MRS. SMITH: Of course, Harry. My goodness, don't you remember how peculiar you seemed to your parents when you were that age?

MR. SMITH (*Thoughtfully*): I remember my sister had a boyfriend once who was something like Alfie.

MRS. SMITH: You see? But everything turned out all right for her. She married a television tycoon and is happy as can be. Come to think of it, Harry, you ought to have a little more appreciation for television just for the sake of family ties.

MR. SMITH (*Smiling*): I guess you're right. (*He stands, walks to set*) Shall I warm up the set for the news? (*He removes cloth from set.*)

MRS. SMITH: Why don't you? I still have a little more sewing to do.

JUNIOR (*Rushing in*): I'm home! Pater, sir, I'm home. I will be in bed by ten. I will!

MRS. SMITH (*Taking out her sewing*): I think you can relax, Junior. The storm clouds have passed.

JUNIOR: Already?

MR. SMITH (*Walking to* JUNIOR *and clapping him on the shoulder*): Glad you're back on time, son. I knew you would be. Why don't we go out in the kitchen and make some popcorn? You can tell me about the TV shows you saw over at Ace's house.

JUNIOR (*Protesting*): But, Dad! I was helping Ace with his homework!

MR. SMITH (*As* MRS. SMITH *looks on approvingly*): I know. I remember when I was your age, I had a friend named Charlie Hart, and, whenever my father decided the time had come to ban the radio in our house—those were the days before television, of course—I'd decide that the time had come to borrow a book from Charlie Hart. Oddly enough, Charlie not only had a radio but a phonograph and a ton of records, too. (*Curtain*)

THE END

Production Notes

ANOTHER MAN'S FAMILY

Characters: 9 male; 4 female; 2 male voices; 3 female voices; singers (for radio and television commercials).

Playing Time: 40 minutes.

Costumes: Scenes 1 and 3: Modern, everyday dress. Mrs. Smith wears a gingham apron, and Mr. Smith wears casual clothes. Junior, Stephanie, Ace, and Alfie wear extreme versions of the latest fad in teen-age dress. Mr. Phillips-Birt wears a business suit. Scene 2: Appropriate dress of 1939. Mom wears a gingham apron. Young Harry, Charlie, and Robbie wear collegiate sweaters, saddle shoes, and Harry has a crew cut. Gwen wears saddle shoes and bobby socks, pleated plaid skirt, and a man's shirt with shirt-tails out.

Properties: Popcorn, newspapers, dress for Mrs. Smith, pins, knitted dress for Mom, bulletin board, paper cup tops.

Setting: Scenes 1 and 3: The Smiths' typical American living room. There is a wall calendar showing that it is the present, and a clock shows that it is 8 o'clock. The room is comfortably furnished with chairs, lamps, bookcases, etc. There is a table with a tablecloth and a footstool, and at one side is a television set with the picture out of view of the audience. A bulletin board is added in Scene 3 and the clock reads 9:45. Scene 2: The living room of Harry Smith's home as a teen-ager. The setting is similar to Scene 1, but old-fashioned, overstuffed chairs and sofa are used in place of modern furniture. A 1939 calendar hangs on the wall, and the television set has been replaced by an old-fashioned radio. In both scenes, there is an exit right to the rest of the house, and an exit up center to the outside.

Lighting: No special effects.

Sound: Voices and music from radio and television, as indicated.

Bailey, Go Home

Characters

MR. PHIPPS-TRIMBLE, *a gentle Englishman*
MRS. PHIPPS-TRIMBLE, *his wife*
FELIX ⎱ *their teen-age children*
JESSICA ⎰
MR. PADDINGTON ⎤
MRS. PADDINGTON ⎬ *neighbors*
MISS NEVILLE ⎦
FRANK BAILEY, *a TV personality*
JIM BARTLETT, *ace cameraman*
ANNA-BELLE, *a teen-age movie star*
MRS. THELMA BRASHLEY, *her mother*
THREE SINGERS
THREE VENDORS
MONKEY

SCENE 1

SETTING: *The garden of the Phipps-Trimble estate on El Paradiso, a small, unspoiled Caribbean island.*

AT RISE: MR. *and* MRS. PHIPPS-TREMBLE, MR. *and* MRS. PADDINGTON, *and* MISS NEVILLE *are seated in the garden, having tea. They are well-dressed and have elegant manners.*

Miss Neville (*Putting down her cup*): Delicious tea, Mrs. Phipps-Trimble.

Mrs. Phipps-Trimble: Thank you, Miss Neville. I do think cook is improving. (*To* Mrs. Paddington) More tea, Mrs. Paddington?

Mrs. Paddington: Oh, no, thank you, Mrs. Phipps-Trimble. Mr. Paddington and I must be off.

Mr. Paddington: We want to see the sunset over the coral reef. We find it so serene.

Mr. Phipps-Trimble: I know exactly how you feel, Paddington. (Mr. *and* Mrs. Paddington *and* Miss Neville *stand up.*)

Miss Neville: I must be on my way, too. Thank you so much for the lovely tea, Mrs. Phipps-Trimble.

Mrs. Phipps-Trimble: Do come again soon, all of you. (*The* Paddingtons *and* Miss Neville *exit.*) Such charming people, aren't they?

Mr. Phipps-Trimble: Indeed. There isn't another island in the Caribbean that can boast such delightful company and peaceful settings. (Felix *and* Jessica *enter.*)

Mrs. Phipps-Trimble: Ah, children. Do have some tea.

Felix: No, thank you, Mother. Cook still makes the iced tea too weak.

Mr. Phipps-Trimble: Anybody who puts ice in tea deserves what he gets.

Jessica: Don't be so stuffy, Father. Everybody in America drinks it that way.

Mr. Phipps-Trimble: And how do you know what everybody in America does?

Jessica: Well, this island isn't completely cut off from the rest of the world. The last time a cruise ship passed here we got a whole stack of magazines.

FELIX: They sure ran the gamut—*Jack and Jill, The Public Utilities Fortnightly*—

JESSICA: And *Seventeen,* and the *Vogue Pattern Book. (She turns to show off her dress.)* This is the latest thing in New York.

MRS. PHIPPS-TRIMBLE: Lovely, dear.

FELIX: We haven't had a cruise ship pass by in quite a while now.

MRS. PHIPPS-TRIMBLE: How long has it been?

MR. PHIPPS-TRIMBLE: A matter of months, I think.

JESSICA: I'd love a new magazine.

MR. PHIPPS-TRIMBLE: That's all well and good, Jessica, but magazines don't swim ashore by themselves. Somebody has to bring them.

MRS. PHIPPS-TRIMBLE: And you know what that means.

FELIX *and* JESSICA *(Hopefully)*: Tourists?

MRS. PHIPPS-TRIMBLE *(Distastefully)*: With their cameras and their jazzy sports shirts and the crazy hats they picked up at the last port of call.

FELIX *(Somewhat dreamily)*: Nassau, Haiti, Jamaica . . .

MR. PHIPPS-TRIMBLE: You know, whenever we have an afternoon like this—which is almost every day—I think our great-grandfathers scuttled their ship off this island on purpose. How idyllic it is. How peaceful. How civilized.

FELIX: How dull!

MR. PHIPPS-TRIMBLE *(Amused)*: Dull, indeed! You don't know what dull is.

FELIX: Sure, I do. This is it.

MRS. PHIPPS-TRIMBLE *(To* MR. PHIPPS-TRIMBLE*)*: That's all right, my dear. The young people of the island always go through a stage of thinking the place is dull. They're too young to appreciate what they have. (*To* FELIX) There's an advantage to living in an out-of-the-way place like El Paradiso. People leave you alone.

FELIX: Well, we certainly don't attract a swinging crowd.

MR. PHIPPS-TRIMBLE: When it comes to swinging crowds, my dear boy, there are enough anthropoids in the jungle already.

JESSICA: But sooner or later somebody's going to discover us, and make this island a tourist attraction.

MR. PHIPPS-TRIMBLE: Nonsense, Jessica. For the past two hundred years, the population of this island has effectively resisted all attempts to be discovered. The world likes to think of our island as primitive, if it thinks of the place at all. Let the cruise ships sail by, let all the itineraries bypass our charming harbor. No one here will complain. (*Noise of an approaching helicopter is heard.*)

MRS. PHIPPS-TRIMBLE (*Looking up*): Good heavens! What is that?

FELIX: It's a helicopter! (*All look up, as if following helicopter's progress.*)

JESSICA: Funny! It looks as though it wants to land right here on El Paradiso.

MR. PHIPPS-TRIMBLE (*Incensed*): Funny! We never built an airport so that we could avoid this kind of thing.

FELIX: Helicopters don't need airports, Father. Say, it has something painted on the side—U.S.A. and WKZ-TV.

MRS. PHIPPS-TRIMBLE: TV? That's television!

MR. PHIPPS-TRIMBLE: And that means we are being invaded. (*He begins to gather up tea things for a hasty retreat.*) Felix, run into the village and tell everybody. Jessica, find the Paddingtons and Miss Neville and tell them.

FELIX: Tell them what?

MR. PHIPPS-TRIMBLE: Tell them to stand by—just say, "Here we go again!" (*They all hurry off left; sound of helicopter stops. Then* FRANK BAILEY *enters right, paces about eagerly, then stops at center, looking very self-satisfied as* JIM BARTLETT, *loaded down with movie camera, light meters, tripod, staggers in right.*)

FRANK: Just what I said it would be, Jim Bartlett, ace cameraman. How about starting this travelogue with a shot of me leaning against this palm tree?

JIM (*Struggling with tangle of equipment*): Will you wait a minute?

FRANK: Wait? Millions of Americans are waiting—at their television sets for this week's Frank Bailey Travelogue Show. Millions of people are waiting to see one of the last natural paradises left on earth.

JIM: Well, if millions of Americans can't wait until I set up the camera, it's just too bad.

FRANK: Look at this place! Exactly what I knew it would be. Simple. Unspoiled. What a story we'll do here, Jim. What a story! And for this trip, a new gimmick! A sweet, unspoiled teen-age movie star, beloved throughout the U.S.A., looks at all this sweet, unspoiled scenery and interviews all the sweet, unspoiled natives.

ANNA-BELLE (*Entering right, sucking lollipop*): Golly, Mr. Frank Bailey, you sure picked a dumperoo for my debut into the field of public service flicks. (*Throws away lollipop stick*)

MRS. BRASHLEY (*Following* ANNA-BELLE): Mr. Bailey? My daughter Anna-Belle is a star! She doesn't have to go on a two-bit safari for publicity!

FRANK: Mrs. Brashley, she's here, isn't she? Take my word for it—your daughter Anna-Belle will emerge from this stint on my show more beloved by the American public than Lassie and the Fourth of July put together.

ANNA-BELLE: Why couldn't we have done a human-interest bit about the natives on the Riviera?

FRANK (*Grandly*): I discovered the Riviera last year.

ANNA-BELLE: Well, if I don't get back to some normal teen-age living before long, I'm going to break my contract. Then what will happen to Frank Bailey's travelogue with Anna-Belle, America's teen-age sweetheart, and her own lovable viewpoint of this Caribbean jungle?

FRANK: O.K., Anna-Belle, pipe down. Here's another lollipop. (*He takes one from his pocket.*)

ANNA-BELLE (*Petulantly*): What flavor is it?

FRANK: It's green! How do I know what flavor it is?

MRS. BRASHLEY: Seriously, Mr. Bailey, how long do we have to stay in this forsaken trap?

FRANK: Until we can capture all the color, all the drama, all the heart of these people for the American television audience . . . for the world! Think of it! And, Anna-Belle, don't you get goose bumps to think how much more you're going to be loved by all the kids in America? (ANNA-BELLE *smiles.*) And by all their mommies and daddies, too?

ANNA-BELLE (*Seriously*): Well, yeah, kinda. And I think they love me 'cause I'm such a nice, regular kid.

FRANK (*Patting* ANNA-BELLE's *head*): There's the humility of a real star!

ANNA-BELLE: But I can tell you one thing. This is the last travelogue I do. From here on it's back to exciting things like blueberry picking and blowing bubble gum.

FRANK: Remember! The Frank Bailey Travelogue Show must go on!

MRS. BRASHLEY: Oh, for goodness' sake, why?

FRANK: Because, if it doesn't, Anna-Belle won't earn her salary, and *you* won't have enough money for a new wiglet. Now, let's slip off and interview some natives.

JIM: I've just set up all this stuff! (*He starts loading himself down with photographic equipment.*)

FRANK: Do you have everything there, Jim? Camera? Film? (JIM *groans.*) Come, pioneers. Let's get to the heart of the island and meet people. (*Calling*) Hello out there, all you undiscovered natives! (MR. PHIPPS-TRIMBLE *appears left and blocks their path. He wears torn and ragged shirt and pants.*)

MR. PHIPPS-TRIMBLE (*Haughtily*): Hello to you!

FRANK (*Nervously*): Don't panic! (*They all cower and retreat.*) Don't panic! Jim will protect us!

JIM: Me! (*Looking about as* FRANK *falls to ground*) Protect you from what?

FRANK: We're not afraid, O noble chief of noble tribe.

MR. PHIPPS-TRIMBLE: Do get up. You're going to get smudges on your jodhpurs.

FRANK (*Staggering to his feet*): Anything you say, chief. We're just ambassadors of good will.

MR. PHIPPS-TRIMBLE (*Dully*): I know. I've seen your type before.

ANNA-BELLE (*Coming forward*): Chief, I'm Anna-Belle, America's teen-age sweetheart. How about a lovable little interview?

MR. PHIPPS-TRIMBLE: Well, first of all, I think I should clarify a point. I am not a "chief." Words like "chief" and "tribe" have connotations of spears and war dances and missionaries being boiled in huge pots. (FRANK *hides behind* JIM.) We simply don't do that sort of thing here.

FRANK (*Coming forward again*): Well, then. I guess we can proceed. (JIM *starts to leave.*)

MR. PHIPPS-TRIMBLE: But I *am* more or less the head of this community simply because no one else wants the job. (JIM *puts down equipment.*)

JIM (*To* MR. PHIPPS-TRIMBLE): He's going to call you

"chief" whether you like it or not, so you might as well get used to it.

FRANK (*Ignoring* JIM): You know how it is, chief. It looks better on TV. Gets across the idea that this place is kind of primitive.

MRS. BRASHLEY (*Insincerely*): It's so natural . . . so untrampled by progress. Just the sort of place everybody would like to visit.

MR. PHIPPS-TRIMBLE (*Shouting*): Oh, no! No! It's too . . . too remote!

MRS. BRASHLEY: But these days, with jets and helicopters and things, no place is too remote.

MR. PHIPPS-TRIMBLE: This one is. It's awful here! Awful!

MRS. PHIPPS-TRIMBLE (*Entering left, dressed in ragged clothes*): Was that you screaming, dear?

FRANK (*Extending his hand to her*): And this must be the chief's little squaw. (*She ignores him.*) I'm Frank Bailey, world-famous traveler.

MR. PHIPPS-TRIMBLE (*Nervously, to his wife*): I'm sorry I startled you, dear, but this woman just said everybody wants to visit our island.

MRS. BRASHLEY (*Introducing herself*): Thelma Brashley, mother of that excruciatingly popular teen-age movie star, Anna-Belle.

ANNA-BELLE: That's me.

MRS. PHIPPS-TRIMBLE (*Ignoring* ANNA-BELLE, *who curtsies, then concentrates on her lollipop*): Mr. Bailey, I'm sure no one would want to come here. Our ways are very primitive. We eat only wild berries and wear these dreadful frocks.

MR. PHIPPS-TRIMBLE: We put up with this revolting place because we have no choice. And now (*Dismissing them*), I'm sure you have better tropical islands to visit.

FRANK: Not on your life. I owe it to my public to bring

them something new, something different. And I'm going to make a film on El Paradiso for one reason . . .
nobody else has done it.

JIM: Shall I set up the equipment here?

MR. PHIPPS-TRIMBLE (*Vainly protesting*): Now, one moment here!

FRANK: And by the time we're through showing America
what a colorful place this is, I'll bet we'll have you sold
on it, too. (*Starting to "stage" his show*) Now, let's see.
Chief, you sit on this rock and smoke your pipe.

MR. PHIPPS-TRIMBLE: But I don't smoke!

FRANK: And squaw? What will you be doing?

MRS. PHIPPS-TRIMBLE: I never do anything!

ANNA-BELLE: Maybe she should be mending a grass skirt.

MRS. PHIPPS-TRIMBLE: Nobody here wears grass skirts!

FRANK (*To* JIM): Roll 'em! (JIM *starts to film the "interview" from many angles.*) And we are here, ladies and
gentlemen, on El Paradiso, undiscovered paradise of the
Caribbean.

ANNA-BELLE (*Pushing forward*): Undiscovered until we
got here, you mean, Mr. Bailey. (*Upstaging everybody*)
Hi, out there, teen-age America. Come on down!

FRANK: You'll find that things here are still unspoiled. (*He
shoves microphone at* MR. PHIPPS-TRIMBLE.) Aren't they,
chief?

MR. PHIPPS-TRIMBLE: That's putting it mildly, Mr. Bailey.

FRANK: A little modernizing, a little Americanization
wouldn't hurt, eh?

MR. PHIPPS-TRIMBLE (*Almost shouting*): We live in a
jungle tangle that would frighten Tarzan!

MRS. PHIPPS-TRIMBLE: And wait till the monsoons set in.
They start tomorrow and last until about this time next
year.

ANNA-BELLE: I'll bet the kids have a ball swimming and surfing.

MRS. PHIPPS-TRIMBLE: If they're really tired of El Paradiso, they do. With all the *sharks*, it's like a nautical game of Russian roulette!

FRANK (*Waving his arms*): Wait a minute! Cut, cut, cut! Now, come on, chief. I don't think you and your squaw are giving this place much of a pitch.

MR. PHIPPS-TRIMBLE (*Standing*): Frightfully sorry. Perhaps you should interview someone else.

FRANK (*Waving to* JIM *to pack up again*): All right. We'll do the rest of the island and leave you till last.

ANNA-BELLE (*Blowing kisses*): See you later, chief.

MR. PHIPPS-TRIMBLE (*Weakly*): We can hardly wait.

ANNA-BELLE: 'Bye! (*To* MRS. BRASHLEY) Come on, Mumsy. This way. (*She leads* MRS. BRASHLEY *by the hand.*)

FRANK: Onward, onward, onward! (*They exit.*)

MRS. PHIPPS-TRIMBLE: I don't think we got our message across.

MR. PHIPPS-TRIMBLE: Whenever they talk about Americanization, I break out in a cold sweat.

MRS. PHIPPS-TRIMBLE: Can you imagine what this beautiful place would be like if that . . . that barbarian put it on television and showed everybody how ideal life here really is?

MR. PHIPPS-TRIMBLE: Yes. I can imagine. I can imagine all too well.

MRS. PHIPPS-TRIMBLE: The island would be a honky-tonk amusement park in no time.

MR. PHIPPS-TRIMBLE (*Smiling*): My dear, something just occurred to me. Did you know that El Paradiso has already been "discovered" by the tourists?

MRS. PHIPPS-TRIMBLE: Why, whatever do you mean?

MR. PHIPPS-TRIMBLE: Squaw, I'm not the big chief of this tribe for nothing. Let me take you to the bazaar, where, for the bargain price of two dollars and ninety-eight cents, you may buy a genuine native voodoo doll.

MRS. PHIPPS-TRIMBLE: Have you taken leave of your senses?

MR. PHIPPS-TRIMBLE: My dear, fear no longer. The invading hordes will be driven out—and simply enough. If you can't fight them, join them.

MRS. PHIPPS-TRIMBLE: What?

MR. PHIPPS-TRIMBLE: Join them and go them one better. Chief? Indoctrinate the natives! Spread the news! When it comes to greeting the tourists, El Paradiso has had the course! (*They hurry off left as the curtain falls.*)

*   *   *

SCENE 2

BEFORE RISE: ANNA-BELLE *enters in front of curtain with* FELIX, *who now looks extremely "Americanized." He is dressed in the latest extreme style and is chewing bubble gum.* ANNA-BELLE *carries a small tape recorder and microphone.*

ANNA-BELLE: And yours, then, is the average teen-age opinion?

FELIX (*As they stroll across stage*): You're not just clickin' your teeth, cutie.

ANNA-BELLE (*Uneasily*): And . . . and you simply love it here?

FELIX: Is there another place to be?

ANNA-BELLE: Uh . . . what do you do for dates?

FELIX: We just live it up.

Anna-Belle: In America we go to drive-in hamburger drive-ins and drive-in movie drive-ins.

Felix: Still? We haven't done that old stuff here in years!

Anna-Belle: I thought this paradise was supposed to be a little backward.

Felix: Backward? You don't say!

Anna-Belle: That's why we're here! Mr. Bailey just doesn't bother with places that have been "discovered."

Felix: Kiddo, if you're looking for someplace backward, then you can swing on out of here. We livened up this volcano a long while back.

Anna-Belle (*Delighted*): Really? You mean I'm not stuck in the middle of a tribe of clods after all? (*She starts to dance.*) Well, whoa-whoa-whoa, and yea-yea-yea!

Felix: Uh . . . beg your pardon?

Anna-Belle (*Dancing*): Whoa-whoa-whoa, yea-yea-yea.

Felix (*Following her*): Oh, that! Sure! But here that kind of dancing went out with high-button shoes! Come on, let's go to town and check out the action. (*They exit.*)

Mrs. Brashley (*Entering immediately through center curtain with* Jessica, *who is dressed in a Hollywood idea of Caribbean costume*): And naturally, dear, I don't mean to criticize. It just seems to me that, for an "undiscovered" island, you people look a bit more "discovered" than you ought to look.

Jessica: You don't say!

Mrs. Brashley: Of all the people I've seen here so far, I haven't found one who doesn't seem . . . well . . . sort of hip.

Jessica (*Innocently*): Hip? What does that mean?

Mrs. Brashley: With it. And I thought that we'd be the ones to introduce you to the finer things of civilization . . . like electric toothbrushes and traffic jams and breakfast cereals that crash and go boom.

JESSICA: What a bore!

MRS. BRASHLEY: Listen, hon, I'm a lot more disappointed in you than you are in us. The least you could do is look quaint for Mr. Bailey's sake.

JESSICA: All right. Why don't we go over to that waterfall, and you can interview me while I shampoo my hair in the foam?

MRS. BRASHLEY: But that sounds like a TV commercial!

JESSICA: Where do you think the TV people got the idea? Now, what do you want to talk about? The average El Paradiso opinion of the world monetary crisis and its effects on fashions? Union wages?

MRS. BRASHLEY (*As* JESSICA *pulls her along*): What?

JESSICA: Union wages! If we can't talk about that, we should be able to talk about something. Come on, I'll show you the town. (*They exit as the curtains open.*)

*   *   *

SETTING: *The Town Square. Makeshift but colorful booths are placed about the stage, with signs reading:* SOUVENIRS, EATS, CARIBBEAN-COLA—NO CALORIES, *etc.*

AT RISE: VENDORS, *including* MR. PADDINGTON, *all wearing gaudy shirts, sunglasses, etc., stand near booths, calling out their wares.* JIM *is filming* MONKEY (*man wearing a monkey suit*), *who holds a banana and a tin cup with a dollar sign on it.* MRS. PADDINGTON *and* MISS NEVILLE, *dressed as "hula girls" in a combination of Caribbean and Hawaiian costume, dance in left and swagger across stage, exiting right, as* ANNA-BELLE *and* FELIX *enter left, and stop in front of refreshment stand.* ANNA-BELLE *does a few dance steps.*

ANNA-BELLE: Are you sure this went out with high-button shoes?

FELIX: Right. (*To* 1ST VENDOR, *in refreshment stand*) A hot dog for our guest . . . with mustard, mayonnaise, catsup, sweet and sour relish . . .

ANNA-BELLE (*Stopping her dance*): Uh . . . no, thanks.

FELIX: Oh, come on. Be a sport. (*To* VENDOR) You heard the order, mac. And give her a triple malted.

JESSICA (*Entering, to* FELIX): To think we're going to be on TV. Isn't it a thrill?

ANNA-BELLE (*Looking somewhat green*): Who knows? You may end up a big star like me.

MR. PADDINGTON: Hey, little girl. How about some genuine souvenirs of the island? (VENDORS *begin approaching.*) All big stars get special discounts.

ANNA-BELLE: No, thanks. Hey, what is this?

2ND VENDOR (*Approaching with* MONKEY): Take your picture eating a banana with a trained marmoset? Send it to the folks back home. Use it for a Christmas card.

ANNA-BELLE (*Sternly*): No, thanks! (MONKEY *does a few turns, and* VENDORS *amble back to their booths.*)

JESSICA (*To* ANNA-BELLE): Why don't *we* take a few pictures of *you?* It's been a long time since we've had anybody here who looked so cute and old-fashioned.

ANNA-BELLE: Old-fashioned!

FELIX: Like that dance you were doing. Sort of moldy.

1ST VENDOR (*As* ANNA-BELLE *fumes*): Hot dog and malt here.

JESSICA (*Taking food from him and passing it to* ANNA-BELLE): Thanks, handsome. (ANNA-BELLE *takes food but then puts it down.*)

FRANK (*Entering energetically right*): And here's the town square!

JESSICA (*Quickly*): The town square? No, it's only Anna-Belle. (*Turning, gesturing to booths*) Oh, you mean this!

JIM (*To* FRANK, *as* ANNA-BELLE *glowers*): Are you sure somebody didn't get here before we did?

FRANK (*Ignoring him*): It looks as though we're in time for market day.

FELIX: Every day is market day around here.

MR. PADDINGTON: Hey! How about a genuine shark's tooth key ring? Glows in the dark! Helps you drive on foggy nights!

FRANK: No, thanks.

MR. PADDINGTON: Aw, come on. Help out the cottage industries. (FRANK *reaches into pocket.*) Three dollars and fifty cents American money. We cash travelers' checks. (MRS. PADDINGTON *and* MISS NEVILLE *dance in right.* JIM *busies himself with following action with camera.*)

MRS. PADDINGTON *and* MISS NEVILLE (*Singing*):
Come with me, to El Paradiso
Where you can break your necks
In native discothèques. Cha-cha-cha.

JIM (*Putting down camera*): What was that?

BOTH (*In unison*): We said, "Cha-cha-cha!" (*They exit left, as* MR. PHIPPS-TRIMBLE, *now dressed in gaudy shirt, sunglasses, and straw hat, enters.*)

MR. PHIPPS-TRIMBLE: Ah, there you are, Mr. Bailey. I've taken the liberty of arranging a few typical local amusements so that you won't waste too much of your time. Time's money, we say here on El Paradiso. That's why life here gets somewhat frantic now and again.

FRANK: Hey, chief, what's up?

MR. PADDINGTON (*Interrupting*): How about a genuine reproduction of Gilda, the native moon goddess? (*Holds up hideous statue*) Guaranteed to bring you good luck. And if she doesn't bring you good luck, just release your hostilities by smashing her against the wall. (*To* FRANK) How many, sir? Cheaper by the gross. You can use 'em as door prizes for the next P.T.A. shindig. They make great lamp bases. We ship air freight.

FRANK: Stop it! (3RD VENDOR, *holding "shrunken head" suspended from string, sneaks up on* FRANK, JIM, *and* ANNA-BELLE.)

3RD VENDOR: You can't leave El Paradiso without a genuine shrunken head.

FRANK, JIM *and* ANNA-BELLE (*Turning and screaming*): Ugh!

FRANK (*Sputtering, to* MR. PHIPPS-TRIMBLE): But I thought you said you didn't do that sort of thing.

MR. PHIPPS-TRIMBLE: Oh, we don't—not anymore. But we have a rather large stockpile in the deep freeze and . . .

FRANK: Uh, chief. I hate to interrupt, but I'll do it, anyway. Are you putting on some kind of act or something?

MR. PHIPPS-TRIMBLE: Act? What do you mean?

FRANK: You seem so . . . so happy.

MR. PHIPPS-TRIMBLE: But that's what we are . . . happy, happy, happy!

FRANK: I thought you said life here was awful.

MR. PHIPPS-TRIMBLE: Awful happy, Mr. Bailey. And awful discovered, too. You know, you may think you're filming an island that nobody's ever heard of before, but this place has been a tourist trap for years. Pretty soon there's going to be a Hilton hotel over here, and a Sheraton hotel over there . . .

FRANK: Not before *I* show this place to the world, there isn't.

MR. PHIPPS-TRIMBLE: Then you'd better hurry up. I think the world may be one step ahead of you so far as El Paradiso is concerned.

FRANK: What do you mean by that?

MR. PHIPPS-TRIMBLE: Just take your little pictures, Mr. Bailey.

MONKEY (*Sneaking up on* ANNA-BELLE): Have a banana?

ANNA-BELLE (*Screaming*): Mama!

MONKEY: I'll sell it to you cheap.

ANNA-BELLE: Mama! (MRS. BRASHLEY *enters right. She has so many souvenirs—crazy hat, leis, shell jewelry, etc.— that she is barely recognizable*)

FRANK (*To* JIM, *indicating* MRS. BRASHLEY): There's a typical native character, Jim. Get a closeup.

MRS. BRASHLEY (*Pushing* JIM *aside*): Don't you dare! Just get me out of this place before these sharpies sell me the Brooklyn Bridge.

MR. PHIPPS-TRIMBLE: As I was saying, Mr. Bailey, we've arranged some amusements for you. A Little League tournament, the Rotary Club is doing a combination war dance and rain dance, and the Campfire Girls are giving you a jazzy little cookout.

MRS. BRASHLEY: And what are they cooking, native pizza?

MR. PHIPPS-TRIMBLE: They threatened to cook a Girl Scout. Bit of friendly rivalry, you know.

MRS. PHIPPS-TRIMBLE (*Rushing in on one skate, from left*): Track! Fore! Out of my way! (*She stops suddenly in front of* FRANK.) You would! Messed up the longest downhill run I've had in weeks. (THREE SINGERS *with guitars bounce in right and serenade* ANNA-BELLE.)

SINGERS:
I loves ya, little baby,
I loves ya like mad,
An' when my eyes don't see ya,
I feel sad, sad, sad.
An' a whoa-whoa-whoa, an' a yea-yea-yea
Feel sad. Like mad.
(ANNA-BELLE, FELIX *and* JESSICA *dance, then* MRS. PADDINGTON *and* MISS NEVILLE *reappear, left. They dance across stage, singing their song while* SINGERS *sing theirs*

and the VENDORS *hawk their wares.* JIM *leaps about to get pictures.*)

FRANK (*His hands on his ears, jumping up and down*): Stop it, stop it, stop it! (*The noise subsides. To* MR. PHIPPS-TRIMBLE) Look! Don't you ever let me catch you luring any more tourists down here under the pretext that this place is "undiscovered."

MR. PHIPPS-TRIMBLE: It's a shameful practice, isn't it? But a buck's a buck, as you say.

FRANK: Why, this place is a mixture of every tourist trap going on the globe!

MR. PHIPPS-TRIMBLE: But I did warn you about that, didn't I?

FRANK (*To* JIM): Come on. Let's get out of here.

ANNA-BELLE (*Gaily*): Are we going home?

MRS. BRASHLEY: To Hollywood?

FRANK (*Angrily*): We still have to find an unspoiled island for this week's show!

MRS. BRASHLEY *and* ANNA-BELLE: Oh, no!

JIM: You mean we're not going to use all these pictures? (*He holds out camera, film.*) I've done all this for nothing. (*He cries.*) All this film?

FRANK: We'd be laughed off television. (*He takes film from* JIM *and hands it to* MR. PHIPPS-TRIMBLE.) Here. Take this. It's all yours. (JIM, *sniffing, packs up his equipment.*)

MR. PADDINGTON (*As* VENDORS *converge on* FRANK): You'll never forgive yourself if you go away without Gilda, genuine island moon goddess.

1ST VENDOR: Have some hot dogs before you leave. Take some along on the trip.

2ND VENDOR: Why not buy the marmoset? We have more where he came from. I'll throw in a peck of bananas and some green stamps.

FRANK: Out of my way!

MRS. PHIPPS-TRIMBLE: Oh, dear! I suppose this is farewell.

MR. PHIPPS-TRIMBLE: Too bad we won't be on your show, Mr. Bailey.

FRANK: Well, don't think I won't tell everybody what I found here. You won't get another sucker here if I can help it.

MR. PHIPPS-TRIMBLE: Pity.

ALL (*Calling*): 'Bye, Mr. Bailey. 'Bye! Aloha. *Hasta la vista!*

FRANK: Aloha yourself!

ALL: 'Bye, Anna-Belle. (*They wave.*)

ANNA-BELLE (*Crying, as she exits with* FRANK, JIM, *and* MRS. BRASHLEY): I wouldn't do this again for all the lollipops in the world!

FELIX: And so, as the sun sinks slowly into the sea, we leave fair El Paradiso. (*Helicopter noise is heard.*)

JESSICA: But, before boarding our silver jet, we tossed our last nickel into the genuine native wishing fountain, so we know we'll return some day. (*They all look up to watch the progress of helicopter's takeoff and flight.*)

MRS. PHIPPS-TRIMBLE: Well, shall we clean up? It's almost time for tea, and I want to get out of these clothes. (*Helicopter noise fades out.*)

MR. PHIPPS-TRIMBLE: Lovely idea. You know, I think that Mr. Bailey and crew amounted to what is known as a rather close shave. (*To* VENDORS, *who start to clean up some of their wares*) Well, thanks a lot, everybody. Another crisis has been met. (MR. *and* MRS. PHIPPS-TRIMBLE *and* VENDORS *exit.*)

FELIX (*To* SINGERS): You kids were great.

1ST SINGER: I don't know that it's such a compliment to be great at giving such a repulsive performance.

MRS. PADDINGTON: I can't imagine that people really sing and dance like that.

MR. PADDINGTON: Well, thank goodness things here are more civilized.

MISS NEVILLE: Thank goodness, indeed. (*The* PADDING-TONS *and* MISS NEVILLE *exit.*)

FELIX: Thank goodness.

JESSICA: Indeed. (*There is a slight pause.*) Uh . . . did you write that song yourselves?

1ST SINGER: Touching lyrics, don't you think?

2ND SINGER: How did that go? That whoa-whoa business?

JESSICA (*Starting to dance*): You mean this?

2ND SINGER (*Imitating* JESSICA): Yes.

FELIX: There are a few hot dogs left.

3RD SINGER (*Starting to strum on guitar*): I thought they tasted quite good, myself. Passable anyway.

FELIX (*Dancing also*): You know, Father is right. How lucky we are to live in a place that's really civilized!

SINGERS (*While all dance*): I loves ya, little baby . . . (*Curtain*)

THE END

Production Notes

BAILEY, GO HOME

Characters: 6 male; 6 female; 6
male or female for Singers and
Vendors.
Playing Time: 40 minutes.
Costumes: The Phipps-Trimbles,
the Paddingtons, and Miss Neville are well dressed in appropriate tropical clothes when play
begins. Mr. and Mrs. Phipps-
Trimble later put on ragged
clothes, then change to gaudy
Caribbean "tourist" clothes, as
does Jessica. Felix changes to
clothes in the extreme of modern
fashion. Mr. Paddington and
Vendors wear gaudy flowered
shirts and sunglasses. Mrs. Paddington and Miss Neville appear
as "hula girls." Singers are dressed
as an American pop singing
group. Frank is dressed in style of
old-time movie director—jodhpurs, pith helmet, etc. Anna-Belle
and Mrs. Brashley wear modern

dress—appropriate for "movie
star." Monkey is actor dressed in
monkey suit.
Properties: Tea service, movie camera, light meters, tripod, tape recorder and microphone, banana,
tin cup, hot dog, soda, statue,
papier-mâché "shrunken head,"
skate, guitars.
Setting: Scene 1: The garden of the
Phipps-Trimble estate on El Paradiso. A few chairs and a table
with tea things are at one side.
Palm trees and tropical plants
may be placed about to suggest
Caribbean setting. Scene 2: The
Town Square. Makeshift but colorful booths, selling souvenirs,
food, etc., are set up about the
stage. Exits are at right and left.
Lighting: No special effects.
Sound: Offstage helicopter motor, as
indicated in text.

Way, Way Down South

Characters

MRS. EVERLY, *owner of a hamster plantation*
DUSTIN, *her butler*
BLOSSOM, *her granddaughter*
YARBOROUGH BLAIR, *Blossom's boyfriend*
PHINEAS FRAUD, *plantation manager*
PETUNIA PLOTAFOOT, *a spy*
THE COUNT, *her flunky*
REPORTER
TV CAMERAMAN
TROOPS
POLICEMAN

SCENE 1

SETTING: *The living room of the Everly Hamster and Gerbil Plantation. A couch is downstage, center, and on all the walls are memorabilia of the Everly enterprises: a portrait of the late Max Everly, trophies and ribbons awarded his hamsters, and a large photo of a gerbil.*

AT RISE: MRS. EVERLY, *the plantation founder's elderly but lively widow, is draped on the couch, sobbing and daub-*

ing her eyes with an enormous handkerchief. Her butler,
Dustin, *flies about the room with a feather duster.*

Mrs. Everly: Oh, woe is me! All is gloom and despair!

Dustin: Why not open up your heart and let the sun shine in?

Mrs. Everly: Oh, shut up! You're nothing more than the butler around here, and you're making me sick!

Dustin (*Bowing*): Madam, if I'm the cause of all your dyspepsia and despair, there's nothing for me to do but kill myself . . . not, however, until I get all the back wages you owe me.

Mrs. Everly: Oh, Dustin! How could you!

Dustin: Easy. I'm flat broke and fed up. All this gloom and doom is beginning to take the zing out of me.

Mrs. Everly: I'm entitled to my woe. I'm the widowed grandmother in this farce. (*Waving her handkerchief*) Starvation is leering at me from behind every souvenir of my glorious hamster and gerbil plantation.

Dustin: We all have our little ups and downs.

Mrs. Everly (*Standing*): Remember the good old days, Dustin? Remember my late husband (*She flicks her handkerchief at portrait*), Miserly Max Everly, who wrested these thousands of acres from the claws of Mother Nature, and turned them into the happiest hamster haven this side of Hackensack?

Dustin: A tyrant, but he had his little ways.

Mrs. Everly: What vision he had . . . turning a bunch of rotten rodents into an empire! "A hamster for every hearth, a gerbil for every garage." That was his motto.

Dustin (*Opening his shirt to show a Mickey Mouse T-shirt*): I have it woven into all my undershirts. (*Rebuttons his shirt.*)

Mrs. Everly (*Touring the room*): Trophies . . . blue

ribbons (*With a sweeping gesture*) . . . trash. And all that lovely money! (*Moaning*) Oh, where is the bread of yesteryear? We're flat broke, Dustin.

DUSTIN: Maybe people don't dig the little beasties these days.

MRS. EVERLY: Maybe. I never could get within slingshot range (*Slapping the gerbil photo*) of their beady eyes without breaking out in a rash.

DUSTIN: On the other hand, you may have a culprit in your plantation manager, true-blue Phineas Fraud.

MRS. EVERLY (*Eagerly*): Maybe Phineas Fraud would be willing to take a mortgage!

DUSTIN: He's not named "Fraud" for nothing, you know.

MRS. EVERLY: There you go again. One minute you're full of sunshine, and the next you're making nasty slurs.

DUSTIN: It was no slur, Madam.

MRS. EVERLY: I don't have time to debate the fakery of Phineas. I have lots to do. (*Proudly*) Blossom's coming home today!

DUSTIN: Blossom! Not your darling granddaughter, Blossom Everly, the dainty, dimpled and demure!

MRS. EVERLY (*Nodding*): Home from State U. Aggie Farm and Finishing School. (*Briefly, more serious*) She called me last night. She's dropped out of school. (DUSTIN *feigns a swoon*) I confess the news rattled me a trifle at first, but, after a sleepless night, I realized that every cloud has a silver lining. Why shouldn't Blossom put the plantation back on its feet?

DUSTIN: I hardly think that Blossom's one course in cage-cleaning makes her a budding hamster tycoon.

MRS. EVERLY: You forget that Blossom's been learning a few other things—like how to be a smashing chick, and . . .

DUSTIN: A smashing chick?

MRS. EVERLY: Yes, and she's sure to snag the richest swain in town. (*Carried away by her own fantasy*) Then, we'll pay off the creditors and I'll nag my new grandson-in-law until he packs me off to the Riviera with a pension.

DUSTIN: Oh, Madam. How could you? You! An ex-suf-fragette!

MRS. EVERLY: How could I what?

DUSTIN: Use Blossom as a—a commodity (*Putting his hand on his head melodramatically*) . . . put her on the auction block! (*Throwing himself onto the couch*) Oh, no!

MRS. EVERLY (*Clutching at him*): Have pity, Dustin! My back is to the wall. (*Doorbell rings.*)

DUSTIN (*Rising, going to door*): First bill collector of the day, I suppose? (MRS. EVERLY *flops on couch.* DUSTIN *opens door to reveal* YARBIE, *dressed in jeans, sweat shirt and beads; he carries a guitar.*) Oh! (*In a bored tone, to* MRS. EVERLY) Madam, it's your hired hand, Yarborough Blair. (YARBIE *enters.*)

YARBIE (*Smiling*): You were expecting the Avon lady? (*Closes the door*) Hi, Mrs. Everly. What a beautiful day!

MRS. EVERLY (*Pulling herself up*): Just how much of this syrup and joy do you expect me to take?

YARBIE: What's wrong, man?

DUSTIN: Madam has a bad case of the blahs!

YARBIE: Sure, man. Today her rising sign shows that Capricorns should have stayed in bed. But, fear not. I'll clear away all the bad vibes by strumming a few lines of my latest protest song.

MRS. EVERLY (*Icily*): And what, pray tell, are you protesting now?

YARBIE: The enslavement and exploitation of the lemon. Part of my interest in ecology. The way I see it. . . .

MRS. EVERLY: No explanations, please. (*Wearily*) Strum your lemonade serenade . . . and scram.

YARBIE: I wrote this one in ragtime . . . to get the message across to you . . . uh . . . older folks.

MRS. EVERLY: Oh, brother!

YARBIE (*Singing*):
Lemons are like you and me,
All they want is to be free.
(DUSTIN *begins a cakewalk dance.*)
Still they're crushed in cakes and drinks.
Soaps for beards and kitchen sinks.
Though they perfume greasy stoves,
Lemons love life best in groves.
There's just one solution—
Citrus revolution—
Liberate the lemon, liberate the lemon,
Liberate the lemon . . . ra-a-ag!

MRS. EVERLY (*Approaching* YARBIE, *then pushing him into a chair*): Yarbie, dear . . . do sit down. Down! (*He sits.*) Now for the nitty-gritty. (*Sweetly*) Yarbie (*She pats his hand*), for the next few weeks I want you to make yourself very scarce. Go on some kind of love-in, or camp-out, or something. In other words, don't do your thing around *my* pad.

YARBIE: You hate me.

MRS. EVERLY: Not exactly. It's just that you're such a mess. You understand, don't you? (*Shrugs*) Of course you don't.

YARBIE: Sure, I do. Blossom's coming home.

MRS. EVERLY (*Surprised*): How did you know?

YARBIE: It's in the stars. Besides, I know the signs—you always treat me like the purple plague whenever Blossom's within fifty miles of here.

MRS. EVERLY: You're being very unfair. (*Pacing*) I realize that you and Blossom were good friends when you were tots, but it wasn't so serious when Blossom was that age for her to be cavorting with the hired help.

YARBIE: It isn't my fault that my pappy was chief hamster groom.

MRS. EVERLY: And a groovy groom he was, Yarbie. Absolutely aces.

YARBIE: I'm following in his tracks. (*Sighs*) It's the only way I know to pay my fare to rock festivals.

DUSTIN: Why don't you thumb like the rest of your crowd?

MRS. EVERLY: Quiet, Dustin. Yarbie, Blossom has been promised to another.

YARBIE: Like, who's the cat?

MRS. EVERLY (*Flustered, hesitatingly*): Er—well—we don't quite know.

YARBIE (*Jumping up*): You mean Blossom's up for bids?

DUSTIN (*Snorting*): You hit the nail on the head.

YARBIE (*Banging the table*): Well, I think that rots.

MRS. EVERLY (*Sternly*): It's for her own good, Yarbie.

YARBIE: Yeah? And what will Blossom think of all this?

MRS. EVERLY: She'll think it's divine. Dustin, show him the door.

DUSTIN (*Giving* YARBIE *a gentle push*): You heard the wrought-up widow, Yarbie. Buzz off!

YARBIE (*Going to door*): Man! What a protest song this will make! (*He exits, slamming the door after him.*)

MRS. EVERLY (*Hand to forehead, moving right*): I think I shall repair to my chambers for some sarsaparilla and a caraway biscuit. Should we be favored with any more visitors, just say that Madam has retired. (*She exits dramatically.* DUSTIN *starts to dust again, when doorbell rings.* DUSTIN *goes to door and opens it, revealing* PHINEAS FRAUD *in doorway.*)

PHINEAS (*Smoothly, with sinister laugh*): Well, Dustin, you baleful bag of bones. (*Enters and closes door*)

DUSTIN (*Icily*): If it isn't Phineas Fraud, our beloved plantation manager.

PHINEAS: And where's the worried widow, if I may ask?

DUSTIN: Nursing her neuroses.

PHINEAS: Pity. I bring tidings of deeds so dire, they'd really make her neurotic. No reason why I shouldn't let you in on the little secret, though.

DUSTIN: I can think of one good reason, *Mister* Fraud. I will not be your accomplice. Poor madam. I could not betray her.

PHINEAS: She's poor, all right. (*Hastily*) But I could change all that. Why, she could subdivide this pea-patch, put up little ticky-tacky lean-to's, toss in a few tamale stands and a surplus sauna . . . and she'd be in clover.

DUSTIN (*Stiffly*): To her, this plantation is sacred.

PHINEAS: So much the better for me. I've been stuffing those hamsters with so much wheat germ and vitamin B-12 that they've been multiplying like dandelions.

DUSTIN: But what do you do with them all?

PHINEAS: Stockpile 'em, dumb-dumb. I've been holding 'em off the market for years.

DUSTIN: I know, but aren't they getting a bit . . . ripe?

PHINEAS: You're forgetting my added ingredient . . . monkey glands! Why, those hamsters will go on forever . . . and climb trees besides.

DUSTIN: And what's all this going to get you?

PHINEAS: Power! And a lot of kicks.

DUSTIN: My head is spinning.

PHINEAS: Dustin, old buddy, all you have to do now is talk her into letting me take the mortgage, and I'll be set for negotiations.

DUSTIN: I told you I'm no accomplice. (*Curious, in spite of himself*) What negotiations?

PHINEAS: Be my accomplice, Dustin, pal, or you may never get your back salary.

DUSTIN: It gives me the twitches to think about it, but I may compromise. After all, I have nothing to lose but my self-respect. And besides . . . Blossom's coming home.

PHINEAS: Marvy. She must be old enough to wear braces by now.

DUSTIN: Beware of Blossom, that's all I have to say. 'Tis said she has turned into a ravishing beauty, with a plan or two up her sleeve.

PHINEAS: No female ever fooled or foiled Phineas Fraud! Ah, but I sense that you're not telling all.

DUSTIN: Well, phooey on you. When I asked you about your nefarious negotiations, all you did was change the subject. I'm not playing my last card.

PHINEAS: You're so petty!

DUSTIN: It's your move, brother.

PHINEAS: O.K. I'll level with you. I *need* the title to this pelt preserve because I've developed a secret weapon that I'm about to let loose on the world—through a foreign power which shall be nameless and whose unscrupulous agent is due to arrive here on the hour.

DUSTIN: You're not only crooked, you're crackers. They should call you Pretzels!

PHINEAS (*Shaking his finger*): Laugh if you will, but you'll see. The proof of the pudding is in how many cooks spoil the broth.

DUSTIN: Which reminds me that I must repair to the pantry to put a potato in the pot. The chef quit yesterday.

We're down to our last potato. What a cop-out! (*He exits.*)

PHINEAS (*Calling after him*): Keep the winsome widow out of here while I'm negotiating. (*A gong sounds.*) Ah, the hour has arrived. (*Doorbell rings, and he darts to door*) And so has the unscrupulous secret agent! (*He opens the door, and* BLOSSOM *enters. She is dressed in jeans, a sweat shirt, Indian headband and beads. Her hair hangs loose and wild. She is barefoot and carries a megaphone.*) Perfect! What a disguise!

BLOSSOM: I'm for women's liberation!

PHINEAS (*Admiringly*): Me, too. The customs agents must have thought you were nothing but a harmless hippie. (*She ignores him.*)

BLOSSOM (*Using her megaphone*): Up with Liberation! Down with the Establishment!

PHINEAS (*Rubbing his hands together*): Maybe we can change all that once we get down to business.

BLOSSOM: As soon as my troops arrive.

PHINEAS (*Jumping*): Troops?

BLOSSOM: You're kind of up tight, aren't you, mister?

PHINEAS (*Gulping*): Me? I'm just an average, easy-come, easy-go villain, that's all.

BLOSSOM: You're just a male chauvinist.

PHINEAS: A what?

BLOSSOM (*Moving in on him*): You think I'm inferior, don't you?

PHINEAS (*Retreating*): On the contrary. As long as you have the cash, you hold all the cards.

BLOSSOM (*Throwing up her hands*): All you guys ever think of is money.

PHINEAS: What foreign power do you represent, anyway?

BLOSSOM: You'll see.

PHINEAS: Do you want to rule the world, or don't you?

BLOSSOM: Man, are you off the deep end!

PHINEAS (*Almost pleading*): Can't a villain be vile any more without one double cross after another?

BLOSSOM: These aren't the good old days, you know.

PHINEAS: You're telling me! Time was when an unscrupulous agent from an unknown foreign power would know her place.

BLOSSOM: Her *place?* Times have changed, buddy. Get out of my sight! (*She pushes him to the door*) And the quicker the better.

PHINEAS: Someone else will want my secret weapons. In the meantime, I'll let a few of them loose on you! (*He exits.*)

BLOSSOM (*Laughing*): Poor old Phineas. Just as nutty as ever. (*She goes to telephone and dials.*) I guess I've changed. He didn't even recognize me. (*Slight pause.*) Hi, Yarbie? Hi. It's me. Blossom! Yeah, man. I'm home! (*Curtains close.*)

*   *   *

SCENE 2

SETTING: *The Everly home, the same as Scene 1.*

AT RISE: MRS. EVERLY *is sitting on the couch.*

MRS. EVERLY: Oh, woe is me! (*Looking around*) Where is that girl! (*Doorbell rings.*) Perhaps I'll get some sympathy at last. (*Calling*) Come in, if you have a tender heart. (PETUNIA *opens door and slinks onstage, followed by a dapper* COUNT, *who carries suitcase. Both speak with foreign accents.*)

PETUNIA (*Aside*): Put my suitcase down, please, darling.

Now where is this Phineas Fraud we're supposed to meet here?

COUNT: I'm sure he'll make an appearance. . . .

MRS. EVERLY (*Breaking in, tearfully*): Is that you, Blossom? I can barely see through my veil of tears.

PETUNIA (*To* COUNT): What's this "Blossom" bit?

COUNT: Blossom? A kind of flower.

PETUNIA: Then she knows that I'm Petunia Plotafoot, unscrupulous agent! She must be the doll to deal with.

MRS. EVERLY: Please don't mumble, Blossom. Come and console me. It is Blossom, isn't it?

PETUNIA (*To* COUNT): So I'll go along with the gag. (*To* MRS. EVERLY) Of course, darling, it's Blossom. You're in distress, no?

MRS. EVERLY (*Sitting up, looking at* PETUNIA, *then doing a double-take*): Wow, baby! They've really done you over.

PETUNIA (*Comforting her*): You've been crying, darling. Too many tears make the face puffy.

MRS. EVERLY: They taught you everything at good old State U., didn't they!

PETUNIA: It was a crash course, but a mind-blower.

MRS. EVERLY: They've even changed your accent.

PETUNIA: There are no half measures when you're dealing in destinies. May I present the Count?

COUNT (*Kissing* MRS. EVERLY'*s hand*): Charmed, Madame. Seldom in this country does one encounter such delicacy of feeling, such tenderness, such . . .

PETUNIA: You're overdoing it, darling.

MRS. EVERLY: But Blossom . . . he's cute!

PETUNIA: Also a million laughs.

MRS. EVERLY (*Aside, to* PETUNIA): Tell me . . . is he rich?

PETUNIA: He can pay my tab at the pizza parlor, if that's what you mean.

MRS. EVERLY (*To* COUNT): Tell me, Count, do you and Blossom have serious intentions?

COUNT: Nothing can stop us now!

MRS. EVERLY (*Jumping about*): Whoopee!

PETUNIA: I would like to freshen up, please. The trip was . . . how you say . . . a drag.

MRS. EVERLY: I'll come with you. The Count won't mind. He knows we have things to talk about. You know, Count (*Giggling*), girl talk? (PETUNIA *and* MRS. EVERLY *exit.*)

COUNT (*To himself*): Why can't they just sell you secret weapons like a can of sardines and be done with it? But, no, they have their agents freaking out all over the place. (*Doorbell rings repeatedly.*)

DUSTIN (*Entering, wiping his hands with a towel*): How can anybody boil a potato with all these interruptions! (DUSTIN *opens the door.* YARBIE *bounds into room, slamming the door behind him.*)

YARBIE: Have you seen Blossom?

DUSTIN: Look, yokel, if Widow Everly sees you around here, she'll feed you to the pussy cat. And, to answer your question, the answer is I don't think so.

YARBIE: You'd know if you saw her, man!

COUNT: Blossom, as you call her, is upstairs.

YARBIE (*Indicating the* COUNT): Who's he?

DUSTIN: Blossom must have brought him home.

COUNT (*Putting his thumbs to his ears and wiggling his fingers*): I'm a spy, of course!

DUSTIN: Well, everybody knows who I am, and I'm off! (*He starts out to the kitchen, singing*) "Polly put the kettle on, we'll all have tea . . ." And if anybody asks who let you in here, Yarborough Blair, you just stormed the gates yourself. (*He exits.*)

YARBIE (*To* COUNT): Are you really Blossom's latest?

COUNT: No . . . just a suave flunky who's going off his rocker.

YARBIE: Yeah? . . . And what's with Blossom?

COUNT: With Blossom is a giggling reject from the Geritol Follies. You know, I think I'm getting tired of playing this "Blossom" game.

YARBIE: She used to be kinda sweet.

COUNT: Deep down under that satin-swathed façade beats the heart of a feminine feline. Smart as a whip, though.

YARBIE: You know what she wants to do? She wants to set them free . . . liberate them, that's what she wants to do.

COUNT: Don't you believe it. She wants every man to be her slave.

YARBIE: I mean the hamsters! It's a symbolic crusade! (BLOSSOM *slams into room. She carries her megaphone and a "*CAN THE CAGE*" sign.*)

BLOSSOM: Liberate them all!

YARBIE (*To* COUNT): I thought you said she was upstairs!

COUNT (*Pointing at* BLOSSOM): You mean . . . *that's* Blossom?

YARBIE (*Nodding weakly*): Sure is.

BLOSSOM: Just wait 'til my troops get here.

COUNT: Troops? (*Charging stage right, calling offstage frantically*) Petunia!

PHINEAS (*Rushing in after* BLOSSOM): You're dashing my designs, foiling my fantasies!

COUNT (*Louder*): Petunia!

PHINEAS: I've been training those tiny rodents for years! They're going to jumble the jets, put cogs in the computers . . . create chaos!

COUNT (*Still louder*): Petunia . . . it's a trap!

PETUNIA (*Entering, followed by* MRS. EVERLY): What's the din all about, darling?

COUNT (*Pointing to* BLOSSOM): *That's* the secret weapon, and it's calling the fuzz on us!

PETUNIA (*Calmly*): This may call for a change in plan.

BLOSSOM (*To* MRS. EVERLY): Hi, Granny. I'm home. It's me. Blossom.

MRS. EVERLY (*Dumfounded, pointing to* PETUNIA): But, I thought *she* was you!

PETUNIA: I'm a fake.

MRS. EVERLY: I thought so, when you didn't even recognize your old Barbie doll. Sling me a seltzer, somebody. (*Sound of motorcycles, sirens and martial music is heard from offstage.*)

BLOSSOM (*Going to window*): Here they come!

PETUNIA (*Starting to door*): And here we go, Count.

PHINEAS (*Blocking them*): Nobody goes until I deal my deal!

YARBIE (*Looking out window*): What a scene!

BLOSSOM (*As noise grows*): We're on the move!

MRS. EVERLY: I wanted the Riviera, not a revolution!

BLOSSOM (*Using her megaphone*): Free the hamsters! Right on, rebels! (*As the curtain falls,* MRS. EVERLY *grabs* BLOSSOM *by her beads and pulls her offstage left.* BLOSSOM *continues her slogan-shouting and the offstage noises boom as the curtains close.*)

*   *   *

SCENE 3

BEFORE RISE: MRS. EVERLY *leads* BLOSSOM *onstage, in front of the curtain.*

MRS. EVERLY: When those famous troops of yours arrive, you're just going to have to get rid of them.

BLOSSOM: I don't care what you say. This is a symbolic crusade.

MRS. EVERLY: Let the hamsters romp free in the forest, and your darling grandmother will have to pop off to the poorhouse.

BLOSSOM: Affluence from caged animals is wicked.

MRS. EVERLY: They paid for your tuition, and bought a few knickknacks for you as well. And how do you expect to harpoon a husband when you're decked out like the dregs of a grab bag?

BLOSSOM: This is my uniform. I want no part of your scheming. And you of all people—an ex-suffragette. Look at you! What are you now?

MRS. EVERLY: There's one thing I know I am, and that's broke.

BLOSSOM: Have hamsters brought you happiness? Have gerbils brought you joy?

MRS. EVERLY: I despise the blasted things.

BLOSSOM: See? They've made you bitter. In the long run, all you've done is turn these beautiful acres into a blight on the environment.

MRS. EVERLY: I have?

BLOSSOM: Yarbie was the one who pointed it out to me.

MRS. EVERLY (*Knowingly*): Oh, did he!

BLOSSOM: And he gave me the idea.

MRS. EVERLY: He did?

BLOSSOM (*Nodding*): He wrote me letters all about it. You should give him credit for that, even if he is only a man.

MRS. EVERLY (*Somewhat tenderly*): My Max was a man, too. I rather liked that about him.

BLOSSOM: Besides, Yarbie found out about Phineas. He's a fraud.

MRS. EVERLY: Of all the nerve!

BLOSSOM: He's taken you for your last trolley token.

MRS. EVERLY (*Yielding*): I've been such a fool.

BLOSSOM (*Rapidly, almost without pauses*): Yarbie suspected something was suspicious when he was taking off for a music festival last fall, and Phineas asked him to see whether he could contact some unscrupulous agents from an unknown foreign power who might be interested in paying a pretty penny for a haul of hungry hamsters that could be used as a secret weapon (*Taking a breath*) . . . because they could gum up the intricate insides of anybody's military-industrial complex by weaseling through the wires of the most complicated computers and making a general mess. (*Gasps for breath*)

MRS. EVERLY: So Yarbie surmised that Phineas was a traitor? (*Shaking her head*) What's a granny to do?

BLOSSOM: Yarbie wasn't sure, either, but I've figured the whole thing out. Give Phineas the heave-ho, free the hamsters, and you still have this paradise of a plantation. It would make a dandy commune.

MRS. EVERLY: A what?

BLOSSOM: A commune. (*Looks at watch*) We can talk about that later. The troops have taken their stations by now, and in a few more minutes they'll open the cages. You'll see. I've thought of everything.

REPORTER (*Entering, carrying a pad and pencil*): Oh, Mrs. Everly? I'm a reporter from the *Daily Blatt*. We've heard of your concern for ecology, your animal altruism.

CAMERAMAN (*Entering, carrying a TV camera*): I'm from KTV-TV, Mrs. Everly. You're going to make a mint. We've scheduled you for "Meet the Public," and three night talk shows. (*Curtains open behind them.*)

*   *   *

SETTING: *The Everly living room.*

AT RISE: PETUNIA, COUNT, *and* YARBIE *watch as* TROOPS,

girls in outfits similar to BLOSSOM's, *mill around.* PO-LICEMAN *holds* PHINEAS *by the collar.* BLOSSOM *and* MRS. EVERLY *enter, followed by* REPORTER *and* CAMERAMAN.

BLOSSOM (*To* MRS. EVERLY): Now don't worry, Granny. I told you I'd thought of everything.

POLICEMAN (*To* PHINEAS): Just hold still until the wagon arrives.

COUNT (*Aside*): How I long for the salt of Siberia!

MRS. EVERLY (*To* PHINEAS): Well! I always thought you were a snake!

PHINEAS: We'll see who has the last laugh. Those hamsters know their master.

TROOPS (*Chanting, ad lib*): Liberation! Can the cage! Free the hamsters! Right on! (*Etc.*)

PHINEAS: One word from me, and they'll nibble you all to nubbins.

YARBIE: Hamsters aren't vicious.

PHINEAS: Neither is a hungry shark. (*Jeers*)

CAMERAMAN: The camera's all set.

PHINEAS: If you're smart, you'll pack it in an armored truck, and get out of here as fast as you can.

BLOSSOM (*Consulting her watch, her right hand held high*): Time for the countdown.

MRS. EVERLY: Are we really in danger?

BLOSSOM: Five!

PETUNIA: Guess I'll miss this year's reunion . . .

BLOSSOM: Four!

PETUNIA: . . . of the Mata Hari Society.

BLOSSOM *and* TROOPS: Three!

PHINEAS: You won't foil Phineas!

BLOSSOM *and* TROOPS: Two! One! (*There is a second of silence.*)

YARBIE (*Weakly*): Like, zero? (*Silence*)

MRS. EVERLY: Nothing's happening!

REPORTER: Say, is this for real?

BLOSSOM: It's for real, all right. (*Gradually, scuffling and squeaking sounds are heard from offstage.*) Ah, listen to their freedom song. (*The sounds increase.*) They're free! Free! (BLOSSOM, YARBIE *and the* TROOPS *cheer.*) Right on, hamsters! (MRS. EVERLY *laughs nervously;* PHINEAS *chuckles and twirls his moustache. Door bursts open, and noises become very loud as the invisible hamsters and gerbils rush onstage. Everyone jumps on chairs and tables or scurries for shelter except* PHINEAS. REPORTER *takes notes furiously, and* CAMERAMAN *tries to record the scene.*)

PHINEAS (*Shouting*): Down, baby. Nice gerbil. There's a good hamster. Hey! Ouch! I'm your friend. Bite somebody else, why don't you! (*He screams for help, does a mad dance about room, then heads for door and darts offstage. As he disappears, animal noises fade, and gradually everyone gets down from chairs, etc.*)

CAMERAMAN: I hope the camera got all that.

REPORTER: This is one story I'm handing to the editor personally. (*He exits.*)

CAMERAMAN (*Following him*): If this hits the six o'clock news, I have it made. (*He exits.*)

POLICEMAN: Where is everybody?

MRS. EVERLY: I think Phineas has flown.

POLICEMAN: We'll catch up with him; don't worry. (*Spotting* PETUNIA *and the* COUNT) Ah . . . there's the pair I'm after.

PETUNIA: I surrender. A firing squad is one thing, but hamsters on the lam I don't dig. (*They exit with* POLICE-MAN.)

BLOSSOM (*Through megaphone*): Troops, victory is ours.

(*They cheer.*) You may all disperse. (TROOPS *exit, cheering.*)

YARBIE (*To* BLOSSOM, *as he crosses toward door*): Well, old buddy, it looks as if that's that.

BLOSSOM: Yarbie! You're leaving? And what's this buddy bit?

YARBIE: I'm going to split. I mean, I'm still a guy, and I still like girls, but all this liberation stuff, with troops— (*Shrugs*)

BLOSSOM (*Going over to him*): Don't go, Yarbie. Right after dinner I'll give you all my pamphlets, and we can have a real rap session. What I want, you know, is liberation for everyone. (*She takes his hand.* MRS. EVERLY *beams at them.*)

DUSTIN (*Entering with a single potato on a silver tray*): Madam, potato is served.

BLOSSOM: Yarbie, play me a protest song, will you? (*Quick curtain*)

THE END

Production Notes

WAY, WAY DOWN SOUTH

Characters: 7 male; 3 female; as many female extras as desired for Troops.
Playing Time: 35 minutes.
Costumes: Blossom, Yarbie and the Troops wear jeans, sweat shirts, T-shirts, etc., ropes of beads and Indian headbands, and other appropriate "with-it" clothes. Phineas wears a loud suit. Petunia has a slinky gown, and the Count wears a business suit with suave touches—a bowler, an umbrella, spats, etc. Dustin wears black cutaway suit, snap-on bow tie which can be easily removed when he opens his shirt to reveal Mickey Mouse undershirt. Mrs. Everly wears a flowing gown, shawl, ropes of pearls, and other touches of vanished elegance.
Properties: Feather duster and towel, handkerchief, guitar, megaphone, watch and CAN THE CAGE sign, similar signs for Troops, suitcase, pad and pencil, portable TV camera, potato, silver tray.
Setting: The living room of the Everly Hamster and Gerbil Plantation. Couch, chairs, table and decorative screens are placed around the room, and on the walls are memorabilia of the Everly enterprises: a portrait of the late Max Everly, trophies and ribbons, large photo of a gerbil. There are doors to the kitchen, left, and to the outside, right.
Lighting: No special effects.
Sound: Doorbell, gong, recorded sounds of motorcycles, sirens, marching music, and sounds of scurrying animals, as indicated in text.

Young Forever

Characters

AUNT ZOE
RUDY, *her nephew, seventeen*
MR. HACKER ⎤
MRS. HACKER ⎦ *tourists*
GILBERT ⎤
MERRILEE ⎬ *teen-agers*
JOAN ⎦
PEPE PONCE DE LEON

SETTING: *Lonely strip of beach on Florida coast. At left stand a palm tree and tropical plants. At right is a roadside stand, with a counter and several stools in front of it. A large sign on stand reads,* RUDY THE BEACHCOMBER. *Other signs read,* FLORIDA SOUVENIRS, COCONUT MILK 10¢ —SPECIAL FORMULA FOR ETERNAL YOUTH, *etc.*

AT RISE: MR. *and* MRS. HACKER, *tourists, sit on stools in front of counter, examining wallets.* RUDY *stands beside them. Out of sight of audience, and unknown to the* HACKERS, AUNT ZOE *is hiding behind counter, listening.*

MR. HACKER: Don't tell *me* these wallets are genuine lizard!

185

Rudy: You doubt my word, sir? Why, you can ask anyone!

Mrs. Hacker: Who's "anyone"? I don't think there's a house around here for miles.

Rudy (*Pointing toward audience*): Yes, there is—that big castle over there.

Mrs. Hacker (*Turning, squinting*): That ruined house in back of the sand dunes? You call that a castle?

Rudy: I do, madam, because that's exactly what it is, and the dear lady who owns it cleans all seventy rooms herself.

Mrs. Hacker: That woman must be off her rocker.

Rudy: She's a woman of intelligence, madam. You ask her about the wallets if you don't believe me.

Mr. Hacker: I've tried to make it clear, Mr. Beachcomber. We don't want to buy anything. All we want are directions—so that we can get back to the main highway for Miami.

Rudy (*Pointing to sign*): What about some of my special formula coconut milk to maintain youth?

Mr. Hacker: A ten-cent youth potion? Ha! A fake.

Rudy (*Assuming pose*): Well, how old do you think I am?

Mr. Hacker (*Looking closely at* Rudy): I don't know. Sixteen?

Rudy (*Pretending to laugh*): Sixteen! Old Rudy looks sixteen! Wait till the boys at the Senior Citizens' Club hear about this!

Mrs. Hacker: Come on, Homer. This kid's wasting our time.

Rudy: Wasting your time? Why, madam, the lady who lives in the castle drinks this coconut milk constantly. She's 93, but you'd never know it.

Mrs. Hacker: We only want to get out of here!

Rudy: How about some guava jelly?

MR. HACKER: We hate guava jelly!

RUDY (*Bringing out some rocks*): A few bits of Indian lore?

MRS. HACKER: Why, those are nothing but a bunch of dirty rocks.

RUDY (*Desperately*): But *what* dirty rocks, madam! Left here by the Indians when Ponce de Leon explored the Florida coast.

MR. HACKER: You know, you're beginning to make me angry!

RUDY (*Producing samples*): Some driftwood, then? How about a genuine jellyfish preserved in an old mayonnaise jar?

MR. HACKER (*Angrily*): Look, kid, or Rudy the Beachcomber, or whoever you are, we're due in Miami at noon tomorrow, and we have to inspect a lot of real estate on the way.

RUDY (*Eagerly*): Real estate? You're not, by chance, looking for investment property? Sure you are! You want to buy a bit of Florida and make a mint!

MRS. HACKER (*Tugging at her husband's arm*): Come on. I'm hot.

RUDY (*Jumping in their path*): It just so happens, sir, that I am the exclusive broker for the magnificent coastline you see before you.

MR. HACKER: This forsaken sand strip? If we hadn't taken the wrong turn, we'd never have blundered along here to begin with.

RUDY: But think of the possibilities, sir! And I'm sure the little lady who owns all ten miles of this land would listen to an offer of about five hundred dollars an acre.

MRS. HACKER: Is that a lot, Homer?

RUDY (*Briskly*): No, madam, not five hundred a lot, five hundred an acre! Think of the bargain!

MR. HACKER (*Gruffly to his wife*): It's a bargain, all right.

This Rudy the Beachcomber would try to sell an Eskimo a refrigerator and a freezer!

RUDY: All it takes is vision, sir. Maybe if you'd rejuvenate your brain by drinking some of my coconut milk you'd have some of that vision! (*Gesturing to include the whole stage*) One day you'll drive along this cowpath— only it will be a magnificent boulevard then—and you'll see the skyscraper hotels and the free-form swimming pools, and you'll turn to your wife and say, "Honey, I could kick myself from here to Jacksonville for scoffing at the word of that poor old beachcomber."

MR. HACKER (*Taking his wife's arm*): Come on, Primrose, let's get out of here.

MRS. HACKER: But, Homer, you still don't know how to get back to the Miami highway!

MR. HACKER (*Furiously*): Let's go! I'll find the way myself! (*They storm off.*)

RUDY (*Weakly*): 'Bye! (*Suddenly* AUNT ZOE *pops up behind counter. She shakes her fist angrily in direction of* HACKERS *as sound of automobile starting and driving off is heard from offstage.*)

AUNT ZOE (*Shouting*): Have a nice trip, you cheapskates! (*Sarcastically*) You're the last of the big spenders! (*To* RUDY) Never you mind, boy. They'll be back. Nobody was ever known to find his own way out of this territory.

RUDY: Aunt Zoe, I wish you wouldn't hide under the counter this way when I'm trying to close a big business deal.

AUNT ZOE: But I like hiding there!

RUDY: I don't care. You mumble nasty remarks about the customers and distract me from my sales pitch.

AUNT ZOE (*Pouting*): Rudy, you're scolding me! (*She walks out from behind counter.*) Anyway, that woman did look grotesque—don't deny it.

RUDY: Even if she did, looks aren't everything.

AUNT ZOE: Don't nod in my direction when you say that, boy.

RUDY: I wasn't referring to you.

AUNT ZOE: I'm pretty well preserved for 93 . . . isn't that how old you said I was?

RUDY: You know I didn't mean anything by that!

AUNT ZOE (*Returning to stand*): You're just looking for an excuse, that's what you're looking for . . . somebody to blame for your bumbling salesmanship.

RUDY: Selling anybody anything is hard work.

AUNT ZOE (*Sitting on stool in front of stand*): You know, you *would* try to sell an Eskimo a freezer. But, Rudy, something has to be done about you before we both are consumed by dry rot and eaten by sand fleas.

RUDY (*Protesting*): I'm doing the best I can!

AUNT ZOE: You'll have to do better. For one thing, there's no point in trying to sell anybody your special formula keep-'em-young-forever coconut milk at ten cents a cup.

RUDY (*Weakly*): Five cents?

AUNT ZOE (*Loudly*): One dollar!

RUDY: What? Who'd pay a price like that?

AUNT ZOE: At least as many people as are willing to pay ten cents! Give me a crayon, Rudy. (*He does so.*) And another thing. (*She goes to sign and changes price.*) You have to start quoting my property at five or ten *thousand* an acre, not five *hundred*. People like to pay a lot of money for things, Rudy. Makes 'em think they're getting something goldplated and glamorous.

RUDY: Then why not twenty thousand an acre?

AUNT ZOE: Why not? When you're really desperate to sell something, up the price . . . I learned that in a crash course in salesmanship long before you were born. And

I'm desperate to sell this place, Rudy. It's my nerves. Your Aunt Zoe isn't what she used to be.

RUDY: You seem the same to me.

AUNT ZOE: Oh, no. No matter how young I think these days, I can't seem to stir up any of the old zing. (*She takes out handkerchief.*) Pretty soon I'll be feeling creaky and feeble, Rudy. But don't let that bother you! (*She sniffs.*)

RUDY (*Concerned*): Don't cry, Aunt Zoe.

AUNT ZOE (*Dramatically*): You have your life to live. Why should you want a wrinkled old albatross around your neck? (*As* RUDY *starts to protest*) Wait a minute! Wrinkled . . . creaky . . . feeble. . . . How old did you tell those tourists I was?

RUDY (*Puzzled*): I said you were 93.

AUNT ZOE: Well, just hold on a minute, Rudy. (*She goes behind counter and brings out sack of flour, piece of charred driftwood, mirror, old shawl and her purse.*)

RUDY: What are you doing with the flour? And the charred driftwood?

AUNT ZOE (*Beginning to powder her hair with flour*): I'm making myself into a first-class little old lady, because I have to get out of here and make my way to the big city before I snap. (*She draws lines on her face with charred wood during the next speeches.*)

RUDY: Aunt Zoe, we can't leave here until we sell the place, you know.

AUNT ZOE (*Sputtering*): Rotten poverty! Makes me sick!

RUDY: But Aunt Zoe! This is all we have!

AUNT ZOE (*Still making up her face*): I know, and I'm going to make it pay. Oh, I don't mean to chide you, boy. I just want to give things a little push. You see, there isn't much time left to me.

RUDY: Nonsense, Aunt Zoe. You'll go on forever.

AUNT ZOE (*Brightly*): You think so? There isn't really some power in the coconut milk, is there?

RUDY: No. It's barely more than water.

AUNT ZOE: Too bad. (*Turning to face* RUDY *and showing that she is now made up to look much older*) Well, how do I look?

RUDY (*Laughing*): You look at least 93! How did you do it?

AUNT ZOE (*Putting away her materials*): A little driftwood charcoal for the complexion and for wrinkles and shadows, some flour for white hair, and a spine bent at the thought of spending the rest of my life here waiting for you to sell the place, and there you have it! (*She pretends to walk with a limp.*)

RUDY: What do you expect to accomplish?

AUNT ZOE: Everything, Rudy! Just everything! (*Suddenly she grabs* RUDY *and pulls him back into stand.*) Be careful! (*Pointing off*) Some kids are coming. See? They have weapons! (GILBERT, JOAN *and* MERRILEE *enter, with a bicycle and surfboards.*)

RUDY: Relax, Aunt Zoe.

AUNT ZOE (*To teen-agers*): Halt! You're trespassing on private property!

GILBERT (*Dumfounded*): We're sorry. Honest! We didn't know it was private property!

MERRILEE (*Climbing on stool*): Just to show we don't mean any harm, we'll take a double round of cheeseburgers and malts.

RUDY: Sorry, we don't sell food here. Not that kind. No demand for it. Now, what will you have? Kumquat marmalade? Pickled mango in avocado juice?

AUNT ZOE: I pickle a mean mango.

GILBERT: Then I'll take *two* pickled mangoes.

AUNT ZOE: Oh, no, you don't. No buttering up a wise old

gal like Aunt Zoe. You were down on that beach because you wanted something.

MERRILEE: Actually, we did want something, but we'll forget about it and be on our way.

AUNT ZOE: Wait a minute. What did you want?

GILBERT: Just a place to surf.

MERRILEE: We're advance scouts for the surf club.

GILBERT: We've been exploring the coast all morning.

AUNT ZOE: Surfing, you say?

RUDY (*To* AUNT ZOE): Surfing's a sport.

JOAN: It's become so popular that everybody's getting in everybody's way.

GILBERT: The beaches are too crowded.

MERRILEE: And people are starting to complain.

GILBERT: I guess it isn't the sort of sport older ladies would go in for.

AUNT ZOE (*Bouncing out of stand*): A real young sport, is it?

MERRILEE: More or less. You have to be fairly agile.

AUNT ZOE: Why? Tell me more!

MERRILEE: Because you have to be able to stand up and balance on the board while you ride the wave into shore.

AUNT ZOE: Whee! That sounds like a blast!

GILBERT (*Cautiously*): You know, we'd be glad to pay a fee if you'd let the club use your beach. It is your beach, isn't it?

AUNT ZOE: It is. Ten miles of it. That should give you enough room for riding the waves, don't you think?

JOAN: You mean you really might let us use the place?

RUDY: We should be able to work out a reasonable fee for you. We're looking for something to . . . to tide us over.

MERRILEE: We promise we won't leave any litter.

JOAN: We'll even help you beachcomb if you want . . . or mind your stand for you when you take a day off.

GILBERT: Once word gets around that surfers are welcome here, you might do quite a business!

AUNT ZOE (*Walking to stage center*): It's all O.K. with me on one condition. (*Flatly*) Teach me to surf, too!

GILBERT: Oh. Well, now. I have no objections to teaching you, but I'm afraid I don't see how . . .

AUNT ZOE (*Emphatically*): Then the deal's off.

GILBERT: It's just that I wouldn't want to be responsible.

AUNT ZOE: Responsible for what? (*Taking out handkerchief*) For giving an old lady a little happiness in her twilight years?

RUDY: Come off it, Aunt Zoe.

JOAN: He just wouldn't want to be responsible for your going out there and breaking your neck, that's all!

AUNT ZOE (*Sternly, putting away handkerchief*): Well, think no more of it. I'll just have to be content to while away my remaining time on a trampoline.

GILBERT: After all, people have slower reflexes when they reach middle age.

AUNT ZOE (*Flattered*): Middle age?

GILBERT: I don't mean to insult you, ma'am.

AUNT ZOE (*Batting her lashes*): How old do you think I am?

GILBERT (*Embarrassed*): I don't know.

RUDY (*To* AUNT ZOE): It's mean to put him on the spot.

AUNT ZOE (*To* GILBERT): Tell me, boy.

GILBERT: Well, you must be old enough to be my mother.

AUNT ZOE (*Patting* GILBERT's *cheek*): Sweet!

MERRILEE: And who'd risk teaching his mother how to surf?

RUDY: Nobody's mother is like Aunt Zoe.

AUNT ZOE (*Darting to stand*): If it'll make you feel any better, I'll sign a statement releasing you from all responsibility. (*She whips out pen and paper and writes.*)

RUDY (*To* GILBERT): Don't worry. She knows what she's doing. She decided a long time ago she was going to stay young forever, and sometimes I think she will.

AUNT ZOE (*Returning*): There you are. (*She hands* GILBERT *the paper.*) Now, one of you girls can zip back and tell your surf club you've found your beach. (*Sound of automobile approaching is heard.*) And you, young man . . . (*She hears the automobile, looks to the right and speaks to* RUDY) There they are again, Rudy dear. I told you they'd come back. (*To* GILBERT) I'm sorry, kids. I have a little business to transact right now. But you run down to the beach and warm up a surfboard for me. As soon as I'm through here, I'll tear home, put on my bikini, and whoopee!

GILBERT (*To* AUNT ZOE *as they move off stage left*): The kids sure will be glad they're welcome here, ma'am.

AUNT ZOE (*Assuming an "old" position on a stool and shooing the surfers off*): Think nothing of it. See you!

GILBERT (*To* JOAN *and* MERRILEE): I hope you have a first-aid kit.

JOAN (*To* GILBERT): Do you think we're doing the right thing? (*He shrugs.*) She looks ancient! (*They exit.*)

MR. HACKER (*Puffing in, stage right*): Now you look here!

RUDY: Ah, my rapidly aging friend who's looking for a good buy in real estate.

MR. HACKER: Now don't start that again! I'm back here for one reason!

RUDY (*Innocently*): And what, pray tell, could that be?

MR. HACKER: Get me off this rocky trail and back on the main highway! I'm hot (*He chokes*) and my throat is parched!

RUDY (*Pouring from bottle into paper cup*): Then have a cup of my coconut milk!

AUNT ZOE (*Feebly*): Excuse me, son. I was here first. (MR. HACKER *gulps the milk, then looks horrified.*) Would you give me two cups of your special formula coconut milk? (RUDY *pours.*)

MR. HACKER: You'll be sorry, granny.

AUNT ZOE (*Ignoring him*): I heard about its therapeutic powers from my sister-in-law. You may remember her. The old hag who was on her way to St. Petersburg to wait out her last days in the sunshine? Felt the shadow of the grim reaper, she did. (*To* MR. HACKER) Eighty years young . . . and a frail thing . . . convinced her days were numbered. (*To* RUDY) But now she's joined a crowd of ski bums and headed for Switzerland. (*To* MR. HACKER) And don't think it's not a relief to me, mister. There were days when I thought she and I would be taking each other's blood pressure all afternoon.

MR. HACKER: Rudy! Please! Give me the directions.

AUNT ZOE: Don't interrupt! It's rude, and old ladies like me won't put up with it.

RUDY (*Giving her two cups*): Here you are, ma'am. That will be ten, twenty . . .

AUNT ZOE (*Immediately*): Two dollars! It's one dollar per cup. I see your sign!

MR. HACKER (*Looking at changed sign*): What?

AUNT ZOE: I don't blame you for upping your price, Mr. Rudy. Fame of your magic potion has spread as far as Atlanta. (*To* MR. HACKER) That's where I come from, mister. Sped myself along the scenic route in my own wheelchair, I did. It broke down two miles from here, and I crawled the rest of the way.

MR. HACKER: Now just a minute!

AUNT ZOE: Well, here's to youth! (*She drinks rapidly.*)

MRS. HACKER (*Entering right*): Homer, what *are* you doing? Can't you ask for some simple directions?

MR. HACKER: That's all I've been trying to do.

MRS. HACKER: We've just been going around in circles!

MR. HACKER (*Shouting*): You're telling me?

MRS. HACKER: Don't shout at me, Homer Hacker. It's not my fault!

MR. HACKER: I've had to stand here and wait while this . . . this . . .

AUNT ZOE (*Smiling*): This dear old lady . . .

MR. HACKER: This dear old lady guzzles that curdled soup.

AUNT ZOE: And you know, I feel better already. (*She slowly slides off stool.*) Sure! (*She drags herself about the stage.*) Used to be I could barely get out of my wheelchair to switch on "The Old Folks at Home Hour." (*She shows improvement.*) I never thought these old bones would click in harmony again. That special formula coconut milk! It's the living end! He-he! (*She begins to act more sprightly.*)

RUDY: Now, don't overdo it, ma'am.

AUNT ZOE: Don't tell me how to skin a cat, sonny.

RUDY (*To* MR. HACKER): You never know. Sometimes the stuff works like magic. Depends on the metabolism and the genetic setup.

AUNT ZOE (*Kicking up her heels*): Not bad for a girl my age, eh?

MRS. HACKER: How old *are* you?

AUNT ZOE: How'd you like it if I asked you that question? (*She gradually straightens, at first with effort, then almost with relief.*) There! The old spine's like a ramrod again!

MRS. HACKER: Homer, do you suppose that coconut milk would do something for us?

MR. HACKER: It could kill us!

MRS. HACKER: But, Homer! Look at her! I must be seeing things.

MR. HACKER: It wouldn't be the first time.

MRS. HACKER: Homer, I want some of that milk!

MR. HACKER: But it's terrible! I just had a cup.

RUDY (*Filling cup*): Try a sip before you buy a gallon. The price may go up again. Nothing to lose but your old age.

MR. HACKER: And my hard-earned money. (MRS. HACKER *drinks.*)

AUNT ZOE (*Now almost leaping*): Zowie!

MRS. HACKER: This stuff tastes like medicine!

MR. HACKER (*Childishly*): I told you so.

RUDY: But you'd be suspicious if it tasted yummy, now, wouldn't you?

MRS. HACKER (*To* MR. HACKER): Well? How do I look?

MR. HACKER: How does anybody look after a dose of poison?

MRS. HACKER (*To* RUDY): Do I look any different?

RUDY: The question is, how do you feel?

MRS. HACKER: Well . . . not bad . . . not bad at all! Rudy, I'll take a gallon of that stuff, and if it keeps on working, we'll stop by on our way home and buy more.

AUNT ZOE: I think I'll go swimming! Sure! Why not? Maybe I could even surf and ride the waves. Yahoo! (*She exits left.*)

RUDY (*Calling*): Don't forget to come back and place your permanent order, ma'am! (*To the* HACKERS) That will be twenty dollars, please.

MR. HACKER: Twenty dollars!

RUDY: You can see, it's cheaper buying it this way.

MRS. HACKER (*A little giggly*): Anything that expensive *must* be good. Pay him, Homer. I'm dying to start my treatment. (*He pays reluctantly.*)

RUDY: But you already started your treatment, madam.

And as you continue, keep telling yourself that with every sip and every glass you're getting younger!

MRS. HACKER (*As* MR. HACKER, *jug in hand, drags her off stage*): You'll see me again, Rudy. Maybe by that time I'll look like fifteen!

MR. HACKER: If you don't stop blabbering, we'll never see Miami.

MRS. HACKER: I didn't look bad when I was fifteen, Homer. You'll see someday. (*They exit right.*)

RUDY (*Waving*): And they still don't have directions. (*Sound of automobile starting, then driving away*) Oh, well. I guess that means they'll be stopping by again. (*He sighs happily and takes out two water jugs.*) And I guess I'd better go down to the springs for some more magic-formula spring water. At the rate Aunt Zoe's pushing coconut milk this morning, the demand might exceed the supply any month now. (*He exits, right. At left,* PEPE PONCE DE LEON *sticks his head out of the foliage, looks around, and then tiptoes to center. He wears glasses and the helmet of a conquistador.*)

PEPE (*Weakly*): I claim this land in the name of Spain. (*More confidently*) I said, I claim this land in the name of the King of Spain. (*In a booming voice*) I said it before, and I'll say it again. I claim this land in the name of the King and Queen of Spain!

RUDY (*Returning with jugs, startling* PEPE, *who jumps*): That's not what you said before. You didn't mention the Queen.

PEPE: Well, so what?

RUDY (*Putting jugs on counter*): So plenty. I shouldn't think the Queen would be very happy about being left out when somebody's going around claiming land. And I should think the King would be happier if you didn't forget about the Queen, too. Save him a lot of nagging. (*Falsetto*) "Why did you claim that land for you and not me, Alfonso?"

PEPE (*In a huffy tone*): So all right.

RUDY: But then Spain doesn't have a king and queen.

PEPE: I was talking about Spain in 1514.

RUDY: Oh. Well, since history never was one of my strong points, you can handle 1514 any way you want.

PEPE (*Bowing*): Thank you two times. Not that I'm any authority on Spain in 1514, either, exactly.

RUDY: But this land has already been claimed by Spain and bought by the United States. I mean, don't you think you're wasting your time?

PEPE (*Sitting on a stool*): Oh, drat. I hope not. Could somebody give me a smidge of guava jelly on a biscuit? I'm famished. (*He sits down.*)

RUDY: Sure. We're pushing coconut milk today, too.

PEPE: Well, you can push it on somebody else. Any kind of milk makes me nauseated. (*Changing tone*) I suppose you think it's odd, my popping out of the palmetto scrub in an antique sombrero.

RUDY: Not at all. Happens every day. (*Moving behind counter*)

PEPE (*In a burst of exasperation*): Rats! Don't tell me somebody's beaten me to the trail!

RUDY (*Giving* PEPE *a cracker*): What trail, may I ask?

PEPE: It's very complicated. All tied up with family heritage and honor and so on. You know, they fed me that stuff all my life . . . my family did, I mean. What else could they expect?

RUDY: Sure. What else?

PEPE: Deep down beneath this timid façade beats the stout heart of a man with a quest, an explorer who seeks treasure in the new world.

RUDY: O.K., but I somehow have the feeling that you're a little behind the times.

PEPE: But if you were the umpty-umpth grandson of Juan Ponce de Leon, how would *you* feel?

RUDY: Gee! I'm impressed! Have a biscuit on the house.

PEPE: Thanks. Well, how would you feel, Rudy? You are Rudy, aren't you? (RUDY *nods.*) I thought so because of the sign. (*Nibbling*) I'm Pepe Ponce de Leon, in from Puerto Rico to clear up some old business. I can tell you how you'd feel. You'd feel proud of old Juan for his explorations and sorry he was done in. But what about the Fountain of Youth? Everybody knows that water never did anything for anybody.

RUDY: It's still a nice old legend.

PEPE: So you think it's a legend, too. (*Getting up and pacing theatrically*) Oh, the trials, the tribulations! Imagine what it must have been like in the old days, to have embarked for the west in an old wooden barge with a couple of crummy sails . . . not knowing whether you would meet friend or foe . . . perhaps not knowing in your heart whether you were right in thinking the world was round . . . whether it would be over the edge and curtains! (*He shudders.*)

RUDY (*Coming out of stand*): Do you consider yourself an explorer?

PEPE: Of course! My family thinks I'm nutty. "These days the only place left to explore is outer space," that's what they all told me. Naturally, that kind of thing is out. I get the squeamies if I so much as look out the upstairs window. Anyway, I became obsessed with the idea of checking out the Ponce de Leon story. He knew there was a fountain of youth around here somewhere. He was just so anxious to find it he probably did nip-ups over

the first fresh-water puddle he saw. And that turned out
to be the no-good spring in St. Augustine. Would you
mind if I had another biscuit?

RUDY (*Returning to stand and offering biscuits*): Take two.

PEPE (*Returning to his seat*): Thanks. Well, it all doesn't
really make much difference except that once the legend
had been disproved to everybody's satisfaction, it made
old Juan look like some kind of a nut.

RUDY: Maybe he was.

PEPE: Please! The thought of it gives me a headache.
(*Sound of car approaching, then stopping, is heard.*)
There's a fountain of youth around here somewhere, all
right, or my name isn't Ponce de Leon!

MR. HACKER (*Bustling onstage from right*): Now you look
here!

RUDY (*Innocently*): How do you do, sir? Another lovely
day in the Florida sunshine. How about a glass of coconut milk? Its rejuvenating powers will astound you.

MR. HACKER: I just paid twenty bucks for a jug of that
stuff.

RUDY: You? Oh, no!

MR. HACKER: Yes, me! Me! And all I want to know is how
to get on the road for Miami. My car's almost ruined!

RUDY: Pepe, you wouldn't believe that this is the same man
who was in here before.

MR. HACKER (*Raging*): How do I get on the road for Miami?

PEPE (*Recoiling*): Nobody's going to tell you if you scream.

RUDY: You have to go that way . . . the way you came.

MRS. HACKER (*Entering right*): Rudy! Yoo-hoo! We're
back.

MR. HACKER (*To his wife*): I told you to stay in the car.

RUDY: But this is astonishing! Pepe, not half an hour ago

this lovely lady (PEPE *removes glasses, polishes them*) and her dashing husband dropped by for a visit.

PEPE (*Putting glasses on*): It's even hotter than I thought.

RUDY: They looked—well—let's say they looked tired.

MRS. HACKER: Oh, we were, Rudy. I felt so run-down. But now, after drinking your special formula coconut milk, I almost feel young again. Maybe I should stay here forever!

MR. HACKER: Primrose, we're leaving!

MRS. HACKER (*Resigned*): All right, honey. 'Bye again, Rudy.

MR. HACKER (*As his wife and* RUDY *wave to each other, he stops short, seeing something offstage, right*): No! Two flat tires!

MRS. HACKER: Hello again, Rudy.

MR. HACKER: Where's the telephone? Where's the nearest garage?

RUDY: The phone's in back of the stand. And the garage is up the road somewhere. (MR. HACKER *goes behind the stand.*)

MRS. HACKER: Gee, Rudy. Maybe I'll be a teen-ager before I leave here after all. (*She sits at counter*) Do you really think I look younger? I don't think Homer looks younger.

RUDY: Of course he does.

PEPE: Who's Homer?

MRS. HACKER: My husband.

RUDY: Of course he is.

PEPE: Of course.

RUDY (*Clapping* PEPE *on the shoulder*): You see? Pepe Ponce de Leon agrees. (PEPE *looks confused.*)

MRS. HACKER: Ponce de Leon? You're not one of *the* Ponce de Leons!

PEPE (*With a bow*): The very same.

MRS. HACKER (*In a huff*): I think that was a mean trick your family pulled . . . finding an old water hole and telling everybody it was a fountain of youth. I drank that water on every vacation for three years. It never did anything for me.

PEPE: It never did anything for anybody, madam, because the real fountain of youth remains undiscovered.

MRS. HACKER: You mean there *is* a real one?

PEPE (*Proudly*): I'm out to prove it.

MRS. HACKER: It couldn't be better than Rudy's coconut milk.

MR. HACKER (*Peeking around corner of stand*): The guy from the garage wants to know how to get here.

RUDY: Tell him it's near the castle at Golden Springs.

PEPE (*Eagerly*): Golden Springs? You have springs here?

RUDY: Lots of them. (PEPE *claps his hands.*)

AUNT ZOE (*Running in left, wearing a terrycloth robe and flowered bathing cap, her makeup washed off*): Rudy? Call the sports store and order me a surfboard. Next to having wings, this is *it!* (GILBERT, *looking exhausted, staggers in.*) Oh, and order hamburgers and supplies for the surfers. They're beginning to pour in by the dozens. Did you see me on that last wave?

GILBERT (*Leaning against stand*): You're a champ, Aunt Zoe. You've just about worn me out. (MR. HACKER *returns.*)

AUNT ZOE: I love wild water sports. Swam the English Channel in 1885. Not that I can prove it. In those days nobody stood around with cameras and stopwatches. (*She takes off cap to show her dark hair*) Oh, Rudy. What I owe to you! (*Aside*) And to a good scrub in the ocean.

GILBERT (*Reviving*): You swam the Channel in 1885?

AUNT ZOE (*To the* HACKERS' *bewilderment*): Give or take a year. I never was much good at dates and figures. I was eighteen at the time.

RUDY (*Taking her aside*): Come on, Aunt Zoe. That would make you . . . 99 years old!

AUNT ZOE: Give or take a year. Well, don't look so surprised. You pegged me at 93. (*She beams.*)

RUDY: But I was only joking!

MR. HACKER: Now just a minute. You don't mean to tell me you're the same woman who was here before—the pale, white-haired old girl from Atlanta!

AUNT ZOE: The very same. (*Spotting* PEPE) Who are you?

MRS. HACKER: He says he's descended from Ponce de Leon.

PEPE: I am. And I'm looking for the magic spring that Juan Ponce de Leon never found . . . the real Fountain of Youth.

AUNT ZOE: You don't say! The magic spring, hm? But who needs a fountain of youth with Rudy's magic-formula coconut milk around? You wouldn't want to tell us what makes this formula of yours so special, would you, Mr. Rudy?

RUDY (*Uncertainly*): It's a secret.

AUNT ZOE (*Firmly*): But I know you'll want to tell us all about it.

RUDY (*Getting the point*): Ah, yes! The basic ingredient that turned this old woman into a surfboarding youngster is water . . . water from our own, special, private, golden springs.

PEPE: Spring water! I knew it. I've found it! The lost fountain of youth!

AUNT ZOE (*Knowingly*): Say, you really think so? That should make this place pretty valuable.

PEPE: This will be the greatest tourist attraction this side of Disneyland.

RUDY: I can see the skyscraper hotels, the free-form swimming pools!

GILBERT: But the surfers would be driven out!

AUNT ZOE: Oh, no, they wouldn't. I'd see to that. You kids have first claim on this beach. Why, now that I've found surfing . . . and Rudy's special formula youth potion . . . I feel the old zing coming back!

PEPE (*Rubbing his hands together*): Where's the water?

AUNT ZOE (*Waving*): Out there! An ocean full of it.

PEPE: Not that water. *The* water. My fountain! Oh, I could cry. Now I know how Juan must have felt.

MRS. HACKER: You mean this is for real? I *am* getting younger?

MR. HACKER: You look the same to me.

RUDY: Are you sure? Look again!

MR. HACKER (*Looking again*): Sure I'm sure.

RUDY: Closer. Look closer!

MR. HACKER: At least I think I'm sure.

MRS. HACKER: Then it's true!

RUDY (*Pouring water into paper cups*): And, if all of you want to try some more of the basic ingredient, here's a jug of water I just brought back from the springs.

MRS. HACKER (*Almost throwing herself on counter*): Give it to me!

RUDY: We'll pass it around. (*He does*) And I'll even try some myself.

PEPE: A toast to Ponce de Leon . . . and the fortitude and determination of his noble descendants!

GILBERT: And to the best lady surfer on the Florida coast!

AUNT ZOE (*Aside*): You know, Rudy, now that things are starting to swing around here, I don't know that I want to go to the big city after all.

MERRILEE (*Entering left, followed by* JOAN): We have sixty surfers down there and more on the way.

JOAN: Plenty of customers, Rudy.

AUNT ZOE (*To* RUDY): You'd better start ordering supplies.

GILBERT: Rudy, if we can get everybody to pay a dollar a day each, that should make this worthwhile for you, don't you think?

MRS. HACKER (*As* RUDY *smiles, nods*): Look! The water does look golden. Yes! Like liquid gold!

MR. HACKER: Uh, how much did you want for this land, Rudy?

RUDY: I'll have to convey your offer to the lady who lives in the castle.

MR. HACKER: Tell her I want an option on six waterfront acres for a start.

AUNT ZOE: Better order those supplies, Rudy. (*She and* RUDY *move to center*) I tell you, Rudy, surfing is the greatest. I'll bet I rode fifty yards (*Gesturing*) just like that!

RUDY (*Aside as others fill their cups, toast, drink*): Uh, Aunt Zoe, do you really expect them to believe you're 93 years old?

AUNT ZOE: Give or take a year. Well, do you expect anybody to believe that's a Ponce de Leon? But what a ploy! I think you're catching on. The undiscovered Fountain of Youth! That's salesmanship, kid! (*Loudly, for all to hear*) Well, anyway, Rudy, this surfing bit is the end. You've got to try it! Come on, Gilbert. Come on, girls. (*Loudly to* RUDY) With all the surfing business and the Fountain of Youth to boot, I'll bet the old lady who lives in the castle might even up her price. Get me, Rudy?

RUDY: Got you, Aunt Zoe.

AUNT ZOE: I'll race you, Gilbert.

RUDY (*As* AUNT ZOE *and* GILBERT *line up*): Strange. I suddenly feel a craving for a lollipop. And a ride on a merry-go-round. I haven't wanted lollipops since I was . . . six years old?

AUNT ZOE: Say, you know I feel about sixteen again? Great!

RUDY: But I hated being six years old!

AUNT ZOE: Ready?

RUDY: I even hated seven!

AUNT ZOE: Set?

RUDY: And I hated five even worse than that!

AUNT ZOE: Go! (*All take off,* AUNT ZOE *well in the lead, with* RUDY *bounding after them as the curtain falls.*)

THE END

Production Notes

YOUNG FOREVER

Characters: 4 male; 4 female.
Playing Time: 45 minutes.
Costumes: Modern beach wear. Rudy wears frayed but clean jeans and T-shirt. Aunt Zoe first appears in gaudy Florida-style clothes with much jewelry, as if she were trying too hard to appear young. She carries a handkerchief. Later she disguises herself with makeup and old shawl to look very old; finally, she appears as if just back from surfing wearing a terry cloth robe and flowered bathing cap. The Hackers wear summer tourist clothes, he a drab sport shirt and slacks, she a garish sports dress or slacks and blouse. Mr. Hacker carries dollar bills in his pocket. Surfers wear jeans cut off above the knee and sweat shirts or sweaters. Pepe wears Bermuda shorts, sport shirt and a conquistador's helmet, which can be fashioned from a pith helmet decorated with plume and insignia such as a coat-of-arms. Pepe wears glasses.
Properties: Wallet, bicycle, two or three surfboards. Inside stand: rocks, driftwood, jellyfish in jar, crayon or marking pen, sack of flour, charred driftwood, purse with makeup inside, mirror, old shawl, rags, pen, paper, paper cups (at least 8), pitcher or bottle of "coconut milk," gallon jug, 2 water jugs, crackers.
Setting: A lonely strip of beach in Florida. Backdrop of sky, beach and ocean. At left a clump of tropical foliage, such as palm tree or banana plant, large enough for Pepe to hide behind. At right a roadside stand with counter and at least 2 stools. Counter should be large enough to contain a variety of hidden props and to hide Aunt Zoe.
Signs: "Rudy the Beachcomber," "Florida Souvenirs," "Coconut Milk 10¢—Special Formula for Eternal Youth," "Land for Sale," "Guava Jelly," "Genuine Indian Lore," "Shells—All Kinds," etc.
Lighting: No special effects.
Sound: An automobile starting, driving off, approaching and stopping, as indicated in text.

The Reluctant Columbus

Characters

PRINCE COLUMBUS
PRINCESS INGA, *his fiancée*
QUEEN MOLTOBELLA, *his mother*
DR. SHRINK
CHRISTOPHER THE CARTOGRAPHER
MARGUERITE
TWO PAGES
FOUR POCOVIANS
CROWD
EXTRAS

SCENE 1

TIME: 1492.

SETTING: *The palace of Pocovia, minuscule kingdom on the Mediterranean coast. A throne is at center, flanked by two screens with royal emblems.*

AT RISE: PRINCESS INGA *is pacing nervously while* DR. SHRINK, *an intense man with spectacles, strikes a casual pose next to throne.*

PRINCESS: So that's the way it is, Dr. Shrink. I came all the way down here from Scandinavia. . . .

DR. SHRINK (*With an accent*): Quite a trip these days, kid. After all, it's only 1492.

PRINCESS: You said it. I wouldn't take the return jaunt for anything. Besides, I fell in love with the Mediterranean climate . . . and . . . frankly, there's an oversupply of princesses in the North.

DR. SHRINK: You mean you have a better chance of finding a royal husband among the palm fronds.

PRINCESS (*Lightly, but with pride*): I found one!

DR. SHRINK: Felicitations and all that sort of thing, but you certainly didn't ask me to come here all the way from Vienna just to share some crumbs from your wedding cake. It's no easy trip. After all, this is 1492. Travel's slow, and we psychiatrists charge by the hour.

PRINCESS: I'll pay you anything!

DR. SHRINK: Ha! That's what they all say until they get my bill.

PRINCESS: But, Dr. Shrink, I have problems!

DR. SHRINK: You and everybody else. Oh-ho, is this world sick!

PRINCESS: I don't know about the world, I just know about my fiancé. He's the Prince of Pocovia.

DR. SHRINK: You *did* find a title. Good girl.

PRINCESS: I'm very fond of him. I really am.

DR. SHRINK: That's nice. Makes it cozy.

PRINCESS: And he's fond of me.

DR. SHRINK: Makes it cozier yet. So what's the trouble?

PRINCESS: The Prince doesn't want to be a Prince anymore.

DR. SHRINK: So tell him to go out and get himself crowned King!

PRINCESS: Dr. Shrink, I don't think you're taking me seriously.

DR. SHRINK: I'm trying not to. No reason I should go berserk, too, baby.

PRINCESS: Columbus—

DR. SHRINK: Columbus?

PRINCESS: The Prince. That's his name. Prince Columbus feels that kings and queens and princes are out of date . . . that monarchies have had it.

DR. SHRINK: Very interesting. Tell me more.

PRINCESS: The Queen is frantic, and so am I. There's a lot of unrest here in Pocovia, you see. Prince Columbus feels the only way to solve it all and bring back prosperity is to give the country to the people.

DR. SHRINK: Look, it's his country. But we have to admit it isn't much. So, if he's nuts enough to give it away, maybe he isn't so stupid after all. He-he! The point is (*Baffled*) . . . ja . . . we should get to the point.

PRINCESS: The point is that if Columbus is my husband and he's not a Prince, I won't be a Princess, let alone Queen.

DR. SHRINK: Find someone else.

PRINCESS (*Firmly*): I thought I made that clear. I didn't travel this far to escape an excess crop of available males. After all, I'm royalty. I'm not going bourgeois just to find a husband.

DR. SHRINK (*More thoughtfully*): I see, I see. Well, I'll try to fix you up.

PRINCESS (*Kissing him*): You're a sweetie pie.

DR. SHRINK (*Embarrassed but pleased*): You're O.K. yourself. Now, first we must realize that any ideas Prince Columbus might have about political reform are the thoughts of a real nut.

PRINCESS (*Alarmed*): You really think so?

DR. SHRINK: Of course not, but it gives us a start on selling the notion that the only reason he wants to ditch the monarchy is his lack of security and self-confidence. You see, if he thinks he's going to be a flop as the King, he could get real paranoid and think of all kinds of kooky excuses to get out of the job.

PRINCESS: I understand. How clever!

DR. SHRINK: Sure! Especially if he can come up with an excuse that makes him popular with the people at the same time. Great builder-upper for a puny ego.

PRINCESS: You're going to solve all our problems, I'm sure!

DR. SHRINK (*Blankly, to audience*): She must be kidding.

PRINCESS: And now I must be off before Columbus wanders along. Good luck! (*She exits left.*)

DR. SHRINK (*To audience*): That must mean that the Prince is about to make an appearance. (*Brightly, as he spots* PRINCE *entering right*) And here he is! (PRINCE COLUMBUS, *wearing the clothes of a commoner, walks casually to center.*) Uh, you are the Prince?

PRINCE: My name is Columbus.

DR. SHRINK (*Bowing and scraping*): You are the Prince . . . one day the King . . . mightiest in all Europe!

PRINCE: I don't want to be King.

DR. SHRINK (*Slapping him on the back*): Nonsense! What a king you'll make. A world-beater! A tiger!

PRINCE: You don't seem to understand. You see, I feel that kings and kingdoms are soon going to vanish . . . that we're passing into a new era.

DR. SHRINK: Maybe yes, maybe no, but you shouldn't let it vanish here so fast. That's why you see before you Herr Dr. Shrink from Vienna. Things were slow in Vienna, and so I thought I'd soak up some sun and fun on the Riviera. Sit down, but not on the throne. That would put you above me and wreck my image.

PRINCE: I wouldn't sit on the throne as a matter of principle . . . no matter what Mommy says.

DR. SHRINK (*Distastefully*): Mommy?

PRINCE: My mother. Queen Moltobella of Pocovia.

DR. SHRINK: Boy, you sure have some weirdos around here. But sit. (PRINCE *sits on a bench*.) Relax and tell me about yourself. (*He takes out a pad and pencil.*)

PRINCE: Are you a reporter?

DR. SHRINK: Sort of. I'll let you talk your head off, ask you a few questions, maybe, and then decide how much of a ding-a-ling you are. Do you have troubles relating to Mommy?

PRINCE: Nothing compared to her troubles relating to me.

DR. SHRINK (*Writing*): Complex number one!

PRINCE: The world is changing. She thinks I don't know what I'm talking about.

DR. SHRINK: Complex number two. We're really racking them up here, kid. Tell me, were you a happy baby?

PRINCE: How should I know?

DR. SHRINK: Well, if you don't know, who does?

PRINCE: Ask my mother.

DR. SHRINK: Look, boy, you'd better get off this kick.

PRINCE (*Standing, pacing*): The trouble with my mother is that she's over thirty and always has been.

DR. SHRINK: Now you've lost me. (*Writes*) What kind of king do you think you'll make?

PRINCE: Lousy.

DR. SHRINK (*Writing*): "At least patient doesn't kid himself."

PRINCE: I'd be a lousy king because I don't believe in it.

DR. SHRINK: But you certainly have obligations to your country.

PRINCE: Right!

DR. SHRINK: Obligations as Prince . . . King!

PRINCE: Wrong! Say, who did you say you were?

DR. SHRINK: You young people never listen! I'm Herr Doctor Shrink, the famous psychiatrist, and I'm here to make you well and strong.

PRINCE (*Laughing*): There's nothing wrong with me.

DR. SHRINK: That proves you're nuts. Everybody's miserable these days.

PRINCE (*Moving left*): I've had enough of this scene.

DR. SHRINK (*Following him*): You're not leaving without me, you're not. I'm going to make you King of Pocovia if it's the last thing I do! (*Curtain.*)

*   *   *

SCENE 2

SETTING: *A cafe. The throne has been removed, and the screens are turned to show* CAFE *and street signs. A few cafe chairs and tables have been added.*

AT RISE: MARGUERITE *is sitting at a table drinking coffee. To her right and left are two groups of* POCOVIANS, *discussing their politics.*

1ST POCOVIAN: But where's our future? That's what I want to know.

2ND POCOVIAN: Yeah. This place is a drag.

3RD POCOVIAN: And getting poorer every day.

4TH POCOVIAN: The Queen doesn't care.

3RD POCOVIAN: You don't know that for a fact.

4TH POCOVIAN: If she cared, she'd do something about it.

1ST POCOVIAN: All the Queen cares about is how beautiful she is.

2ND POCOVIAN: She'll care when we all revolt.

1ST POCOVIAN: And Prince Columbus . . . what hope do we have in him?

4TH POCOVIAN: I hear that the Prince wants reform.

2ND POCOVIAN: Ha! I'll believe it when I see it.

3RD POCOVIAN: What good is reform without prosperity?

4TH POCOVIAN: It could *lead* to prosperity.

3RD POCOVIAN: I'd rather have the prosperity first, thanks.

2ND POCOVIAN: Revolt. That's the answer.

CHRISTOPHER (*Entering right and going to* MARGUERITE'*s table; he carries rolls of maps*): Marguerite! I'm sorry I'm late.

MARGUERITE (*Looking about*): So am I.

4TH POCOVIAN: Prosperity . . . not revolt.

2ND POCOVIAN: Revolt! (*Talking excitedly,* POCOVIANS *exit.*)

MARGUERITE (*As* CHRISTOPHER *sits down and places maps on table*): Christopher, I've just been hearing the most awful talk . . . all about how bad things are and how the only answer is to revolt.

CHRISTOPHER: That's just talk.

MARGUERITE: Don't be so sure. Everybody isn't as lazy as you are, Christopher.

CHRISTOPHER: I don't see what a revolt has to do with . . . and what makes you think I'm so lazy?

MARGUERITE: Maybe that's not the right word, but that's what I wanted to talk to you about. I've thought it all over, and I don't see how I can possibly marry a man who doesn't have a better chance of success than you have.

CHRISTOPHER: Success? What do you mean by that?

MARGUERITE: I mean I can't help it if I want certain things out of life. I want a nice house in the suburbs and a few pesos in the cookie jar. You don't even have a job!

CHRISTOPHER: I'm self-employed.

MARGUERITE: Great. All you do is sit around and draw maps and maps and maps. . . .

CHRISTOPHER: That's my profession. I'm a cartographer.

MARGUERITE: How are your maps selling these days?

CHRISTOPHER (*Sheepishly*): Well. . . .

MARGUERITE: Exactly.

CHRISTOPHER: But the world is expanding. There's a great future in my field. I know it.

MARGUERITE: Perhaps you know it. But who else knows it?

CHRISTOPHER (*Opening map*): Look. I have here the latest product of my intensive research. It proves beyond a doubt that over the horizon lies a pot of gold for Pocovia.

MARGUERITE (*Bored*): Do go on.

CHRISTOPHER: You bet, because the secret lies in my discovery that the world is round.

MARGUERITE (*Jumping up*): Have you blown your mind?

CHRISTOPHER (*Firmly*): The world is round!

MARGUERITE: Brother! Marrying a pauper is bad enough, but a lunatic! What will my sorority sisters think?

CHRISTOPHER (*Pleading*): Listen, Marguerite, it's true. (*Using map to demonstrate*) If I were to sail out of Pocovia and head West . . .

MARGUERITE: You can't sail, and you know it.

CHRISTOPHER (*Defending himself*): I could, if I didn't get so seasick! If *somebody* were to sail out of Pocovia and head West, that *somebody* would end up in the East.

MARGUERITE: Sure! (*Mocking*) And if I sailed North, I'd end up South.

CHRISTOPHER: Well, actually, if you could do it, yes, you would.

MARGUERITE: What's to stop me? I'll just hop into my little dinghy and paddle away!

CHRISTOPHER: I think you're making fun of me.

MARGUERITE: Never, Christopher dear. Just walk around your padded cell and make yourself at home! You know perfectly well we were taught that the world is flat. What are you trying to do, bug the Establishment?

CHRISTOPHER: I'm trying to show you my discovery! (1ST POCOVIAN *walks across upstage, carrying a placard read-*

ing, BUG THE ESTABLISHMENT) We could discover a direct trade route to the East and become rich! (2ND PO-COVIAN *enters with sign reading,* SHARE THE WEALTH. *He is followed onstage by* 3RD POCOVIAN *with sign reading,* WHAT WEALTH?)

MARGUERITE (*Turning*): Say, what is this? Some kind of demonstration?

1ST POCOVIAN: Right you are, senorita. Want to join?

2ND POCOVIAN: The world's about to pass us by.

3RD POCOVIAN: Either we become involved, or it's curtains for Pocovia.

MARGUERITE: This makes me feel very uncomfortable. Very!

1ST POCOVIAN: It's supposed to.

3RD POCOVIAN: If somebody doesn't get things moving around here, Pocovia won't be on anybody's map.

CHRISTOPHER: As a matter of fact, it's hard enough to find it now. (*Indicating his map*) See this little dot? That's us. Magnified!

MARGUERITE: Why, that's awful! I never thought we were *that* insignificant.

CHRISTOPHER: But we needn't be, Marguerite. That's what I'm trying to tell you. A few sturdy ships, some sound, sturdy men, and the riches of the East will be ours!

1ST POCOVIAN: We want gold!

MARGUERITE: Well, so do I!

CHRISTOPHER: And I can show you the way to get it.

4TH POCOVIAN (*Entering right with sign reading,* GET GOLD OR GET OUT): Go tell it to the Queen.

MARGUERITE (*Pointing at* CHRISTOPHER): That's exactly what you should do, Chris. Tell your story to the Queen!

CHRISTOPHER (*Meekly*): Me?

2ND POCOVIAN: Nobody's ever been able to tell the Queen anything except how beautiful she is.

MARGUERITE: Maybe he can be the first one.

CHRISTOPHER: But . . . but what will I *say?*

MARGUERITE: Tell her everything you told me.

CHRISTOPHER: But what if she doesn't believe me? *You* don't believe me.

MARGUERITE: Past tense, Christopher. I didn't believe you, and the Queen may not, either, at first. But the Queen wants pesos for her cookie jar, too. What does she have to lose? (*Aside*) You do know what you're talking about, don't you—about the world being round? I believe in you and all that, but. . . .

CHRISTOPHER: I'm positive. (*They move toward exit at left.*)

POCOVIANS (*Chanting*): Gold or revolt!

MARGUERITE (*As they exit*): Are there really great riches in the East?

POCOVIANS (*Chanting*): Gold or revolt! Gold or revolt! (*Curtain.*)

*   *   *

SCENE 3

SETTING: *The palace.*

AT RISE: PRINCESS INGA *awaits* QUEEN MOLTOBELLA'*s arrival.* 1ST PAGE *stands right,* 2ND PAGE *left of the throne.*

PRINCESS: It seems to me the Queen gets later every day.

1ST PAGE: She gets older every day.

2ND PAGE: What he means is that . . . uh . . . it takes her a little longer to pull herself together every day.

1ST PAGE: To put on her make-up.

2ND PAGE: And all her jewelry.

1ST PAGE: And all the things that make her . . .

PAGES (*In unison; wearily*): The most beautiful queen in

the world! (QUEEN *enters right. She carries a hand mirror and wears as much jewelry as she can possibly carry.*) And here she is . . . the one and only Queen Moltobella! (QUEEN *poses triumphantly.* PAGES *bow.*)

PRINCESS: Well, now that's out of the way. . . .

QUEEN: That's one thing that is never out of the way in Pocovia, my dear. Fortunately, my subjects absolutely adore me. (*To* PAGES) Don't they, boys?

1ST PAGE: And how!

2ND PAGE: You bet!

PRINCESS: Oh, I don't doubt that for a sec, Queen, but I did want to talk to you about Columbus. I really can't see that Dr. Shrink is doing him much good.

QUEEN (*Sitting on throne*): I don't know about these head doctors. Seems to me that all Columbus needs is a little applause from his people. Let him find out it's fun to be royal. If we can find him a challenge that's really a pushover to perform, he'll come out looking like a hero and his subjects will adore him.

PAGES: Long live the Prince!

QUEEN: See what I mean? A challenge . . . yes, but what? (*Archly*) Frankly, Princess Inga, I thought that between a Scandinavian cutie like you and Dr. Shrink, you could come up with something.

PRINCESS (*Annoyed*): Well, I hope somebody comes up with something soon! My royal future is beginning to look pretty pedestrian.

1ST PAGE: Why don't you call in the doctor and get the straight pitch?

QUEEN: You're meddling, but it's a good idea. (*She claps her hands and calls lightly.*) Dr. Shrink. (*She claps and calls louder.*) Dr. Shrink! (*She stands up and yells full-voice.*) Dr. Shrink! (DR. SHRINK *enters right.*) Come here at once!

DR. SHRINK: Cool it, will you, schatzie? I have nerves, too, you know.

QUEEN: Bow from the waist, when you say that!

DR. SHRINK (*Bowing and muttering*): Royalty! Touchy, touchy!

QUEEN: Now, give me a report on Prince Columbus.

DR. SHRINK: What's to report?

QUEEN: Are you making him forget his silly idea about abolishing the monarchy? Are you showing him that giving the country to the people is the nightmare of a maniac? Are you convincing him that prosperity is a commodity of the ruling class? Are you making him proud of his heritage, proud to be Prince of Pocovia? Well, speak up!

DR. SHRINK: You have a nice kid in that Columbus.

2ND PAGE: Pardon me for meddling, but he may be nothing but a quack.

QUEEN (*Shaking her mirror at* DR. SHRINK): You're nothing but a quack!

DR. SHRINK: I'll decide that. Who's the doctor around here? You? (*To* PRINCESS) You? (*He paces.*) You have Columbus, who isn't turning out the way you want, so you call in a famous expert like me and right off expect me to—well—remold his personality as if it were cookie dough. (*Nostalgically*) Ah, the cookies they make in Vienna!

PRINCESS: Why don't you stick to the point?

DR. SHRINK: I'm beginning to miss the old place.

1ST PAGE: He'd better stick to the point.

DR. SHRINK: The food you have here has as much zing as last year's strudel.

QUEEN: He'd *better* stick to the point, or I'll have his head lopped off!

DR. SHRINK (*Astonished*): What?

2ND PAGE: And she's not kidding, buster.

DR. SHRINK: I thought this place was supposed to be civilized!

PRINCESS: There's not a civilized country in the world where people haven't had their heads lopped off at some time or other.

1ST PAGE: Or been hanged.

2ND PAGE: Or run through with swords.

QUEEN: Or thrown to man-eating plants. We have a lot of those around here.

DR. SHRINK (*Quickly moving left*): I just quit civilization. Bye-bye.

QUEEN (*Gesturing to* PAGES, *who move to stop* DR. SHRINK): Oh, no, you don't! If you ever want to see all those cookies in Vienna again, you'd better deliver.

DR. SHRINK (*Meekly*): The trouble is . . . those ideas Columbus has . . . *you* may not like them, but . . . and he's a nice kid.

QUEEN: Of course he's nice. He's my son.

PRINCESS: My fiancé.

PAGES (*Together*): The Prince of Pocovia.

DR. SHRINK: You don't dig me. Columbus has a guilt complex about being a Prince, and so he develops these ideas to get himself out of it. Or maybe it's vice versa.

QUEEN: You don't know?

DR. SHRINK: You think I'm a magician?

QUEEN: Magic is exactly what I'm looking for!

PRINCESS (*Sweetly*): A little magic, doctor? (*Indicating* QUEEN) You know what she said.

QUEEN (*Slowly and sweetly*): Lop, lop, lop!

DR. SHRINK: *Auf Wiedersehen*, Vienna! (*Offstage, a chant of "Gold or Revolt"—"Get Gold or Get Out"—begins softly.*)

PRINCE (*Entering at left*): Mother . . . (*Quickly, to others*) Oh, hello. (*To* QUEEN) Something's wrong.

DR. SHRINK (*Holding his head*): You should be me.

PRINCE: There's a crowd forming outside the palace.

QUEEN (*Pleased*): They've come to pay me homage and admire my beauty, no doubt.

PAGES: Long live the Queen!

PRINCE: They're not here to admire you today, Mom. They're fed up.

DR. SHRINK: Me, too.

PRINCE: They want prosperity.

QUEEN: What's that? (*Chanting grows louder, and the* QUEEN *stands up and commands.*) Columbus, go out there like the Prince of Pocovia and tell them to stop that at once! (PRINCE *pauses briefly, then walks, with air of authority, off right. Chanting reaches peak, then fades. Brief silence.*) My! (QUEEN *smiles.*) He actually silenced the mob.

PRINCESS: He's probably promised to give them the right to vote and the contents of the royal treasury to boot! (*Suddenly, offstage booing is heard, and shortly,* PRINCE, *out of breath, runs back onstage. Booing fades*).

QUEEN (*Furiously*): And what was that all about?

PRINCE: Prosperity plus.

PAGES: Long live prosperity plus!

QUEEN (*To* PAGES): Silence! (*Turning to* PRINCE) What do the people want? They have enough to eat, haven't they?

PRINCE: Whether they have or they haven't, *enough* to eat is not enough. And getting rid of the monarchy is not enough. What they want is gold.

QUEEN: Why, the greedy little things.

PRINCE: And they want power.

QUEEN: Well, I want gold and power, too.

PRINCESS: So do I.

QUEEN: But we're the ruling class. We're supposed to have these things.

PRINCE: They're talking about revolt.

QUEEN: And it's all your fault. You've been putting those ideas into their heads. If you were any kind of prince, you'd go out in the world and get some gold for them. They'd adore you then, and there'd be monarchy forever. But, no! All you do is spout your theories, and all they do is boo!

PRINCE: I don't think they were booing me personally.

QUEEN: Never in the history of Pocovia . . . (*Exasperated*) Oh, go away. Leave me alone!

DR. SHRINK (*Escorting* PRINCE *off left*): Come on, boy. I think we have a dilemma to discuss.

PRINCE: I certainly understand the people's point of view, Dr. Shrink. If they felt Pocovia had a real future, then they wouldn't expect all their problems to be solved by gold. According to my theory. . . .

DR. SHRINK: Ja, ja. Come on. (*They exit.* QUEEN *moves right and looks off, and* PRINCESS *goes left and looks off.*)

QUEEN: Who in the world do they think they are? Gold, indeed! Look at them milling around down there. (*Both turn and walk to center.*)

PRINCESS: Why don't you call out the palace guards?

QUEEN: I don't have any. They quit. Imagine, I don't have enough silver to pay the palace guards, and (*Gesturing*) *they* want gold.

PRINCESS (*Horrified*): You mean I'm to marry into a royal family that's *poor?*

QUEEN (*Grinning*): We put up a pretty good front, don't we? (CHRISTOPHER, *clutching his maps, enters with* MARGUERITE. *He is speaking nervously to her.*)

CHRISTOPHER: I hope this is the right thing to do. She lops off heads, you know.

MARGUERITE (*Calling*): We must see the Queen! (PAGES *rush to grab* CHRISTOPHER *and* MARGUERITE; PRINCESS *cowers behind throne.*)

QUEEN: Seize the rebels! Throw them into the dungeon!

CHRISTOPHER (*To* MARGUERITE): I told you so!

MARGUERITE: We are no rebels, Your Highness. This is the famed Christopher the Cartographer, and I am his agent.

CHRISTOPHER (*To* MARGUERITE): You *are?*

QUEEN: If he's so famous, why have I not heard of him?

MARGUERITE: Because I have been remiss in my agenting, Your Highness. That is why I present him to you now, without a further day's delay.

QUEEN (*To* PAGES): In that case, let them go. (PAGES *release* CHRISTOPHER *and* MARGUERITE.) Who's afraid of a map-maker, anyway?

MARGUERITE: Not you, I hope. Your Majesty, these maps illustrate and prove my client's theory. (QUEEN *sits on throne, and* PRINCESS *emerges gingerly from behind it.*)

QUEEN (*To* MARGUERITE): Listen, if this is some kind of audio-visual demonstration, beat it!

PRINCESS: Yes. We have enough problems.

MARGUERITE: Indeed, we know.

CHRISTOPHER: We saw the angry mob.

QUEEN: They're not half as angry as I am! They're greedy! If only people weren't so greedy! It's the root of all the evil in the world.

MARGUERITE (*To* CHRISTOPHER): Go on! Tell her why you're here.

CHRISTOPHER (*Clearing his throat*): Uh . . . I have come, Your Highness, to show you how you can pave the streets of Pocovia with gold.

QUEEN, PAGES *and* PRINCESS (*Eagerly*): Gold?

MARGUERITE: The riches of the East.

CHRISTOPHER (*Unfolding map*): Your Highness, I am convinced that if we sail West from Pocovia, we shall reach the East, because I believe that the world is as round as this orange. (*Takes orange from pocket and holds it up.*)

QUEEN (*Disgustedly*): Round as an orange indeed! I've been losing my beauty sleep worrying about how to pay the bills. I have enough on my mind without listening to the ravings of a crackpot.

CHRISTOPHER: I know that everybody thinks the world is flat and that you'll fall off the edge if you sail far enough—

MARGUERITE: But it just isn't true.

PRINCESS: Of course it isn't. Who would believe such a silly thing?

QUEEN (*To* PRINCESS, *who steps forward*): Oh? And what do you know about it?

PRINCESS: More than all of you. Haven't you ever heard of the Vikings?

QUEEN: No, I've never heard of the Vikings. That makes me a moron, I suppose? (PRINCESS *takes map from* CHRISTOPHER *and traces line with finger as she speaks.*)

PRINCESS: The Vikings sailed West hundreds of years ago . . . somewhere along here . . . (*Points to spot on map*) and then—(*Turning abruptly to* CHRISTOPHER) you don't know much about map-making, do you? The Vikings found land along about in here . . . perhaps a whole new continent.

CHRISTOPHER: It's possible, of course.

PRINCESS: Well, you don't have to believe that if you don't want to. The point is that they sailed West and didn't fall off at all. They landed on the other side, way up North.

QUEEN: Why haven't we heard of this before?

PRINCESS: Why? Why should you? I mean, does Spain tell Portugal?

QUEEN (*To* CHRISTOPHER): Then, what you say just might be true?

CHRISTOPHER: All you need is a few ships, some brave, adventurous men looking for a challenge, and my maps will prove it.

MARGUERITE: With all due respect, Your Highness, what do you have to lose? The people (*Pointing offstage*) want gold, and—

QUEEN (*Rubbing her hands together*): And so do I.

PAGES: And so do we!

QUEEN: Everybody wants to get in on the act.

CHRISTOPHER: That's why there's no time to lose.

MARGUERITE: My client, Christopher the Cartographer, is very loyal to Pocovia, Your Highness. But I have his business interests to consider. There's always Spain or Portugal . . .

QUEEN: All right! But ships, supplies . . . they cost money.

CHRISTOPHER: You could raise it easily. All you have to do is sell your jewels.

QUEEN (*Furiously*): What?

MARGUERITE (*To* CHRISTOPHER): Now you've done it.

QUEEN (*Standing, fingering her jewels*): Sell these? These beautiful jewels that have been in my family for ages and make me look even more ravishing than I am? Never! (*Turns her back*)

PRINCE (*Re-entering left followed by* DR. SHRINK): But there is the will of the people to be considered, Dr. Shrink. (*Noticing the* QUEEN) What's the matter with Mother?

PRINCESS: She's in a huff, Columbus, dear, because this

man (*Pointing to* CHRISTOPHER) asked her to sell her jewels.

PRINCE: Say, there's an idea. We could at least get *some* gold together for the people that way.

DR. SHRINK: You idealist! Some is never enough!

PRINCESS: Not to give to the people. To buy ships and supplies so that men looking for a challenge could by sailing West reach the East and bring back great treasures of gold.

CHRISTOPHER: It is my theory, you see, that the world is round, and the news is about to leak out. If Pocovia takes the lead, we're in.

PRINCESS: And I don't see that you have much choice. If the people have a hope of a golden tomorrow, they might put up with anything. Besides, as I told (*Indicating* CHRISTOPHER) him. . . .

CHRISTOPHER: I'm Christopher the Cartographer.

PRINCE (*As they shake hands*): Glad to meet you. I'm Prince Columbus.

PRINCESS: . . . the Vikings did the same kind of thing long ago.

PRINCE: The Vikings? But that's a legend!

PRINCESS: I believe in legends. Don't you? You have to believe in *something!*

CHRISTOPHER: Any man who undertakes this voyage sails to riches, power, glory. . . .

DR. SHRINK (*Brightening*): Wait a minute here.

MARGUERITE: It's one of the greatest challenges in history.

DR. SHRINK: Sure it is. And here we have one little Viennese doctor who also faces the challenge of saving his neck.

PRINCESS: But the Queen won't sell her jewels, so that's that.

DR. SHRINK (*Quietly, to* PRINCESS): Not if you know anything about psychology, it isn't. (*Loudly*) You know, I was saying to the Prince this morning, "Prince," I was saying, "You have the most beautiful Mommy in Europe. Too bad she hides behind all those rings and things. You can hardly see her for all that glitter."

QUEEN: Doctor, you're playing very dirty pool.

DR. SHRINK: "But worse than that," I was saying, "much, *much* worse than that, there's nothing like a lot of jewelry to make a woman look . . . old!"

QUEEN (*Turning and tearing off her jewelry*): Oh! You sure know how to hurt a queen, you little weasel. (CHRISTOPHER, MARGUERITE *and* PRINCESS *applaud.*)

DR. SHRINK: Now you need ships and supplies? I hear Switzerland is moving inland and has some old hulks up for sale at discount rates. I should have you fixed up before the day is over.

QUEEN: And they can sail at midnight. How romantic! And tonight of all nights—New Year's Eve! What an omen! Of course, Christopher the Cartographer will go along to read the stars and interpret the maps . . .

CHRISTOPHER: Me? But . . . I can't! I get seasick.

QUEEN: Mr. Cartographer? (*Gesturing*) Lop, lop, lop?

MARGUERITE: You might get over it, Chris. This is your big chance.

DR. SHRINK: And my advice is that these guys are going to need a real leader out on all that water. (*He begins moving toward* PRINCE.) Somebody who represents the power, authority, and glory of the monarchy . . .

PRINCE (*Drawing away*): Oh, no, not me. I'm not going chasing rainbows.

DR. SHRINK (*Ignoring him*): Somebody who wants to be the biggest hero prince in the history of Pocovia. . . .

PRINCE: Not me. No thanks.

DR. SHRINK: Someone who wants to be rich—famous—powerful!

PAGES (*Chanting*): Rich, famous, powerful! (PAGES *and others close in on* CHRISTOPHER *and* PRINCE COLUMBUS, *whose cries can be heard above chant, as curtain falls.*)

*   *   *

SCENE 4

SETTING: *A street at dockside. This scene may be played before curtain.*

AT RISE: *Lights have been slightly lowered, and* CROWD *of* POCOVIANS, *some carrying lanterns, stand with their backs to audience.* CROWD *hides prop men, who hold up cardboard masts and sails that stand out against backdrop and can easily be lowered at end of scene. All characters except* PRINCE *and* CHRISTOPHER *are downstage.*

QUEEN: Isn't it marvelous? I can walk among my people without fear!

CROWD: Long live the Queen!

1ST POCOVIAN: She's getting us gold!

MARGUERITE: It was my Christopher who did it! (*Four men carry a struggling* CHRISTOPHER *onstage, and all applaud.* MARGUERITE *blows kisses as he is carried through crowd and disappears upstage in crowd.*) Good trip, Chris. I always knew you'd be a success!

DR. SHRINK: Let's get this show on the sea.

PRINCESS (*Shouting as four men carry* PRINCE *onstage*): And here comes Prince Columbus! (*She blows kisses.*)

CROWD (*As* PRINCE *is carried upstage and disappears into* CROWD): Long live the Prince. Long live the Prince!

QUEEN (*Waving*): You see how they respect the monarchy now?

PRINCESS: I'm so proud.

CROWD: Bring back the gold!

QUEEN (*To* DR. SHRINK): We're so grateful to you, Doctor.

DR. SHRINK: Ach, it was nothing. Threaten people with a little lop-lop, and who knows what results you'll get?

QUEEN: Goodbye. It's going to be a great new year!

CROWD: Goodbye. (*There is a sound of bells from off.*)

QUEEN: And there it is. Midnight!

PRINCESS: The new year. (*Sails are lowered as* CROWD *waves.*)

DR. SHRINK: Off they go, and off I go. (*He moves toward exit, right.*) Who knows? 1493 may be this crazy country's year? (*Exits*)

QUEEN (*Calling*): And don't forget! "I claim this land in the name of Pocovia!"

CROWD (*Ad lib*): Farewell, Christopher! 'Bye! So long! Farewell, Columbus! (*Curtain.*)

THE END

Production Notes

THE RELUCTANT COLUMBUS

Characters: 9 male; 3 female; as many extras as desired for Crowd and men.

Playing Time: 25 minutes.

Costumes: Royal court dress for Queen, Princess Inga, and Pages. The Queen is loaded down with costume jewelry. Prince Columbus wears casual, very informal dress—sandals, peasant shirt, etc. Marguerite, Christopher and Pocovians wear period costumes, and Doctor Shrink may look a bit like an alchemist, with spectacles.

Properties: Doctor's pad and pencil, coffee cups, rolled-up maps, signs reading Bug the Establishment!, Share the Wealth, What Wealth?, Get Gold or Get Out, hand mirror, orange, lanterns, cardboard ship's sails and mast on poles.

Setting: Scene 1: The palace. A throne at center is flanked by two screens bearing royal emblems. Other chairs and benches are at sides. Scene 2: Cafe tables are at sides and center, extra chairs are added, and the screens are turned around to show cafe and street signs. Scene 3: The same as Scene 1. Scene 4: A street at dockside. A backdrop showing ships may be used, but none is necessary, and the scene may be played before the curtain.

Lighting: Lights are dimmed for Scene 4, as indicated in text.

The Best of Sports

Characters

PAT GILBERT, *a high school senior*
DANNY, *her younger brother*
MR. GILBERT ⎫
MRS. GILBERT ⎭ *her parents*
ANNE MARKER, *her friend*
WEBSTER CUNNINGHAM
RICK BENSON
BUD RAWLINGS

SCENE 1

TIME: *Spring.*
SETTING: *The Gilbert living room.*
AT RISE: MR. GILBERT *is helping* DANNY *with his homework at desk at left.* MRS. GILBERT *and* ANNE MARKER *are seated on couch at right center, talking.* ANNE *stands.*

MRS. GILBERT: Wait another ten minutes or so, Anne. Pat only went to play tennis. She should be home soon.
ANNE (*Calmly; sitting again*): Oh, well. It's only a matter of life or death. Pat's the only person who can explain

chemistry so that it makes sense to me. Daddy says if I don't pass chemistry, he's going to send me to basket-weaving school. (MRS. GILBERT *laughs*.) Don't laugh, Mrs. Gilbert. What kind of a boy could I meet in basket-weaving school?

DANNY (*Looking up from his work*): Somebody like me, only I'd flunk out before the first football rally.

MR. GILBERT (*Irritated*): Danny, please! Back to your homework.

MRS. GILBERT: Bill, if helping Danny with his homework is going to ruin another weekend, why don't you just stop?

MR. GILBERT: He has to pass the ninth grade before he can get a job, Marjorie.

DANNY: Oh, Dad—

MRS. GILBERT: You two should at least try to be more patient with each other.

DANNY: How patient can anybody be with a dumb kid like me?

MRS. GILBERT: You're not dumb, Danny. There's nothing wrong with your basic intelligence. (*She walks to* MR. GILBERT'*s side*.) But I do think your father should stop helping you with your homework.

MR. GILBERT: There's only a month left before his final exams, and if I don't help him, who will?

ANNE: There's always Pat, Mr. Gilbert. (*Embarrassed*) Oh, excuse me. I didn't mean to butt in.

DANNY (*Going to center*): There's always Pat, 'cause Pat's so smart! (*Mocking*) "Why can't you be smart like your sister, Danny?" I know what everybody's thinking.

MRS. GILBERT: You don't know what anybody's thinking at all. I think Anne's idea should definitely be considered.

ANNE (*Flattered*): Why, thanks, Mrs. Gilbert.

DANNY: I wouldn't let a girl help me with my homework ever. And that goes double for my smarty sister.

MR. GILBERT: If she's smart, it's because she applies herself.

DANNY: Sure. Just wave some competition in front of her nose, and she's off to the Olympics.

ANNE: The Olympics? How divine! Think of all the dates!

MR. GILBERT (*Ignoring* ANNE): Come on, Danny. You're going up to your room, and you're going to finish that page of algebra, and get everything right.

DANNY (*Grabbing book and papers from desk*): Yes, sir! But if you ask me, some people ought to learn to live and let live.

MR. GILBERT (*Escorting* DANNY *to door center*): Nobody asked you. (*They exit, and doorbell rings.* MRS. GILBERT *goes to window right, and looks out.*)

MRS. GILBERT: Why, it's Pat—and Webster came back with her. How nice.

ANNE (*Jumping to her feet*): Webster? Webster Cunningham, the boy? (MRS. GILBERT *nods, then goes to door at right.* ANNE *crouches behind chair at left.*)

MRS. GILBERT (*Opening door*): Why, hello, Webster, come on in. (PAT *and* WEBSTER, *wearing tennis outfits and carrying rackets, enter.*)

WEBSTER: Hello, Mrs. Gilbert.

PAT: Hi, Mom.

MRS. GILBERT: You two must be thirsty after your game. I'll fix you something cool and refreshing. (*She starts toward exit left.*)

WEBSTER: No thanks, Mrs. Gilbert. I mean, I'm thirsty, but I have to be home by five.

MRS. GILBERT: Then you have plenty of time. Oh, Pat, Anne's here. (*She looks around.*) At least I think she is. (*She exits.*)

WEBSTER (*Gulping*): Anne Marker? Uh, come to think of it, I should be home right now.

PAT (*Disappointed*): Are you sure you can't stay?

WEBSTER: Sorry, Pat. Thanks for the game. (*He goes to door.*) It couldn't have been much fun for you, though, playing with somebody you can beat hands down. (*She follows him to door.*)

PAT: You have the makings of a really good tennis player, Webster. All you need is someone to give you a few pointers. (*As she opens door*) I'll be glad to teach you this summer, if you'd like.

WEBSTER (*Nervously*): I'm going to be pretty busy this summer. (*Starts to edge out*) Well, thanks again. Sorry I can't stay. See you in school. (*Exits*)

PAT (*Disappointed*): Sure. (*She walks dejectedly to chair at right, and slumps down in it.* ANNE *peers around corner of chair, then stands up.*)

ANNE: Hi! (PAT *looks up, startled.*) Has Webster gone?

PAT: Yes. He couldn't wait to dump me at the door so that he could rush off to get ready for a big date. Isn't that the most gallant thing you ever heard?

ANNE (*Pleased*): A big date? How do you know?

PAT: Because he told me so! (*She stands and paces, then turns to* ANNE) What were you doing hiding behind that chair, anyhow?

ANNE (*Trying to be casual*): Oh, just waiting for you. (*Starting toward door*) But I have to get right home, to get ready for a big date. I mean, I didn't realize it was going to be a big date, until now. Oh, what's the use— you know what I mean.

PAT (*Slumping into chair again*): You mean Webster's big date is with *you.*

ANNE (*Going to* PAT): How did you know I was going out with Webster?

PAT: It wasn't hard to figure out. Those boys only bother with *me* when they want to be tutored in chemistry, or when they want a game of tennis or golf.

ANNE (*Awkwardly*): Speaking of chemistry, Pat, I was wondering if you might have time to help me a little. Final exams are only a month away, and I just have to have a good grade to graduate.

PAT: Sure. Why not? What else do I have to do?

ANNE: Thanks a lot, Pat. I wish I had your brains.

PAT (*Bitterly, as* ANNE *goes to door*): Why? You're the most popular girl in school. You don't see me getting ready for any big date, do you?

ANNE: Well, I don't know why not. Honestly, you're a mystery to me. I should think you'd be turning them away in droves.

PAT: That's exactly what I *am* doing!

ANNE: You'd think you weren't pretty or something. And you're a better friend than anybody. I just don't under-stand it. (*Shrugging*) Well, I'll see you tomorrow.

PAT (*Weakly*): Have a good time.

ANNE: You, too. I mean—don't work too hard. Oh, you know what I mean.

PAT: Sure, Anne. I know. (ANNE *exits, and* PAT *walks to-ward door at center.* DANNY *rushes in, and runs into her.*) Danny! Why don't you ever watch where you're going?

DANNY: Step on me, and I'll report you to the SPCA.

PAT: Very funny!

DANNY: I just came down for an eraser.

PAT: Then take one and crawl back under your rock.

DANNY (*Bowing*): The human computer has spoken.

PAT (*Backing down*): Oh, I'm sorry for snapping at you.

DANNY (*Taking eraser from desk*): Why? If I heard any kind words out of you these days, I'd drop dead.

PAT: I said I'm sorry! I guess I'm not myself lately.

DANNY: Did you beat Webster Cunningham at tennis?

PAT: How did you know?

DANNY: You're yourself, all right. Off to the Olympics! (*He starts to run out as* MRS. GILBERT *enters left with tray of glasses. He grabs glass.*) Thanks, Mom. (*He exits.*)

MRS. GILBERT: If he could only harness that energy! You know, Pat, he's been having a terrible time with algebra, and Anne thought you might be able to help him.

PAT: Oh, did she! Well, you can tell Anne I have enough problems of my own.

MRS. GILBERT (*Putting tray on coffee table and glancing about*): What's the matter, dear? And where *is* Anne?

PAT: Gone. With Webster Cunningham, to answer your next question.

MRS. GILBERT (*Coolly*): I don't care very much for your tone, Pat. (PAT *stands with her back to her mother.*) Pat, dear. (*Sits on couch and pats place next to her.*) Come here. Sit down.

PAT: I really don't know that I have time, Mother.

MRS. GILBERT (*Calmly insisting*): Sit down, Pat.

PAT (*Sitting*): Well, I'm not going to tutor Danny in algebra, and that's that.

MRS. GILBERT: I'm sorry to hear you won the tennis match today.

PAT: Sorry? And how do you know I didn't lose?

MRS. GILBERT (*Quietly*): Because you never lose, Pat, do you?

PAT (*Tearfully*): Honestly, you'd think it was *my* fault Webster lost the game! Mother, those boys are all alike!

MRS. GILBERT: I doubt that, dear. What about the Benson boy? The golfer?

PAT: Ha! Rick Benson thinks he's Arnold Palmer and Jack Nicklaus all in one, but he couldn't win an amateur tournament for third-string caddies! (*She stands up and paces back and forth, irritatedly.*) And as for Bud Rawlings—sure, he's tops in almost everything, but he asked me to help him with conversational French for the special exam; yet every time I corrected his accent, he blew up!

MRS. GILBERT: I guess it's hard for someone so bright to admit he's having a hard time with something.

PAT: He has to pass an oral exam in French for the scholarship, and to see him react to any correction I make, you'd think *I* was trying to get a scholarship and had asked *him* to help *me!* (*Slumping onto couch*) Oh, I could just die!

MRS. GILBERT (*Dryly*): It's hardly worth going that far.

PAT (*Standing, with resolution*): Mother, I'm going to show those two. I'll win the All-Girl Golf Tournament, and I'll go after the scholarship that Bud's applying for. Besides, I'm sure to be class valedictorian as well. (*Brokenly*) That will take care of them.

MRS. GILBERT (*Calmly*): I don't think it will, Pat.

PAT (*Crying on her mother's shoulder*): Why do men have to be such babies? Such awful, awful sports?

MRS. GILBERT: Most men aren't, Pat; particularly when they're playing a game; they go by the rules. And one rule of any game is that the players should be evenly matched.

PAT: But Webster is supposed to be a first-rate tennis player!

MRS. GILBERT (*Standing*): Sometimes you have to play down your abilities a bit. Men have feelings, too.

PAT (*Agitatedly, getting to her feet*): You mean I have to go through life pretending I'm dumb or can't play tennis very well, or do anything else better than men, just to be popular with them?

MRS. GILBERT: No, Pat. I want you to be the best you can in anything that means a lot to you. But you don't have to play the liberated woman *all* the time. The woman who is *always* superior in everything she does may be admired, but she may also be very lonely.

PAT (*Defiantly*): If there isn't a boy in this world who won't take me just as I am, then I'll just have to be an old maid! (*She wails, and collapses on couch, as* MR. GILBERT *enters at center, shaking head, muttering.*)

MR. GILBERT: It's no use, no use at all. (*Noticing* PAT) Say, what's the matter?

MRS. GILBERT: Your daughter has decided that all men are terrible sports. She beat Webster Cunningham at tennis.

MR. GILBERT: Well, that's no surprise.

MRS. GILBERT (*Drawing him aside*): Bill, please, I wish you'd have a talk with her. She doesn't seem to understand that men simply don't like to be beaten by women at their own games.

PAT (*Perking up somewhat*): Daddy, do you think I have to play dumb and helpless to be popular with men? That's what Mother seems to think.

MR. GILBERT (*Going to her*): You? No, that's not what your mother means, I'm sure. Why, I remember that she used to beat *me* in sports from time to time, and I never minded. (MRS. GILBERT *looks at him, amazed.*) Of course, that was before she settled down to being a good little housewife. And a marvelous cook, too, if I do say so. (MRS. GILBERT *looks at him thoughtfully.*) You just haven't found the right boy, Pat, that's all.

PAT: Oh, Dad. (*Going to door at center*) You just don't understand! I'm going up to my room.

MRS. GILBERT: I'll call you when dinner's ready, dear.

PAT: Maybe I won't have any dinner. Maybe I won't come downstairs ever again! (*She exits.*)

MR. GILBERT (*Shaking his head*): Poor kid. But she'll get over it.

MRS. GILBERT: It isn't as simple as that, Bill. I wish there were something we could do.

MR. GILBERT: Oh, you women. Well, I'm more worried about Danny than about Pat. He's a lost cause, completely hopeless.

MRS. GILBERT: Then turn him over to me.

MR. GILBERT (*Surprised*): You mean *you're* going to help Danny with his Spanish and his math? You know it's ninth-grade New Math at that!

MRS. GILBERT (*Dryly*): I passed the ninth grade, as I recall.

MR. GILBERT (*Laughing*): All right. You have more patience than I do, anyhow. (*He picks up newspaper and sits on couch, and reads as she starts left, then pauses, and returns a few steps.*)

MRS. GILBERT: You know, Bill, I think it might be a good idea for you to take up golf again. You need to get out and away from things. As a matter of fact, I might like to go along with you, if you wouldn't mind.

MR. GILBERT (*Looking up*): You? You haven't played golf for years.

MRS. GILBERT: But I was pretty good, you may recall. And I even managed to beat you once in a while.

MR. GILBERT: That you did. And I *didn't* mind it at all then—and I wouldn't now.

MRS. GILBERT: In that case, there's nothing to stop us.

MR. GILBERT: Fine! We'll begin next weekend. (*He returns to newspaper.*)

MRS. GILBERT: Let's make it tomorrow morning. (*She exits.*)

MR. GILBERT: What did you say we're having for dinner?

(*He looks around, sees that she is gone, shrugs and starts to read, as the curtains close.*)

*   *   *

Scene 2

Time: *Three weeks later.*

Setting: *Same as Scene 1. White cap and gown are on chair at right.*

At Rise: Danny *is sitting at desk, studying. After a moment,* Mrs. Gilbert, *wearing attractive sports outfit, enters right, carrying golf bag and tennis racket.*

Mrs. Gilbert: How are you doing with your algebra, Danny? (*Looks over his shoulder*)

Danny: Mom, you must be some kind of genius! You started helping me with Spanish and math only three weeks ago, and now I'll bet I'll breeze through all my exams—just because of you.

Mrs. Gilbert (*Laughing*): Why, Danny, I didn't do much. You did most of it yourself. I just helped with a little explaining. (*She leans golf bag and tennis racket against a chair and notices cap and gown.*) My! Look at this! (*Holds up white mortarboard*) I can't believe Pat's graduation is only two weeks away. (*Turning back to* Danny) How many exams do you have left?

Danny: Just algebra and history. I think I did O.K. in Spanish and English. (*He stands.*) Guess I'll take a break. Where's Dad?

Mrs. Gilbert (*Gaily*): He's coming.

Danny: I suppose Dad lost the golf game again, just the way he has for the past three weekends.

Mrs. Gilbert (*Laughing*): Danny, you men take these

things much too seriously. (MR. GILBERT *drags himself in, right. He carries a badly bent golf club and a broken tennis racket.*)

MR. GILBERT (*Collapsing on couch, dropping club and racket beside it*): Danny, could you get your old dad a glass of water?

DANNY: Sure. Anything else? Ointment? Bandages?

MR. GILBERT (*Clutching his throat*): Water!

DANNY: O.K. I'm going. (*He exits.*)

MR. GILBERT: Why didn't you ever tell me you were such a dynamo, Marjorie?

MRS. GILBERT (*Amused*): Bill Gilbert, you know I'm nothing of the kind. I just like to do my best.

MR. GILBERT: Well, you've done your best to win every game since we started this nonsense. I don't think I'm going to play golf with you any more. Or tennis, either.

MRS. GILBERT: And you're the one who doesn't mind losing? (*Laughs*) Shame on you for being such a bad sport.

MR. GILBERT: I am not a bad sport. (*Weakly*) Not really. I mean, I don't exactly mind losing to you, but—(*Wistfully*) I wish you'd do your best to make a nice steak dinner for tonight.

MRS. GILBERT (*Brightly*): Bill, I completely forgot to go shopping today, because we left so early. Well, never mind. I'm sure we have enough TV dinners to see us through the weekend. (*Picks up cap and gown and moves center.*) I'll hang up Pat's cap and gown. (*As she exits, DANNY re-enters, carrying glass of water.*)

DANNY: Here's the water, Dad. (MR. GILBERT *takes glass and drinks rapidly. Telephone on desk rings.*)

MR. GILBERT: Would you get that, Danny? (DANNY *starts toward phone.*) No, never mind. I'd better keep using these aching muscles before they give out on me. (*He drags himself to telephone.*) If they haven't given out already. (*Answers phone*) Hello? Señor Gonzales? (DANNY *winces visibly*.) What? . . . .You finished correcting Danny's Spanish exam? . . . (DANNY *moves toward door, pauses*.) Have you double-checked? Triple-checked? . . . Well, I'll break the news to him. Thank you. Goodbye. (*He hangs up phone*.)

DANNY: Break it to me gently.

MR. GILBERT (*Stunned*): Señor Gonzales finished correcting your Spanish exam, and he was so excited he had to call up to tell us your grade right away. You got a ninety-seven! (*He sits*.)

DANNY (*Overcome*): In *Spanish*? (*Shouting and jumping*) Boy! Oh, boy! (*He starts to dash out center, and bumps into* PAT *who is just entering*.)

PAT: Don't you *ever* watch where you're going?

DANNY (*Stopping and smiling broadly*): Say, guess what, Pat?

PAT (*Sourly*): You've been elected neighborhood den mother.

DANNY (*Disgusted*): Too bad you can't snap out of your mood and find a place in the sun. I've found mine, and I'm going to stay there. (*He exits*.)

PAT (*To* MR. GILBERT): What did he mean by that?

MR. GILBERT: He meant that he got a ninety-seven on his Spanish exam.

PAT: He *what*?

MR. GILBERT: Ninety-seven. In Spanish. Olé! If you're going to faint, please faint quietly. I have an awful headache.

PAT: He was nearly flunking Spanish at mid-term. Of course, Mother wasn't helping him then. (*Doorbell rings*.) I'll get it, Dad. (PAT *opens door and* BUD RAWLINGS *and* RICK BENSON *enter. Each carries a pile of books*.) Hi, Bud! Hi, Rick! Come in.

RICK: Hi, Pat.

BUD: I'm returning these books you lent me, Pat. I don't need them anymore now that the scholarship exam is over. (*He and* RICK *put books on desk.*)

MR. GILBERT: Hello, boys. Excuse me for not jumping to my feet—I've just had a hard afternoon on the golf course.

RICK: Hi, Mr. Gilbert. I saw you out on the course with Mrs. Gilbert. (*Shaking his head*) The women in your family are almost unbeatable on the fairways.

BUD: And in class, too!

PAT: What did you think of the scholarship exam this morning, Bud?

BUD: Well, it wasn't exactly a breeze, Pat. But I don't suppose you had any trouble at all.

RICK (*Tauntingly*): No challenge is too much for Pat, Bud. She's going to win the All-Girl Golf Tournament tomorrow. Right, Pat?

BUD: Well, we have to be going, Pat. Thanks for all your help. I couldn't have managed that scholarship exam without it. (*He and* RICK *go to door.*) See you later. 'Bye, Mr. Gilbert. (BUD *and* RICK *exit.*)

PAT *and* MR. GILBERT: Goodbye. (MR. GILBERT *looks at* PAT *thoughtfully, as she walks to center, dejectedly.*)

MR. GILBERT: I'm coming to the conclusion that as far as the male animal is concerned, sufferance is the medal of our tribe.

PAT: The *badge*, Dad, not the medal.

MR. GILBERT (*Annoyed*): Oh, so what!

PAT: If you're going to quote Shakespeare, you should quote him correctly. It's only respectful.

MR. GILBERT (*Irritatedly*): I respect Shakespeare. I *love* Shakespeare! I used to be able to recite *Hamlet* from start to finish.

PAT (*Settling into chair*): There was a question on *Hamlet* on the scholarship exam this morning. (*Smugly*) When I left the exam room, poor Bud looked pretty grim.

MR. GILBERT: Pat! I don't think that's the right attitude.

PAT (*Angrily*): And tomorrow I *will* win the golf tournament, and that'll show Rick Benson. He deserves to end up in a sand trap.

MR. GILBERT: Now, why in the world do you say that?

PAT: He's one of the worst golfers I've ever beaten, that's why.

MR. GILBERT: Maybe he had a bad day.

PAT (*Unkindly*): I hope he has another one. I don't care what Mother says, all men are terrible sports!

MR. GILBERT (*Self-righteously*): Men are the best sports in the world.

PAT: Maybe you are, but you're different. I mean, if you were losing a game of golf to a girl, would you take one of your best clubs and wrap it around a tree?

MR. GILBERT (*Quickly pushing his bent club under chair; uncomfortably*): Uh . . . tennis is more my game.

PAT: Then would you smash your racket on the concrete and jump up and down like a child? (*He shoves racket under chair.*) I don't see why women should play down their abilities to flatter the male ego.

MR. GILBERT (*Standing, speaking unsteadily*): Naturally, Pat, it takes a superior man to appreciate the superior qualities of a superior woman, but I don't think any man minds being *fairly* beaten by a woman, even if she is *pushy enough* to be playing the *man's game!* (*He falters, then drops back into chair.*)

PAT (*Rushing to him*): Are you O.K.?

MR. GILBERT (*Valiantly*): Never felt better in my life. (*He struggles to his feet.*) I'm a bit hungry, though. (*He limps toward door center.*) Perhaps there's a wilted lettuce leaf or two in the refrigerator—just enough to calm the hunger pangs until it's time for tonight's TV dinner! (*He exits, and* PAT *shakes her head sympathetically.* MRS. GILBERT *re-enters. She now wears a dress.*)

MRS. GILBERT: Pat, dear! I didn't know you were back.

PAT (*With no enthusiasm*): Congratulations, Mother.

MRS. GILBERT (*Lightly*): Congratulations on what?

PAT: Didn't you hear? Danny had a ninety-seven on his Spanish exam.

MRS. GILBERT: I knew he could do it if he tried. He's really very good at languages.

PAT (*Facing her mother*): You know he couldn't have done it without you.

MRS. GILBERT (*Smiling*): You and your brother. You both love to exaggerate.

PAT: Maybe. But I don't think I'm exaggerating about Dad.

MRS. GILBERT: Oh? What exam did he take?

PAT (*Visibly upset*): Really, Mother. You mean you haven't noticed? Haven't you seen the change in him?

MRS. GILBERT: Yes, now that you mention it. I think getting more fresh air and exercise has done him a world of good.

PAT (*In disbelief*): Good!

MRS. GILBERT: Well, fresh air never hurt anybody. At least I don't *think* so.

PAT: Mother, that's not what I'm talking about, and you know it. (*She goes to center.*) Ever since you started playing golf and tennis with him a few weekends ago, he's changed from a happy, easygoing, confident man into a sad, tired, undernourished *heap!*

MRS. GILBERT (*Trying to frown*): Goodness! Is it as bad as all that?

PAT: It certainly is!

MRS. GILBERT: Now you *are* exaggerating. I'm certainly not the only wife who joins her husband in a game of golf.

PAT: Joining him is one thing. But you beat him every time!

MRS. GILBERT: Maybe I'm the better player.

PAT: What good does it do to beat a man at his own game, if he's going to end up so unhappy?

MRS. GILBERT (*Going to* PAT): No good at all, dear, unless you've been trying to set a bad example for your daughter.

PAT: Example? Example of what?

MRS. GILBERT: An example of what *not* to do. Tell me something, Pat. Do you think your father is a terrible sport?

PAT (*Irritated*): Why? Just because he doesn't like to feel inferior to you?

MRS. GILBERT (*Quickly*): Webster and Rick Benson and Bud Rawlings don't like feeling inferior either. Those boys are sensitive, as Dad is, about losing to women all the time. The only difference is that before now I've never really let your father know how much better at golf and tennis I am. But I've been winning a lot lately, just to show you something, Pat—something you refused to believe when I tried to explain it a few weeks ago.

PAT (*Sighing*): You mean, winning all the time may not be worth the price?

MRS. GILBERT: That's right, and if you understand that, I can relax and tend to a few important matters. Like dinner.

PAT: Poor Dad.

MRS. GILBERT (*Laughing*): Don't worry about him. He's known me long enough not to let a few lost golf and tennis games hurt him—not for long, anyway! But I think it's time I started making it up to him.

PAT: Say! Why don't we make him a really special dinner tonight? We could run down to the supermarket before it closes and buy the best steak they have.

MRS. GILBERT: Good idea. And I'll make his favorite salad.

PAT: And I'll whip up his favorite lemon pie. (*She starts to exit center.*) I'll tell him where we're going, so he can relax, too. (*She stops and turns.*) Mom? If you're so good at sports, why don't you let me take you on? (*Sadly.*) I probably won't be playing much tennis or golf with Webster and Rick, but I do want to keep in practice.

MRS. GILBERT: Fine! But let's wait until after your graduation.

PAT: Thanks, Mom. (*Smiling*) I think I do understand now.

MRS. GILBERT: Good. I'll just get my coat. (*She exits left, as* PAT *goes to door at center and calls.*)

PAT: Dad? How about a nice, juicy steak for dinner? (*Quick curtain*)

*   *   *

SCENE 3

TIME: *Two weeks later.*

SETTING: *Same as Scene 1. Matador's hat and red cape are on desk.*

AT RISE: MR. *and* MRS. GILBERT *enter right.* MR. GILBERT *wears suit, and* MRS. GILBERT *wears coat and flowered hat, and carries white cap and gown.* MR. GILBERT *sits in armchair at left, and* MRS. GILBERT *puts cap and gown on chair and removes her hat as she comes center.*

MRS. GILBERT: It was a lovely graduation, but I do feel sorry for Pat. I was simply shocked when we heard that Bud Rawlings was valedictorian of the class. I knew Pat was very upset, even though she tried not to let it show. And Bud won that big scholarship, too. That boy must have made up his mind he'd beat Pat, no matter what.

MR. GILBERT (*Smiling*): And so he did!

MRS. GILBERT: Well! You seem almost glad!

MR. GILBERT: Glad? Of course I'm not "glad." Pat's my daughter, and I don't like her to lose out on anything, especially on her graduation day.

MRS. GILBERT: I just hope it wasn't too much of a disappointment for her. (*She sits on couch.*) Then Rick Benson had to go and win the boys' golf tournament.

MR. GILBERT: He must be quite a golfer!

MRS. GILBERT (*Ignoring him*): And right after Pat *lost* the all-girl tournament. Bill, what do you suppose happened to her?

MR. GILBERT: Now, Marjorie, you were the one who thought Pat needed to be taught a lesson about being a good sport, and she *has* been a good sport about all this. I noticed how bad she felt about not being valedictorian.

MRS. GILBERT: I'm proud of her, too, but I hate to see her unhappy.

MR. GILBERT (*Slyly*): As for that golf tournament, I'm not so sure she didn't play a bit carelessly just to teach her mother a lesson.

MRS. GILBERT (*Protesting*): What do you mean by that? (DANNY *rushes in right.*)

DANNY: Hi! How's the supply of Coke and cookies?

MRS. GILBERT: Danny! (*Standing*) Where did you run off to right after graduation? I told you to stay with us.

DANNY: I had to invite people to the party this afternoon.

MR. GILBERT: Party? What party?

DANNY: A graduation party. I decided it was time to put my diplomatic talents to work. (*He goes to desk, puts on matador's hat and picks up cape.*) Now that I'm learning to speak Spanish like a native, I think I'll become a matador. (*Doorbell rings, and* DANNY *rushes to open door, bowing with an elaborate sweep of his cape as* WEBSTER *enters, carrying bags of potato chips.*) Ah, Webster. Welcome to the residence of Danny Gilbert, scholar, linguist, bullfighter, and man-about-town.

WEBSTER: Hi, Danny. (*Walks center*) Hello, Mr. and Mrs. Gilbert. I brought some snacks for the party. Anne's coming with the soda.

DANNY: Put the bags in the kitchen, champ. (*To his parents, as* WEBSTER *starts to exit left.*) Did you hear about Webster? (WEBSTER *stops at door, looks back.*) He's in the Men's Tennis Finals next week. Has a good chance of winning, too, I understand.

MRS. GILBERT: Why, that's wonderful, Webster. Congratulations.

WEBSTER (*As he exits*): Thanks, Mrs. Gilbert. (*She sits. Doorbell rings, and* DANNY *opens door.*) Bud Rawlings, class valedictorian, in person! (BUD *enters.*)

MRS. GILBERT: Congratulations, Bud.

MR. GILBERT: Yes. Congratulations to you.

BUD: Thanks. But Pat's the one I really should thank. I wouldn't have won the scholarship without her.

DANNY (*With a sweep of his cape*): Fancy that!

BUD: She sort of . . . well . . . she sort of inspired me.

DANNY: Isn't that touching? (*Doorbell rings again.*)

BUD: I wanted to invite her to my party tonight.

DANNY (*Going to door*): Well, I don't know about that. You see, Rick Benson mentioned something about (*He opens door and* RICK *enters.*)—and here he is, the pride of the fairways!

MR. GILBERT: Congratulations, too, Rick. We certainly have a lot of winners here today.

RICK: Thanks, Mr. Gilbert. Hey, Danny, what are you doing in that outfit?

DANNY: Waiting for the Spanish Ambassador. He's due any minute to take my sister to a fiesta.

RICK: Tell him she already has a date.

BUD: What's this "date" business?

RICK: I have a date with Pat. For tonight.

BUD: But I want her to come to my party.

RICK: Listen, if it hadn't been for Pat, I never would have won that golf tournament. I made up my mind; I was determined to show her that I could . . . well . . . I wouldn't have done it without her. I want to take her to dinner at the best place in town.

BUD: I was here first. (PAT *enters right with* ANNE, *who carries two cartons of Coke.*)

DANNY (*With exaggerated gestures*): Yes, gentlemen of the press, I can tell you what she was like way back when . . . when men weren't throwing themselves at her feet, when she wasn't the power in back of a single throne, when she inspired not even one duel to the death.

MRS. GILBERT (*A bit awkwardly*): Why, Pat, dear.

ALL (*Turning to* PAT; *ad lib*): Hiya. Hi, Pat, Anne. (*Etc.*)

ANNE: See, Pat? I told you Danny invited us to a party. Where shall I put the Coke?

DANNY: In the kitchen—with Webster. (ANNE *beams.*)

RICK: Pat, you will go out with me tonight, won't you?

BUD: I wanted you to come to my party. Everybody's going to be there.

RICK: I won't be there. Pat won't be there.

PAT (*Sweetly*): I'd love to come to your party, Bud.

RICK: But what about me?

PAT (*Sweetly*): I'd love to go out with you, too.

RICK (*To* BUD): See?

DANNY: Come on to the kitchen. We'll serve up the goodies and be all ready for the Spanish Ambassador.

PAT: I'll be out in a minute.

RICK (*To* BUD, *as* ANNE *leads them left*): Look, why don't we compromise? Pat will come to your party, if I can bring her.

BUD: Did she say that? Did she? I don't remember that I invited *you*. (BUD, RICK *and* ANNE *exit left.* PAT *remains.*)

DANNY: And so another crisis fades into oblivion. . . .

MR. GILBERT: All right, young man. That's enough out of you. Why don't you run off and study or something and leave the graduates alone?

DANNY: Huh. That's the thanks I get. O.K., Dad, I'll go, but studying's over for this year. (*He moves to center.*) I have a summer job, helping the less fortunate. You know Jill Haviland?

MRS. GILBERT: The cute girl with the big blue eyes? The one who modeled in the school fashion show?

DANNY (*Nodding*): She has to take a make-up course in algebra this summer. I thought I'd help her—as a kind of favor.

MR. GILBERT: Your charity touches my heart, Danny.

DANNY: And with Joyce Bates taking a make-up course in Spanish, and Diane Powers needing some tennis lessons, I think I'm going to be busy. See you. (*Goes to door, turns briefly*) And Pat—have fun. I guess you're not such a bad kid after all. (*He bows to her with a sweep of his cape, then exits.*)

MRS. GILBERT (*Rushing to* PAT): My poor dear. I'm so sorry the day turned out to be such a disappointment.

PAT: Disappointment? Not really. After all, I do have two dates for tonight.

MR. GILBERT: Don't you hold it against Bud that he won the scholarship *and* was valedictorian, too?

PAT: Dad! Don't you think that's a bit silly? After all, I did do well enough on the scholarship exam to win the smaller scholarship, and I don't really mind that I ended up second in our class instead of first. Bud was so pleased to be valedictorian. (MR. GILBERT *looks at his wife and shrugs.*) I'm even sort of glad I didn't win the girls' golf tournament, and I'm really happy that Rick won the boys' match. (*Sighing*) But I suppose I can't very well go out with both Bud and Rick tonight.

MRS. GILBERT: Well, why don't you do what Rick suggested —go to Bud's party with Rick? I'm sure you won't be forced to choose between them tonight.

PAT: You're right, Mom. (*Starting toward exit left*) I guess I'll join the others. (*Pausing at door*) You know, Mom, if I'd listened to you much sooner, I wouldn't have suffered so much.

MRS. GILBERT: Put away the handkerchief, dear, and enjoy the party your crazy brother cooked up for you. (PAT *exits.*)

MR. GILBERT: Well, to quote Danny, another crisis fades into oblivion!

MRS. GILBERT: Don't be so flippant. Today could have been a complete disaster.

MR. GILBERT (*Laughing, affectionately*): The only disaster I could imagine right now would be eighteen holes on the golf course with you, followed by a TV dinner.

MRS. GILBERT: Not a chance. I'm still exhausted by all that golf we've been playing. I'm going to enjoy sleeping late on the weekends—and I have a lot to do around the house. (MR. GILBERT *smiles.*) And I found a marvelous recipe I'm going to make for us tonight, after Pat goes out. (*She stands and goes to door center, as* DANNY *enters wearing casual clothes.*) Of course, if you still feel like playing golf and don't want to go alone, you could always take Danny.

MR. GILBERT: Danny!

DANNY: Me?

MRS. GILBERT: Well, he *is* a good caddy. And something of a diplomat, too—good at keeping people under control. He might even keep you from ruining another golf club. (*They all laugh as the curtain closes.*)

THE END

Production Notes

THE BEST OF SPORTS

Characters: 5 male; 3 female.

Playing Time: 40 minutes.

Costumes: Modern, everyday dress. In Scene 1, Webster and Pat wear tennis outfits. Others wear casual dress. In Scene 2, Mr. and Mrs. Gilbert wear sports clothes. Mrs. Gilbert later changes into a housedress. Others wear ordinary school clothes. In Scene 3, Mr. Gilbert and the boys wear suits, and girls wear suitable graduation dresses. Mrs. Gilbert wears a coat and a flowered hat when she first enters. Danny later changes into casual clothes.

Properties: Book, papers, eraser, tray of glasses, newspaper, tennis rackets, bag of golf clubs, smashed tennis racket, bent golf club, glass of water, white graduation cap and gown, piles of books, bags of potato chips, cartons of soda, matador's hat and red cape.

Setting: The Gilbert living room. A desk with a telephone on it is at left. At right center is a couch, and there are armchairs at right and left. An exit up center leads to the upstairs, an exit at left leads to the kitchen. The door at right leads to the outside, and there is a window beside it. Other chairs, tables, lamps, etc., complete the furnishings. In Scene 2, a white cap and gown are on the chair at right, and in Scene 3, a matador's hat and cape are on the desk.

Lighting: No special effects.

Sound: Telephone, doorbell, as indicated in text.

Little Jackie and the Beanstalk

Characters

LITTLE JACKIE DARLING
THELMA DARLING, *his mother*
MISS J. B. MINGE, *his agent*
MAX MILLIONS, *his producer*
MR. BROD, *a TV station owner*
MRS. FENSTERMAKER, *a sponsor*
BOSSIE, *Jackie's cow*
DESDEMONA O'BRIAN
MR. O'BRIAN, *her father*
TELEVISION ANNOUNCER

CLARA ⎱ *teen-agers*
GERT ⎰
MRS. VAN LEER
BEN
JUNIOR, *his son*
MR. TWOMBLEY
MRS. TWOMBLEY
MAGIC HARP, *a girl*
STAGEHAND
CAMERAMAN

SCENE 1

BEFORE RISE: STAGEHAND *brings in standing microphone and large sign:* "THE ADVENTURES OF BOSSIE"—STARRING BOSSIE THE COW AND LITTLE JACKIE DARLING. BROUGHT TO YOU BY MIGHTY MEAL, AMERICA'S FAVORITE CEREAL. CAMERAMAN *brings in television camera, and he and* STAGEHAND *work busily as* MAX MILLIONS *rushes in, followed by* MRS. FENSTERMAKER, MR. BROD, *and* ANNOUNCER, *who carries large box of Mighty Meal.*

MAX: All right, now. We have only a few minutes before the end of the program. (*He consults with* CAMERAMAN.)

MRS. FENSTERMAKER: Only a few minutes before Little
   Jackie Darling will be saved once again by his faithful
   cow, Bossie, from impending doom. (*She sniffs.*) For
   the very last time. . . .

MR. BROD: Now, now, Mrs. Fenstermaker. My television
   station can't keep carrying a program with such low rat-
   ings as *The Adventures of Bossie,* and the show's not
   helping to sell your product, either.

MRS. FENSTERMAKER: But Jackie's been a lovable ten-year-
   old on the show for twelve years. It isn't easy to fire him
   after all this time.

ANNOUNCER: My dear Mrs. Fenstermaker, it also isn't easy
   for a talented announcer like me to stand in front of the
   American public week after week and talk glowingly
   about something as revolting as your Mighty Meal.

MRS. FENSTERMAKER: Why, young man, my family has been
   making breakfast cereal for generations.

ANNOUNCER: Some people never learn. (MRS. FENSTER-
   MAKER *glares at him.*)

MAX (*Coming to center*): Quiet, please. Places! (*He takes*
   MRS. FENSTERMAKER *and* MR. BROD *to one side, as* AN-
   NOUNCER *takes his place at microphone.*)

ANNOUNCER: Why couldn't this station give me a boom
   mike? This thing hides my profile.

MR. BROD: My television station has the best equipment
   available. Only some of the shows are far from the best.

MRS. FENSTERMAKER: And some announcers. (ANNOUNCER
   gestures angrily with box of Mighty Meal.)

MAX (*Looking at his watch*): Stand by.

ANNOUNCER: I've been standing by for twelve years. I'm
   tired of standing by for a cow and an aging child star.
   I'm . . . (MAX *gives signal to* CAMERAMAN. ANNOUNCER
   beams at camera.) Once again, dear friends, *The Adventures of Bossie* has been brought to you by the Mighty

Meal folks (*Holds up box*), makers of Mighty Meal Munchies, the cereal that makes your mornings memorable. Remember—the big M on the box stands for "Mush!" (*A loud "Moo" is heard from offstage, and* BOSSIE *and* JACKIE, *a young man of twenty, stroll in.*) Even Mrs. Thelma Darling, mother of our own Little Jackie Darling (*Pats* JACKIE *on head*), has nothing but praise for Mighty Meal. Isn't that right, Little Jackie?

JACKIE: Sure is, Mr. Announcer, friend. (BOSSIE *moos.*)

ANNOUNCER: And now, dear friends, we have a mighty sad message for you. You have just seen the very last show about our simple country boy, Jackie, and his heroic cow, Bossie. (MRS. FENSTERMAKER *sniffles loudly.*)

JACKIE: Do you mean Bossie and I aren't going to work here at the television station anymore?

ANNOUNCER: That's right, Jackie. But we'll be seeing you two around somewhere, over the far horizon. And now, we'll close this last *Adventures of Bossie* show as we've closed every one for the past twelve years, with Bossie and Little Jackie Darling sinking slowly into the West . . .

JACKIE (*Smiling into camera*): See you over the far horizon, folks.

ANNOUNCER: And Little Jackie waving his chore-toughened hand, and saying . . .

JACKIE (*Waving*): Warm up the Mighty Meal, Mommy. I'm coming home! (*Sentimental music, up and out.*)

MAX: O.K., that's it. Wrap it up! (STAGEHAND *removes sign and mike and* CAMERAMAN *takes camera off, as others gather at center.*)

MRS. FENSTERMAKER: Jackie dear, we wouldn't be firing you if we could help it, but I do have to answer to my board of directors, and sales of Mighty Meal have fallen off so . . . (*She sniffles.*)

JACKIE: Now, Mrs. Fenstermaker, don't get all upset. I understand. (*To* MR. BROD) Can't you do something, Mr. Brod? You own the station.

MR. BROD: I'm afraid not, Jackie. You're twenty years old now, and you can't go on playing a little kid forever.

ANNOUNCER (*Sarcastically*): He came as close to forever as he could.

JACKIE: But I like show business. I don't want to go back to the farm. Couldn't Bossie and I do a *big* kid show?

MAX: Not until the memory of this show has faded from the mind of the public. Now, hurry home to Mommy.

ANNOUNCER: I'm going to rush over to the unemployment office before it closes. (*He exits.*)

MRS. FENSTERMAKER: Goodbye, Jackie. Give my love to your sweet, homespun mother. Goodbye, Bossie dear. (BOSSIE *moos.*) Such a *nice* cow. (*She exits.*)

MR. BROD: I must be going, too. I must find something to fill this time slot. (*He starts to exit.*)

MAX (*Following* MR. BROD): What you need, Brod, is one of my original ideas. What about a show set in the Old West? Something about the greatest cowboy who ever lived? (*They exit, talking.*)

JACKIE (*Putting his arms around* BOSSIE'*s neck*): Well, Bossie, here I am—retired at twenty. But we'll make out somehow. Mr. Max Millions, the nice producer, has been saving all the money we've earned for the past twelve years, so you and Mommy and I are really rich. We'll leave New York and buy a nice farm and settle down forever. (BOSSIE *moos wearily.*) I know you're tired and want to lie down in your nice garden and rest. We'll have to walk all the way home, though. Nobody gave us taxi money today. But you won't ever have to walk up Fifth Avenue again, if you don't want to. (BOSSIE *moos and shakes her head.*) And when we get home, I'll fix you a nice, big bowl of Mighty Meal. (BOSSIE *gives an agonized "Moo," and promptly lies down.*) Mighty Meal isn't that bad, Bossie. And even if the Mighty Meal folks and Max Millions and Mr. Brod don't love you anymore, I still love you, girl. Now, come on. (BOSSIE *drags herself to her feet.*) There we go, there we go! (BOSSIE *shuffles along behind* JACKIE *as they exit.* JACKIE *sings brightly.*) Mighty Meal's the Mush for Me, Mush for Me, Mush for Me . . . (*Curtains open.*)

*   *   *

SCENE 1

SETTING: *The Darlings' ground floor garden apartment. Garden can be seen at back, through open French doors.*
AT RISE: THELMA DARLING, *in gingham dress and sunbonnet, is turning off TV set, as* MISS J. B. MINGE *paces nervously, back and forth.*

THELMA (*Happily*): Miss Minge, did the announcer really mean that *The Adventures of Bossie* isn't going to be on TV anymore?

J. B.: That's what he said, Thelma. Your sweet, unspoiled son Jackie is finished in television.

THELMA (*Dancing about*): Oh, goody, goody gumdrops. I'm free at last. I'll have a swinging time, spending all the money Jackie's made for the past twelve years.

J. B.: I have to call the station right away. (*Goes to phone and dials*)

THELMA (*Whirling around room*): Around the world I go —London, Paris, Rome!

J. B. (*On phone*): Hello? This is J. B. Minge, Jackie Darling's agent. Let me speak to Max Millions.

THELMA (*Dreamily*): I'll go to Paris first. I can get rid of this sunbonnet and these corny clothes. Let's pack our duffel bags. Paris, here I come! (*She exits.*)

J. B. (*On phone*): Max? This is J. B. I'm with Thelma Darling at her place. You'd better get over here fast before she gets on a plane for Paris, and finds out she can't buy a ticket because *you* lost all of Jackie's money in bad investments. Jackie and Thelma think they're rich because "nice Max Millions" has been taking care of Jackie's money. I never should have trusted you to handle Jackie's money in the first place. . . . (*Her voice rising*) Just get over here and explain to Thelma that she's flat broke! And explain to *me* why Jackie's show was canceled. I'll be waiting for you. (*She slams down receiver.*)

THELMA (*Re-entering*): Have you seen my hair dryer?

J. B.: No. Max is on his way over.

THELMA: Then I'd better hurry. If there's one man in television I'll never miss, it's Max Millions.

J. B.: He's the biggest producer in the business.

THELMA: I know. He should go on a diet.

DESDEMONA (*Barging in*): Oh, salutations, Mrs. Darling. Salutations and felicitations. I have this very moment witnessed the proclamation of the culmination and fruition of my counseling with your filial offspring, who henceforth shall, I trust, be known as John or Jack, or anything more suitable for a young man of such physical stature, social acumen, and cerebral profundity of titanic potential.

THELMA: That's sweet of you, dear.

J. B.: What is she talking about?

THELMA: She's glad Jackie is out of television.

DESDEMONA: Permit me to introduce myself.

THELMA: I thought you two had met. This is Desdemona O'Brian, the daughter of our building superintendent.

She's kind of Jackie's girl friend. Desdemona, dear, I'd like you to meet J. B. Minge, Jackie's agent and business manager.

DESDEMONA: Enchanted.

THELMA: Desdemona wants to be a psychiatrist, J. B. She took Jackie on as a sort of test case.

DESDEMONA: All I did was offer Jack some advice. "Jack," I said, "you're far too mature to play pre-adolescent roles on television, or even adolescent roles, for that matter. Furthermore," I told him, "the part is far beneath your intelligence." That's all there was to it.

J. B.: You mean *you* told Jackie to quit television?

DESDEMONA: Call him Jack—please! The diminutive is highly offensive.

J. B.: Why, you've done Little Jackie Darling and his homespun mother out of bread for their table!

THELMA: Homespun, my bonnet!

DESDEMONA: Jack's made plenty of money, and mark my words, someday Jack's going to do something really spectacular.

J. B.: Ha!

THELMA: Well, here's one homespun mother who's glad the whole mess is over with. When Jackie and I left the farm to come to New York, I never thought I'd be spending my life baby-sitting for a cow. What I really wanted was a penthouse apartment. And what did I get? A ground floor apartment with a garden big enough to tether Bossie!

J. B.: I'm sure Bossie appreciates it, Thelma.

THELMA: Now it's back to the farm for Bossie, and up to the penthouse for me.

DESDEMONA: The penthouse is rented to Mr. Twombley, Mrs. Darling.

THELMA: Mr. Twombley will just have to move.

MR. TWOMBLEY (*Roaring, from offstage*): Fee, fi, fo, fum!

J. B.: What on earth is that?

DESDEMONA: It's Mr. Twombley.

THELMA (*Going to window and calling, as she leans out*): All right, Mr. Twombley. You don't have to move. I'm sorry.

MR. TWOMBLEY (*Offstage*): Fee! Fi!

J. B.: What is he doing?

THELMA: It beats me. But he does it all the time. Sometimes in the middle of the night, for hours and hours.

MR. TWOMBLEY (*Offstage*): Fo! Fum!

THELMA: I tell you, J. B., Mr. Twombley would frighten a gorilla. He's an ogre!

DESDEMONA: We lose more tenants because of him. The story is that he's seven feet tall and wide as a city block. And dangerous, too.

J. B.: You can't be serious, Desdemona.

DESDEMONA: All I know, Miss Minge, is what I hear. I've never seen him myself, but our leases all have a clause stating that we are not responsible for damage done to persons or property by Mr. Twombley.

THELMA: The man is supposed to be more gruesome, horrible and scary than . . . than . . .

J. B. (*As* MAX *enters*): Max Millions!

MAX (*With false heartiness*): That's me, dolls. Ah, Mother Darling. How sweet you look. All gingham and smiles.

THELMA: Homespun, you mean. Thanks a bunch.

MAX: This is the night to celebrate! Our own Little Jackie is finally off that two-bit kid show with the cow. Now he can relax and be the All-American Boy.

J. B.: He's almost ready for the All-American Home for the Aged.

MAX: If you knew the strings I had to pull to get Jackie out of his contract! But now I'm everybody's friend.

THELMA: Well, I'm not too sure. Bossie never liked you very much, and when a cow doesn't cotton to a feller, something's wrong.

MAX: Believe me, Jackie's a free boy.

THELMA: Then I'm going to finish packing! (*She exits.*)

DESDEMONA: Mr. Millions, I think it was exemplary of you to assist Jack in his determination to shed forever the miasma of that nauseating weekly sojourn in an infantile fantasy world.

MAX: You said it, doll.

J. B.: Desdemona says she made Jackie quit, Max.

MAX: *She* made him quit! (*Laughing*)

J. B.: Then it *was* you, Max. Why, Max! There's only one reason why you'd let Jackie drop that show. You have another show for him. Bigger and better! A quiz program? *Hamlet* in weekly installments? Tell me what it is, Max.

MAX: Look, J. B. Little Jackie was fired. I give you my word. Mighty Meal's sales were dropping so badly that they decided to take a poll. And do you know what they found out? People have been watching the show to make fun of it, and they're making fun of Mighty Meal, too.

DESDEMONA: They certainly are. (*Sing-song*)
Mighty Meal's adhesive,
Mighty Meal's like glue.
If it's good enough for that old cow,
It's good enough for you!

MAX: Little Jackie Darling is all washed up.

JACKIE (*From offstage*): Good girl, Bossie. (BOSSIE *moos.*)

J. B.: There's our wonder boy now. (JACKIE *and* BOSSIE *enter.*)

JACKIE: Remember, I still love you, Bossie baby.

J. B.: I think I'm going to cry.

JACKIE (*Cheerfully*): Hi, all.

DESDEMONA: You poor boy.

JACKIE: Poor? I'm not poor. I've been working and working since I was knee-high to a hoppy toad. I'm just retiring for a while. Shucks, with all the money Miss Minge and Mr. Millions have been saving for me, I'll be ready to go into business for myself, or settle down with Bossie and Ma on a farm. (THELMA *enters with duffel bags.*)

THELMA: Get that cow out of my living room. (BOSSIE *ambles out into the garden and disappears.*)

JACKIE: When can I get my money, Miss Minge?

J. B. (*Backing toward door*): Tell Bossie I'm sorry I had to leave without saying goodbye.

JACKIE: Mr. Millions? When can I have my money, Mr. Millions?

THELMA: Yes, Max. I'm going to need some cash for my trip around the world.

J. B.: Do have a good trip, Thelma.

MAX (*Opening door*): Send us a postcard, Thelma baby.

DESDEMONA: Do you have a feeling they're trying to hide something?

THELMA: Now just a minute here!

MAX (*Smoothly*): Now take it easy, doll. You're going to double your money. It's just that right now your money's all tied up. The only thing I can give you right now is stock.

THELMA: That's all right. We'll sell the stock.

J. B. (*Sarcastically*): If you find a buyer, send up flares.

THELMA: Do you mean you've thrown away my money on no-good oil wells or a lot of phony gold mines?

MAX: I invested everything in a television production company.

J. B.: Panoramic Pictures, Limited—owned, operated and

run into bankruptcy by the one, the only Max Millions. (*She and* MAX *exit.*)

THELMA (*Shaking her fist*): Max, you miserable, fat, sneaky varmint!

DESDEMONA: Well, I'm glad it's all come out! Now you'll see how clever Jack really is. He's going to set the world on fire.

JACKIE: Now, why would I do a mean thing like that?

THELMA (*Dejectedly*): We're left with nothing! Not a cent. We're ruined.

JACKIE: Now, Ma. We have Bossie, and she loves us.

THELMA: Bossie has to go. We won't even be able to feed ourselves, let alone that cow.

JACKIE (*Sighing*): All right, Ma. If that's the way it has to be, Bossie will help us by bringing a real good price.

THELMA: And who's going to give a nickel for a broken-down television star that happens to be a cow?

JACKIE: But Bossie's famous! Lots of people will want to own this fine bovine friend to man. (MR. O'BRIAN *pushes door open. He is carrying large bag of groceries.*)

MR. O'BRIAN: Sorry to interrupt. I just stopped in to remind you that it is the first of the month.

DESDEMONA: You picked an awkward time to ask for the rent, Father.

THELMA: That's all right, Mr. O'Brian. You want your rent money, I suppose.

JACKIE: But we don't have it.

THELMA: All we have is one cow for sale, and who's going to pay good money for her, I'd like to know?

MR. O'BRIAN: Oh, I don't know. It's hard to keep a dog in the city, but a cow—that's different—especially a famous one like Bossie.

THELMA: We couldn't get a handful of beans for that sorry creature.

MR. O'BRIAN: I wouldn't say that. You should be able to get at least that much.

JACKIE: Ma said we'd take anything we could get for Bossie.

MR. O'BRIAN: In that case, sold! (*Reaching into bag*) I'll give you this package of beans, just to show my heart's in the right place. (*Hands* THELMA *package*)

THELMA: Now, just a minute!

JACKIE: There, Ma. Now we don't have an extra mouth to feed, and we have beans for supper besides. If there's one thing I love, it's fresh, homemade bean soup.

THELMA: And this is the yokel who's going to set the world on fire! Out with the beans! (*She throws package out open French doors into garden.*)

DESDEMONA: I think your mother's a bit annoyed, Jack.

THELMA: Give the man his cow, Jackie. And leave me here alone with my tearstained travel folders. (*She rushes out.*)

DESDEMONA: Come on, Jack. I'll treat you to a sandwich.

JACKIE: All I wanted was some bean soup. (JACKIE *shrugs, and he,* DESDEMONA, *and* MR. O'BRIAN *go out through French doors, into garden.* JACKIE *disappears for a moment, then returns with* BOSSIE. *As all exit, a stout green vine is seen rising from the garden. Curtain.*)

*   *   *

SCENE 2

BEFORE RISE: MR. O'BRIAN *enters in front of curtain, leading* BOSSIE, *who keeps looking back.*

MR. O'BRIAN: Come on, Bossie. Don't keep looking back over your shoulder. I'm your new owner. (BOSSIE *moos sadly.*) Don't worry, girl. I'll be good to you. I'll even feed you Mighty Meal, the way Jackie used to. (BOSSIE *gives agonized "Moo"*) Life will be just the same. (BOSSIE *lies down.*) Now, stop being temperamental, Bossie. You're not a TV star anymore. (GERT *and* CLARA *saunter in, talking, as* MR. O'BRIAN *tries without success to get* BOSSIE *to her feet.*)

CLARA: So he says to me, "Clara," he says, "would you consider letting me escort you to the prom?" I mean, so formal like.

GERT: Yeah, Clara, especially for a boy of Myron's unusual directness. I mean, a girl is like a princess if Myron even grunts at her. Gee. You sure must have something special. (*Seeing* BOSSIE) Say! Look at that!

CLARA: Look at what?

GERT: That cow, lying down in the middle of the sidewalk.

CLARA: Oh, that.

GERT: You know, that cow looks kind of familiar.

CLARA: Sure. So I says to him, "Myron, let me consult my already-crammed engagement calendar to see if I'm free that night."

GERT: I knew I'd seen that cow before. That's Bossie.

CLARA: And I'm Ferdinand.

GERT: Bossie! A genuine celebrity! And me without my autograph book.

CLARA: Who's Bossie?

GERT: The cow on that TV show.

MRS. VAN LEER (*Bustling in, waving her umbrella*): Now see here, sir. You've driven my poodle into a state of complete hysteria.

MR. O'BRIAN: Sorry, lady.

MRS. VAN LEER: It's just too bad when a woman of gentility is unable to walk her dog without having to trip over an abandoned and shriveled rump roast. (BOSSIE *moos angrily.*)

MR. O'BRIAN: This cow is not abandoned, madam.

MRS. VAN LEER: My chauffeur had to drag that screaming poodle back into the limousine, and I merely wished to give you a piece of my mind.

CLARA: So you've given it to him. Buzz off!

MRS. VAN LEER (*Haughtily*): Well, really!

GERT: Do you know who this cow is? This is Bossie, probably the most famous cow in the world. (BEN *enters leading* JUNIOR, *who is licking a giant lollipop*)

BEN: Say, Junior, I think you're right about this cow.

JUNIOR: I wanna see Bossie. I wanna see Bossie!

BEN: Hey, Mac. Tell the kid this cow is Bossie, will you? Bossie from TV?

JUNIOR: Isn't that Bossie?

MR. O'BRIAN: That's right, sonny. Only she seems to have collapsed or something.

GERT: Aw. The poor thing.

MRS. VAN LEER: How frightful! Shall I send for a doctor?

JUNIOR: Want my lollipop, Bossie? (BOSSIE *moos weakly.*)

MRS. VAN LEER: The cow is sick enough already!

BEN: The kid's just trying to be helpful, lady.

MRS. VAN LEER: What on earth happened? Did she trip?

MR. O'BRIAN: All I did was offer her something to eat. Some Mighty Meal. (BOSSIE *collapses completely.*)

JUNIOR: Mighty Meal! Ick!

MRS. VAN LEER: No wonder she fell.

CLARA:

Don't use iron, don't use steel.

Just add water to Mighty Meal.

MR. O'BRIAN: You mean you don't like Mighty Meal, Bossie? (BOSSIE *shakes her head sadly.*) Well, then, you won't have to eat it anymore. (BOSSIE *brightens.*)

GERT: Oh, you're such a kind man.

JUNIOR: What will happen to Bossie now that she's off TV?

MR. O'BRIAN: She's going to enjoy life. She's worked hard enough, don't you think?

GERT: Such a kind man!

MR. O'BRIAN: Well, come on, Bossie. (BOSSIE *staggers to her feet.*) That's the girl. Come on, now. (BOSSIE *ambles offstage, as* MR. O'BRIAN *follows.*)

GERT: Remind me the next time we're out to bring my autograph book, will you, Clara? I mean, you never know who you're going to run into. (*They exit.*)

JUNIOR (*Waving*): So long, Bossie. 'Bye. (*To* BEN) Daddy, why can't we have a cow like that?

BEN: Because we can't.

JUNIOR: Why not, Daddy?

BEN: Come on, Junior.

JUNIOR: I want a cow like Jackie Darling's! (BEN *pulls* JUNIOR *offstage.*)

MRS. VAN LEER: What an idol Jackie used to be. (*Shakes her head*) I wonder what will become of Little Jackie Darling now? (*Starts to exit, calling*) Oh, Forbes! You can bring Mimi out now. The cow has gone. (*Exits. Curtains open.*)

*   *   *

SETTING: *Living room of Twombleys' penthouse apartment. Terrace can be seen at rear, through open doors.*

AT RISE: MR. TWOMBLEY, *a mild-looking elderly man, is practicing his voice exercises, as* MRS. TWOMBLEY *sits nearby, stroking Samantha, the hen.* MAGIC HARP, *a girl wearing a triangular frame with strings, resembling a harp, stands at one side.*

MR. TWOMBLEY (*In powerful voice*): Fee, fi, fo, fum!

MRS. TWOMBLEY: Fiddlesticks, Felix. I wish you'd stop practicing that silly exercise.

Mr. Twombley (*Mildly*): It's supposed to give me a deep, powerful voice, my dear, and make me a masterful public speaker.

Mrs. Twombley: But you don't do public speaking, Felix. You hardly ever even leave the penthouse. Public speaking, indeed!

Mr. Twombley: One of these days I might have to do some, Henrietta, and it would be foolish of me to be unprepared. (*Loudly*) Fee! Fi! (*In ordinary voice*) Now why is it that I can say those syllables in a deep, powerful voice, but still speak as softly as ever the rest of the time?

Mrs. Twombley: I guess it just takes time. But, you know, I don't think Samantha likes the noise one bit. (*Patting hen*) Do you, you sweet little hen? She ruffles her feathers when you start practicing.

Mr. Twombley: She's just ruffled because her favorite television show has gone off the air. (*Booming*) Fo! Fum! (*In normal tone*) It was my favorite show, too. Oh, I did enjoy watching that wonderful cow rescue that nice Jackie Darling every week.

Mrs. Twombley: Still, you have to admit that Jackie Darling was getting rather big to play a ten-year-old. Why, he must be getting on to twenty by now.

Mr. Twombley: I feel sad, all the same.

Mrs. Twombley: Well, I feel sad because of Samantha. You know she won't lay any golden eggs unless she's happy, and that silly program made her happier than anything else. She hasn't laid a single golden egg since they announced the program was going off the air. What will happen if Samantha won't lay golden eggs ever again?

Mr. Twombley: Perish the thought! Those golden eggs have supported us in luxury for years. And even if we do have quite a few on hand, our supply will run out. Maybe she's just tired.

MRS. TWOMBLEY: I've been trying for half an hour. (*To hen*) Henny-penny, henny-penny. You see? She just mopes. She was *so* fond of Jackie.

MR. TWOMBLEY (*Angrily*): Those television people can't do this to Samantha.

MRS. TWOMBLEY: What about us? I *like* being very, very rich, which we won't be without the eggs. You'd better write a letter to the television station, Felix. You might be able to make them change their minds.

MR. TWOMBLEY: That's a good idea. Now, how shall I begin? "Gentlemen: By taking *The Adventures of Bossie* off the air, you have caused my magic hen severe grief, and you have thereby imperiled my supply of golden eggs."

MRS. TWOMBLEY: Really, Felix, that's a bit strong.

MR. TWOMBLEY: A more charitable tone, then. "It is wrong to put an upstanding young man like Jackie Darling out of a job."

MRS. TWOMBLEY: Maybe *you'll* have to find a job now, Felix. That might not be a bad idea, at that. It would get you out of the house every day. And then, if Samantha gave up golden eggs completely, we'd have something to fall back on. (*As she speaks, bean vine can be seen rising outside, in front of open door to terrace. HARP begins to make jingling, discordant sounds.*) Oh, do be quiet, Harp.

HARP (*Pointing to vine*): Master, master, master!

MRS. TWOMBLEY: For heaven's sake, Harp, what's the matter now?

HARP: Get a load of that crazy weed outside the terrace.

MR. TWOMBLEY (*Rushing to terrace door*): Good heavens!

HARP: This is the forty-fifth story, you know.

Mrs. Twombley (*Putting hen into basket and going to door*): What is it?

Harp: A weed. I told you. (Mr. Twombley *goes to terrace door.*)

Mr. Twombley: It's some kind of vine, I think. It's coming from down there somewhere.

Mrs. Twombley: Isn't it the loveliest thing you ever saw?

Mr. Twombley: It can't be a vine. No vine in the world could grow that high. Or that fast.

Mrs. Twombley: Now, dear. Obviously there *is* a vine that can grow that high and that fast. There it is! (Jackie *appears, as if he had climbed up on vine.*)

Mr. Twombley (*Stepping back*): Oho! The vine has a passenger.

Mrs. Twombley: How delightful! We haven't had company for years!

Mr. Twombley (*As* Jackie *climbs onto terrace*): Fee, fi, fo, fum!

Jackie: Hi, all. (Harp *plays madly*) Say, there's a right nice welcome.

Mrs. Twombley: It's sweet of you to drop in, young man. I'm Henrietta Twombley, and this is my husband, Felix. Do come in and sit down. (Jackie *strolls into apartment.* Mr. Twombley *looks at him closely, then turns excitedly to* Mrs. Twombley.)

Mr. Twombley: Henrietta, if this young man weren't so big, I'd swear he was that Jackie Darling boy.

Harp: Well, he isn't Rin-Tin-Tin.

Mr. Twombley: Young man, *are* you Jackie Darling?

Jackie: It's me, all right.

Mr. Twombley: Your show was my hen's favorite program.

Jackie: That's right nice of you to say, sir.

Mrs. Twombley: He's serious, young man. You mustn't

doubt that. We're not doubting that you arrived here on that vine, are we? Where in the world did you find that plant, anyhow?

JACKIE: It just grew in our patio from some beans Ma threw out into the garden.

MR. TWOMBLEY: I don't know that I follow you.

JACKIE: That's a bean vine. I sold Bossie for some beans.

MRS. TWOMBLEY: A very smart thing to do, I'd say. Bossie was getting pretty old. It was beginning to show in the close-ups. Surely you made a lot of money in television when Bossie was at her peak.

JACKIE: I did, but Max Millions, my producer, lost it all for me.

MR. TWOMBLEY: Never you mind. Any young man who has the foresight to sell a cow for beans is going places.

JACKIE: Well, I'm all washed up in television. The station owner said I was the joke of the industry.

MRS. TWOMBLEY: And none of the people you worked with will help you find another job?

JACKIE: That's right. Even my agent, Miss Minge, walked out on me. The only person who's stuck with me is Desdemona. She's a girl I know.

MRS. TWOMBLEY: And a very sensible girl she must be. If she's also pretty, you should see that she doesn't get away. Now, you must meet our hen, Samantha. She'll be thrilled to meet her favorite television star. (*Sits and takes hen from basket*) This is Jackie Darling, dear.

JACKIE: Say, that's a right nice yellow hen you have there, folks.

MR. TWOMBLEY: She lays golden eggs. Or she used to. All we had to say was henny-penny.

JACKIE: Henny-penny?

MRS. TWOMBLEY: Oh, Felix, look. She did it! (*Holds up large yellow egg*)

JACKIE: Henny-penny.

MRS. TWOMBLEY: She did it again! (*Holds up another egg*)

HARP: Master, master, don't let this kid out of your sight.

MRS. TWOMBLEY: I think you have the magic touch, Mr. Darling.

JACKIE: Shucks, I always was good with cows and chickens and things.

MR. TWOMBLEY: How can we ever repay you for what you've done?

JACKIE: Don't worry about it, folks.

MR. TWOMBLEY: There must be something we can do to get you back on your feet again. I'll think about it, but right now, let's all sit down and Harp will play us a tune to celebrate Samantha's recovery. (*They sit.*)

HARP: What do you want to hear?

JACKIE: Do you know "The Rain Wrecked the Rhubarb the Day My Baby Said Goodbye"?

HARP: Sure do. (HARP *begins to play and is immediately interrupted by loud knocking outside the door.*)

THELMA (*Calling from offstage*): Jackie! My baby boy! Are you in there?

JACKIE: I'm here, Ma. (MR. TWOMBLEY *goes to door.*)

MR. TWOMBLEY (*In a powerful voice*): Who's out there? Fee, fi, fo, fum! Who is it, I say? (*To* MRS. TWOMBLEY) Did you hear that? My voice is beginning to get stronger at last. (*Knocking is heard again.*)

JACKIE: That lady's my ma, Mrs. Twombley. I guess she's worried.

MRS. TWOMBLEY: Mothers always worry, my dear.

MR. TWOMBLEY (*In powerful voice*): Come in, Mrs. Darling.

THELMA (*Rushing in*): Jackie! Quick! (*Grabbing his arm*) I'll save you! The elevator's waiting.

HARP: What's your hurry, Sunbonnet Sue?

MRS. TWOMBLEY: Jackie's perfectly all right, Mrs. Darling. You needn't fuss.

THELMA: The ogre will get him. I heard his voice. He's here somewhere.

HARP: Ogre? What an imagination! (THELMA *lets go of* JACKIE.)

MRS. TWOMBLEY: Hush, Harp. Felix, I wish you'd teach Harp some manners. Now, Mrs. Darling, we're the only people here. What's all the excitement about?

THELMA: It's about Jackie, actually. Oh, Jackie, if you could see it, down there on the street—fire engines, reporters, cameras, lights, television, crowds of adoring fans. Max just told me that nobody in the history of television has ever done a publicity stunt to match this one. You're a hero, Jackie, a star again!

JACKIE: All I did was climb that old bean vine, Ma.

DESDEMONA (*Rushing in and hugging* JACKIE): Jack! I knew you'd do it. I knew you'd make them sit up and take notice!

JACKIE: Hi, Desdemona. This is the girl I was telling you about, Mrs. Twombley.

MAX (*Rushing in with* J. B.): What a gimmick. It'll make us a fortune.

JACKIE: And this is Max Millions.

MR. TWOMBLEY: I smell the blood of a crooked producer.

JACKIE: And Miss Minge. This is Mr. Twombley.

J. B.: The ogre who scares little children? Marvelous! Sign with me, Twombley, and I'll sell your story to the movies. We'll bring out a whole new line of products with your name—dolls, beanies, sweatshirts! And Jackie —you're back on top again. Those crazy beans will make you rich!

THELMA: Maybe I can take that trip to Paris after all.

Maybe I can even rent this penthouse. (JACKIE *and* DES-
DEMONA *talk together at one side.*)

MRS. TWOMBLEY: Oh, I wish you would! I'd much prefer
a little place in the country. Besides, now that Samantha is feeling better again, we're going to need more
room to store the golden eggs.

MAX: To store *what?*

MR. TWOMBLEY: Eggs. We have this hen, you see. When
she's feeling well and happy, she lays one golden egg
after another. Twenty-four carat, usually.

J. B.: What a story, Max. A midget ogre in the sky with a
magic hen!

MRS. TWOMBLEY: We also have a magic harp that plays
pretty songs. Play something for the people, Harp.

HARP: I wouldn't play "Chopsticks" for these phonies.
(JACKIE *and* DESDEMONA *rejoin others.*)

JACKIE: Say, Mrs. Twombley. You were right about Desdemona. She *is* sensible, and she's going to be my new
agent.

HARP: Now you're talking, sonny.

J. B.: But I was going to help you market your beans.

JACKIE: Only one of the beans grew, Miss Minge. And besides, how many people need a forty-five-story bean vine?

HARP: Good point. (*All except* MR. TWOMBLEY *start talking at once.*)

MR. TWOMBLEY (*His voice more powerful than ever*): One
moment, please. (*All stop talking and look at him.*) This
is the living room of my apartment. It is not a theatrical
office. I'll thank you all to leave. *Immediately!*

MAX (*Admiringly*): What a voice!

MRS. TWOMBLEY: I always thought Felix would make a
marvelous announcer with that powerful voice. Why, he

should be able to sell any kind of product. Even golden eggs!

MAX: Now I've heard everything! (*He starts to leave.*)

MR. TWOMBLEY (*Suddenly, as if getting an idea*): Wait a moment! I have an announcement to make. (*All look at him.*) The product that my magnificent voice is going to sell is—Twombley's Frozen Golden Eggs. It's something brand-new. Let's show them, Jackie.

JACKIE (*To hen*): Henny-penny, Samantha. Henny-penny three times, you little ol' golden hen.

MR. TWOMBLEY (*Displaying golden egg*): And there you are, ladies and gentlemen. Twombley's Frozen Golden Eggs—for those who appreciate the finest things in life, for instant use in omelettes and cakes. They're dandy when used whole for paperweights and doorstops, and easily sliced into instant, hard, cold cash! If your store is temporarily out of Twombley's Golden Eggs, be patient. The demand far exceeds the supply. And remember . . .

HARP (*Singing to tune of "London Bridge Is Falling Down"*):
Twombley's eggs are good to eat.
Can't be beat. Oh, so neat!
Try this novel, special treat!
Instant *money!*

MRS. TWOMBLEY (*Applauding*): Why, Felix! What a clever idea! I'm proud of you, dear. You were good, too, Harp.

HARP: Not bad for an improvisation, if I do say so.

MAX: Twombley, you have a sensational product here. And what you need is to sponsor a good TV show to get your message across. And you'll also need a good producer.

J. B.: And a good publicity agent.

DESDEMONA: You need a top-notch star. Now, I have in mind a seasoned performer who's been the idol of millions.

JACKIE: Who's that, Desdemona?

DESDEMONA: The one and only—Jack Darling!

JACKIE: That sounds right nice. But it sure will seem funny without Bossie. She's retired from show business. (MR. O'BRIAN *enters, leading* BOSSIE, *who is panting heavily.*)

MR. O'BRIAN: No, she hasn't. The minute Bossie saw you in the spotlight, climbing that vine, she couldn't wait to get back into show business. This cow has the theatre in her blood. I would have been here sooner, but we had to walk up to the forty-fifth floor. Bossie wouldn't fit into the elevator.

JACKIE: Bossie! (*Hugs* BOSSIE, *who moos faintly*) We're going to be back together again.

MRS. TWOMBLEY: Isn't that touching! Felix, why don't you sponsor Mr. Darling in a series about a giant who lives in a castle in the sky with a hen that lays golden eggs, and a magic harp that can talk and sing?

JACKIE: What about Bossie?

MRS. TWOMBLEY: The giant can also have a magic cow.

JACKIE: I'd like to play a giant. Fee, fi, fo, fum.

MR. TWOMBLEY: You'll need a lot of practice, but I'll be glad to coach you.

MAX: It'll never work. Nobody would believe it.

J. B.: At least it's more original than a show about cowboys.

MAX: You know, you're right, J. B. Say, we could make this the adventures of a kid who plants some magic beans that he was paid when he sold his cow. And the beans grow into a vine that takes the kid up to the giant's castle . . .

DESDEMONA: If you think that my client Jack Darling is going to play another kid part . . .

MAX: O.K., Jack will be the giant.

HARP: I think you should make it a musical. I might consider playing the role of the harp myself.

MAX: A musical! Harp, you're a genius. It's a great idea! Every week a new adventure in the sky. With guest stars, big production numbers, the works! (*To* MR. TWOMBLEY) Of course, it'll probably cost you, as the sponsor, quite a bit to do this kind of a show.

MR. TWOMBLEY: As long as it makes Jack Darling the biggest star on television, no expense will be spared. After all, we wouldn't have a golden egg to our name if it weren't for him.

MAX: We'll make a million.

THELMA: Paris, I'll see you yet! And London! And Honolulu! New clothes, new jewels, everything!

MR. TWOMBLEY (*Going to center and speaking in his most powerful voice*): Fee, fi, fo, fum! And now, the makers of Twombley's Frozen Golden Eggs present *Jack Darling!*

HARP (*Singing, to tune of "London Bridge"*):
Twombley's eggs are good to eat,
Can't be beat! Oh, so neat!

ALL (*Singing*):
Try a novel, special treat—
Instant money!
(HARP *plays an arpeggio, and* BOSSIE *moos and dances as curtains close.*)

THE END

Production Notes

LITTLE JACKIE AND THE BEANSTALK

Characters: 10 male; 9 female; 1 or more male or female for Bossie.

Playing Time: 40 minutes.

Costumes: Jackie wears blue jeans, checkered shirt, and straw hat. Thelma wears gingham dress and sunbonnet. A two-piece cow costume may be worn by Bossie, or a cow mask may be used. The girl playing the Harp has a triangular frame with strings attached to her back, so that she acts as the pillar of the harp. Others wear appropriate everyday, modern dress.

Properties: Sign: THE ADVENTURES OF BOSSIE, etc., as indicated in text, standing microphone, television camera, box of Mighty Meal, duffel bags, bag of groceries containing box of beans, lollipop, cardboard or papier-mâché hen, basket, several gold-colored eggs, heavy crepe paper vine.

Setting: The living rooms of the Darling and Twombley apartments. The same set may be used for both scenes, with a few changes in decor to indicate the change of scene. Both apartments have wide doors at back: the Darlings' apartment looks out on a patio garden; the Twombleys', on the penthouse terrace. A telephone, television set, and easy chairs, etc., complete the furnishings. Exits are at right and left, and through doors at back. In both scenes, a large green vine is raised against the backdrop outside the apartments.

Lighting: No special effects.

Sound: Recorded music for television program, and for harp; offstage knocking. If desired, Mr. Twombley's offstage voice may be amplified in Scene 1.

The Reform of Sterling Silverheart

Characters

MAMA GHOUL		DUPE DARKLY
VERONICA		FRAUD WILLIE
JASMINE	her children	BELLISSIMA BORGIA
DONALD		WAITRESS
STERLING SILVERHEART		CONSTABLE

SCENE 1

TIME: *Morning.*

SETTING: *The old-fashioned kitchen of the shack which the Ghoul family is currently haunting.*

AT RISE: MAMA GHOUL *is putting ingredients into black pot on stove, as* VERONICA *sweeps the floor.*

MAMA (*Calling offstage*): Jasmine! Help me shred these bats' wings, will you, dear?

VERONICA (*Putting down her broom and going to help her mother*): Bats' wings, bats' wings. I wish somebody would think of something to do with the rest of the bat.

MAMA: Where is that sister of yours, Veronica?

VERONICA: She's probably doing something angelic again,

Mama. Yesterday I caught her studying her Girl Scout Handbook.

MAMA: More likely she's writing love poetry to that Sterling. (*Quotes mockingly*) "Hail to thee, Sterling Silverheart. I hope that we shall never part." (*Shaking her head*) I worry about Jasmine. She's so peculiar.

VERONICA: She and Sterling deserve each other. He's an Eagle Scout, you know. Do you think they'll get married, Mama?

MAMA: I hope not. One misfit in the family is bad enough. (*Calls again*) Jasmine! (*To* VERONICA) I'd like to get her away from Sterling. If we could only pay off the mortgage on this dump—(JASMINE *enters*.)

JASMINE (*Cheerfully*): Oh, what a lovely, sunny morning!

MAMA: Did you get up on the wrong side of the bed again, Jasmine?

JASMINE (*Stretching and speaking dreamily*): No, Mama. I was at my window, watching the sunlight glint on the blue water of our lagoon.

MAMA: Did you see Donald? He was haunting down there last night.

VERONICA: I saw his fire burning when I was shrieking out of the east window on my four a.m. rounds. (*Gleefully*) It's such fun when Donald plays pirate.

JASMINE: It's pretty silly, if you ask me.

VERONICA (*Snapping*): Nobody asked you.

JASMINE (*Paying no attention*): Imagine a grown ghoul sitting on a rock next to the ocean, waiting for a pirate ship loaded with treasure to come in!

VERONICA: What else would you have him do, go to a 4-H Club meeting with Sterling Silverheart?

JASMINE: And why not? One day Sterling will be (*Raising her arms dramatically*) the biggest pig farmer in the country!

VERONICA (*Stopping her work*): Of all the dumb ambitions!

JASMINE (*Impatiently*): Sometimes I think this whole family is crazy.

MAMA (*Affectionately extending her arms to* JASMINE): That's the first nice thing you've said in months.

JASMINE (*To audience, with many gestures*): Someday Sterling will take me away from all this and give me a pretty little house with roses growing beside the door.

MAMA (*As* VERONICA *twists her face in disgust*): Have no fear, Veronica. Sterling would sooner abandon his hogs than ask for Jasmine's hand in marriage. He's too cheap.

JASMINE (*Turning on them*): He's just frugal. You don't like him because he's so decent!

MAMA (*Stopping her work*): You can say that again! He has nothing at all to recommend him.

DONALD (*Running in from outside, right, wearing a pirate's costume*): Hi-ho, hags! What's cooking? (*He looks into the pot.*)

MAMA (*Wiping her hands on her apron*): Morning, dear. I'm marinating some bats' wings for a hex I have to deliver on Thursday.

VERONICA: Did your pirate ship come in, Donald?

DONALD (*Acting out his words*): It passed in the night. But there were plenty of rowboats out there early this morning. "Turn back! Turn back!" I shouted. "Another inch and I'll blast you into the briny!" Those oars spun faster than propellers on a helicopter.

MAMA (*Pleased*): Good for you, Dead-Eye!

DONALD (*Still acting*): I'll guard the treasure. Tonight I'm going to launch some flaming arrows.

MAMA: That's nice, dear. (DONALD *exits.*) He's not very bright, but his heart's in the wrong place.

JASMINE (*Her hands to her head*): Sometimes I have a feeling that I must get way from here.

VERONICA: Your broom's in the corner. Take a little spin!

JASMINE (*Exasperated*): That's not what I mean, and you know it!

MAMA (*As she and* VERONICA *close in on* JASMINE): When are you going to stop playing Miss Juvenile Decency?

VERONICA: You're the laughingstock of the entire spook set, you and your corn-pone boyfriend.

JASMINE: Who cares what a bunch of harpies think?

MAMA (*Pointing her finger in* JASMINE'S *face*): I care! Doesn't that mean anything to you?

VERONICA: Mother's losing status right and left because of you.

MAMA (*Moving away from* JASMINE): I'll tell you one thing, Jasmine. If you don't give Sterling the freeze, I'll be forced to step in and take care of the situation for you.

JASMINE (*Clutching at* MAMA'S *apron*): You wouldn't!

MAMA (*Gleefully*): I'll show that hog-jowl some real fun. Maybe his pigs could get the plague!

VERONICA (*Dancing about*): Oh, lovely! (*There is a heavy pounding on the door, right.*) Oh! That must be lover-boy, now!

JASMINE (*Smoothing her skirt and calling sweetly*): Come in, Sterling!

STERLING (*Entering and smiling*): Good morning, all! Jasmine, I want to show you the map of the new farm I'm going to buy (*Pulls a map from his hip pocket*) with the money I saved from my newspaper route.

JASMINE (*Earnestly*): That's wonderful, Sterling.

MAMA: Oh, bother! Tell me, Sterling (*She walks to his side*), have you done your good deed for the day?

STERLING (*Ashamed*): No, ma'am. Not yet, that is.

MAMA (*Pointing to the door*): Then get lost.

VERONICA: You bother us, boy. (*Door opens suddenly and* DUPE DARKLY *and his accomplice,* FRAUD WILLIE, *carrying picks, shovels, miner's helmets, etc., enter.* WILLIE *stumbles over gear occasionally throughout rest of scene.*)

DARKLY (*To* GHOULS *and* STERLING): Stay where you are!

WILLIE: Yeah! Right where you are! And don't move!

DARKLY: Case the joint for treasure, Willie, while I hold off these dangerous creatures.

WILLIE (*Dumping equipment with a crash*): Right, boss. (*Begins poking around room*)

MAMA (*Gaily rushing to greet* DARKLY): Why, Dupe Darkly! You old clown, you! Don't you know me?

DARKLY (*In joyful recognition*): Griselda! It's been years. (*Gesturing to* WILLIE) May I present my new partner, Fraud Willie? Willie, this is the Ghoul family, all except for that bumpkin (*Pointing to* STERLING) over there.

JASMINE (*Haughtily*): We were just leaving. (*She and* STERLING *go to door right.*)

STERLING (*Dutifully*): I promise I won't keep Jasmine out too late, Mrs. Ghoul.

MAMA (*With a sigh*): I'm sure you won't, Sterling. (*Waving brightly*) See you! (STERLING *and* JASMINE *exit.*) Now, Darkly. (*She pulls up chair.*) Sit down and tell me what you've been doing with yourself. (*She and* DARKLY *sit down.* VERONICA *stands, flirting with* WILLIE.)

DARKLY: Living it up, Griselda. Foreclosing mortgages all over the place. Tying fair maidens to railroad tracks and buzz saws. Just the usual stuff, but lots of it.

VERONICA (*Coquettishly*): My, but Mr. Darkly's a dashing and sophisticated gentleman, isn't he, Mama?

MAMA (*Nodding*): The sort of man Jasmine should marry.

VERONICA (*Hurt*): I'm available, too, you know.

MAMA: But Jasmine's in real trouble! (*To* DARKLY, *in desperate tone*) You must save her from that boy. He's turning her into a sweet little goody-goody. And she had such promise as a child. (*She sobs.*)

DARKLY (*Embarrassed*): It couldn't be that bad.

MAMA (*Wailing*): She hasn't done one beastly thing in months!

DARKLY: That is bad. (*Brightening*) There must be a solution somewhere. (*He stands.*) I'll think about it as soon as I foreclose your mortgage.

MAMA: *Our* mortgage? Why?

DARKLY: Simple. There's pirate treasure on your property.

MAMA (*Aside to audience*): Donald's story must have been more convincing than I thought. (*Eagerly, to* DARKLY) Then why don't you marry Jasmine? (*She stands.*) You can be master of the house and get the treasure, too.

DARKLY (*Walking away*): What fun would that be? I get all my kicks out of foreclosing mortgages. (*Turning to face* MAMA) No. I want to do the mean thing first. Then we'll see about Jasmine. Right, Willie?

WILLIE (*Still eyeing* VERONICA): You bet, boss.

DARKLY (*Grabbing* WILLIE'*s arm*): Off to the town hall, then. We'll start proceedings immediately. (*They exit.*)

MAMA (*Jumping for joy*): Hallelujah! Dupe Darkly will foreclose, and we'll be free of our payments on this old house forever.

VERONICA (*Relieved*): It's been a grind to haunt this one, I'll tell you.

MAMA: We can whisk Jasmine off and away from Sterling Silverheart.

VERONICA (*Moving to left exit*): Help me bring the suitcases down from the attic. Where shall we haunt next, Mama?

MAMA (*Following* VERONICA): Oh, I don't know. What about Buckingham Palace for a change of pace?

VERONICA: Oh, keen! Come on, Mama. Let's pack. (*They skip off as the curtain closes.*)

*   *   *

SCENE 2

TIME: *Following immediately.*

BEFORE RISE: DARKLY *and* WILLIE *enter stealthily.*

DARKLY: What fools! Fools! I don't even hold the mortgage on her property, and she's going to let me foreclose!

WILLIE: Nice if you can get away with it, boss.

DARKLY (*Impatiently*): Of course, I'll get away with it. But it won't be easy. Well, come on, Willie. We have some skulduggery to do.

WILLIE: You bet, boss. (*As they move left,* DARKLY *stops and puts his hand to his ear.*)

DARKLY: Wait! I hear voices. Let's hide behind this convenient and imaginary bush. (*They crouch off left and stick heads out.*) We might be able to learn something. (STERLING *enters right, holding up large map.* JASMINE *follows him.*)

STERLING: This is where it's located.

JASMINE: You're so brilliant, Sterling. (*Glancing at map*) Don't you want to share your good fortune with somebody? A lifetime companion?

STERLING: Good fortune doesn't come easy. (*Pats map*) You have to work hard for it. Dig for it. (DARKLY *winces.*)

JASMINE (*Breathlessly*): You're so strong!

STERLING: Nobody's going to come along and give you a pot of gold. But (*Pointing to map*) that's about the richest piece of land you could find.

JASMINE: It must be if you say so, Sterling.

STERLING: My key to the future, right here on this itty-bitty piece of paper.

JASMINE: Shall we have a malted to celebrate? (STERLING *grunts, still staring at map.*) Mercy, Sterling, what would I do without a man like you to lean on?

STERLING: I don't know, Jasmine. I guess your life would be rough. (*They exit.*)

DARKLY (*Standing*): Aha!

WILLIE (*In imitation*): Aha!

DARKLY: It's always the same. The least likely character has the key to the mystery.

WILLIE: Yeah. Seems to me the thing to do now is get your hands on that kid's map.

DARKLY: Quick thinking! But, first (*He faces audience*), my secret weapon! Wait'll you see her, Willie. Of course, that Jasmine isn't a bad little number, either, eh?

WILLIE: Aha! Sure, boss.

DARKLY (*As he drags* WILLIE *off left*): Dupe Darkly is about to cheat himself into a fortune. (*They exit. Curtain opens.*)

*   *   *

SETTING: *The Malt Shoppe and Sidewalk Café.*

AT RISE: STERLING *and* JASMINE *are seated at a table, as* WAITRESS *takes their order.* STERLING *eats throughout this scene.*

WAITRESS: Three more hot dogs, an anchovy pizza and a piece of pecan pie? (*She looks incredulously at* STERLING.)

STERLING: Not a piece. The whole pie!

WAITRESS: O.K. You're sure making up for all the times you came in and ordered a glass of water. (*She exits.*)

JASMINE: But, Sterling, I don't have enough money to pay for all this.

STERLING (*Innocently*): Gee, Jasmine, you should've told me before. I hate to think of you in that steamy kitchen, washing dishes.

JASMINE: I'd be glad to wash dishes for you, Sterling. (*She stands*) But, instead, I think I'll just run home for more money.

STERLING: I won't order another thing 'til you return.

JASMINE (*Backing into* WAITRESS, *who enters carrying a loaded tray*): Goodbye for now. Until anon!

WAITRESS: Hey! Watch out!

JASMINE (*Flustered*): Oh! Excuse me! He simply carries me away.

WAITRESS (*Calling to* JASMINE, *who runs off right*): Well, pull yourself together before you kill somebody! (*To* STERLING) Here. (BELLISSIMA BORGIA *enters right.*) While you're working on this course, I'll start your bill through the computer. Eat hearty, Romeo.

BELLISSIMA: Romeo? Wherefore art thou? (*To* STERLING) Ah! There thou art!

WAITRESS: Man, they're sure in from the hills today.

BELLISSIMA (*Sauntering to* STERLING's *table*): A romantic soul I can tell from ten kilometers, and a gentleman I can tell from twenty (*She sits.*)

WAITRESS (*To* BELLISSIMA): Want a menu?

BELLISSIMA: Champagne, please.

WAITRESS: This is a malt shop, honey.

BELLISSIMA (*With a wave of her hand*): Then bring me some malt! (WAITRESS *shrugs her shoulders and exits.*)

What does it matter? In the presence of such a man, who can make decisions?

STERLING (*Awkwardly*): How about some pecan pie?

BELLISSIMA: Too many calories, *caro mio*. A movie star has to watch her figure. (*She stands*) You like my figure, no?

STERLING (*Not looking at her*): Sure is a pretty day, miss.

BELLISSIMA (*Grandly*): Signorina Bellissima Borgia, star of the Italian cinema. You've seen my pictures, no?

STERLING (*Still eating*): Don't go to the movies much. Too costly.

BELLISSIMA: Ah, but with me on the screen, who cares? Admit it. Did you ever see a more ravishing woman? But I embarrass you! (*She sits down.*) How gentle! How irresistible! A lion of a man with the heart of a bunny rabbit.

STERLING: Uh . . . what's a famous movie star like you doin' around these parts?

BELLISSIMA: It is just your good luck, Romeo. I was driving my sports car to the coast and lost my way. Could you put me on the right road to Hollywood?

STERLING (*Nervously*): Gee, Miss Borgia.

BELLISSMA (*Laughing*): You're so shy! Ah, that must be the secret of your charm. (*Leaning nearer to* STERLING) Come with me to Italy, and we can watch the moon come up over the catacombs. From my humble little piazza you can see the very spot where Julius Caesar was stabbed in the back.

STERLING (*In a squeaky voice*): How about a pizza?

BELLISSIMA: Romantic! We can listen to the mandolins playing "Come Back to Sorrento—Or Else" and hear the gentle splash of the drain water on our gondola in the Grand Canal.

STERLING: I thought that was in Venice.

BELLISSIMA: I feel faint in the presence of such a brain. I hardly trust myself with you! No. No matter what you suggest, I must keep control of myself. (*Standing again*) Bellissima! Remember your career. Remember your art! (*To* STERLING) Alas, *caro,* I dare not dally with you one second longer. (WAITRESS *enters with empty tray.*)

STERLING: What happened to the pizza?

WAITRESS (*Gathering up dishes*): I only have two hands. (*She exits.*)

BELLISSIMA: Now. The road to Hollywood. Perhaps you have a map. I see you do have a map!

STERLING (*As* BELLISSIMA *grabs map*): That's nothing.

BELLISSIMA: But it is a map, no? A map is a map.

STERLING (*Standing*): That map won't show you how to get to Hollywood.

BELLISSIMA (*Tweaking* STERLING's *chin*): You let me be the best judge of that, you cute little Don Juan, you. (*Looking at map*) Ah. But I cannot see too well. My eyes, you know. They're almost ruined by my years before the spotlights. Let me look at this in the daylight. (*She moves downstage, as* STERLING *follows.*)

STERLING: Listen, lady, that map's no good to you.

BELLISSIMA (*Ignoring him*): Yes! This light is better. Now, if I hold it up like this, I can see the road clearly. Not darkly. Not (*Shouting*) darkly! Not *darkly* at all! (DARKLY *runs in right. As he passes* BELLISSIMA, *he whisks map from her hand, pushes her into* STERLING's *arms, and runs off left.*) Help! (WAITRESS *runs in, carrying pizza.*) Let go of me this instant! Help! (JASMINE *enters right, carrying a large pocketbook. She stops, aghast, as she sees* STERLING *and* BELLISSIMA.)

JASMINE: Sterling Silverheart! What are you doing?

STERLING: I want my map!

BELLISSIMA: Take your hands off me, you small-town fiend. (*Shrieking*) Police!

WAITRESS: Really, Sterling, I didn't know you could be so bold. You should eat out more often.

JASMINE (*Crying*): Oh! I've never been so humiliated in my life!

CONSTABLE (*Entering right*): What's going on?

STERLING (*Protesting loudly*): I just want my map. She stole my map!

BELLISSIMA (*Dramatically*): Search me. Go ahead and search me! If I stole a map, I must have the map, no? Do you see a map?

STERLING: Then that guy with the black cape took it.

BELLISSIMA: You accuse me of committing a crime, and now you see little men in black capes, too.

JASMINE (*Whining*): Sterling Silverheart, I never want to see you again as long as I live.

CONSTABLE (*Pushing STERLING right*): Come on, you wolf in pig's clothing.

STERLING (*Kicking*): There *was* a guy in a black cape. There was, there was, there was!

CONSTABLE: It is my duty to warn you that anything you say may be used against you.

STERLING (*Being led out*): I want my map! (*He continues struggling, as CONSTABLE leads him offstage.*)

WAITRESS: And who's going to pay his check?

JASMINE: He can wash dishes when he's served his sentence. In twenty years! (*She starts to cry.*)

WAITRESS: Phooey. I'll repossess his hogs. (*Exits.*)

BELLISSIMA (*Calling to STERLING*): *Arrivederci*, hot shot. (*To* JASMINE) Too bad, kid, but it's all in a day's work. (*Curtain closes behind* BELLISSIMA. DARKLY *steps out from center of curtain.*)

DARKLY: Good job, Bellissima. You'll receive a fitting reward, some day.

BELLISSIMA: How about a sports car I can drive to Hollywood? I sort of liked that idea.

DARKLY: All in good time, my pretty.

BELLISSIMA: Listen, Dupe Darkly, you cut me in on this one or I spill the beans.

DARKLY: And admit you're my accomplice?

BELLISSIMA (*Pounding her fists to her forehead*): Oh, Bellissima Borgia, will you never learn?

DARKLY (*Amused*): Don't try to double-cross an old double-crosser like me.

BELLISSIMA (*Pulling herself together*): I shall wait one hour for you in the tea room of the Alfalfa Hilton. You may bring my sports car to the door. (*As she strides off right*) Make it black with red leather seats and wire wheels! (*She exits.*)

DARKLY (*Calling after her*): Just give me time. (*To audience*) Like a hundred years. Now! (*Rubbing his hands together*) Off to meet Fraud Willie and break ground. Quite a girl, Bellissima. Too bad she doesn't get smart.

DONALD (*Strolling in from left, still wearing his pirate's costume*): Oh, hi.

DARKLY (*Startled*): Hi.

DONALD (*Matter-of-factly*): I'm a pirate. What are you?

DARKLY (*Dumfounded*): I'm a villain.

DONALD: I never tried being one of those.

DARKLY: I never tried being a pirate. Do you have to wear that outfit?

DONALD: How do you expect a pirate to roam around the streets? I'm certainly not going to put on a pinafore and Mickey Mouse ears. What do you do?

DARKLY (*With authority*): I've been here all day, giving stern warnings to litterbugs.

DONALD (*Moving across stage*): Oh. Well, I don't like to rush away, but I have to check on my treasure. Nice to see you. (*Exits*)

DARKLY: Treasure? Hm-m-m. I have some digging to do. (*Exits*)

*   *   *

SCENE 3

SETTING: *The Haunted House. The same as Scene 1.*

AT RISE: *Suitcases and boxes are scattered about.* VERONICA *packs while* MAMA *tries to console* JASMINE, *who is draped over an old chair.*

MAMA: There, there, Jasmine.

JASMINE: I could die, that's what I could do.

VERONICA: No man's worth that. Especially not Sterling.

JASMINE: You should have seen him with that . . . that flashy floosie with the painted eyes.

MAMA: My! Sterling may have some gumption after all.

JASMINE: I just want to go away and stay away forever.

MAMA: We've already arranged that. But, first, tell me you don't want to be like other girls anymore.

JASMINE (*Groaning*): Who would have dreamed it would all come to this?

VERONICA: Serves you right, I'd say.

MAMA: From now on, you'll stop mixing with the wrong people and concentrate on being a good ghoul instead!

DONALD (*Popping in through the door right*): Supper ready?

MAMA: Quiet, dear. Jasmine's had a bad day.

DONALD (*Brightly*): I know. I hear Sterling's turned out to be quite a cad.

JASMINE (*Melodramatically*): You, too, Dead-Eye? More wretched wounds from brutal barbs of verbal vilification?

DONALD: That's the best laugh I've had in a long time. Now that he's a cad, we might even consider letting him into the family.

JASMINE (*Dramatically*): Oh, torture! Have you no sympathy?

VERONICA: We're not a clinic for the lovelorn.

DONALD: I'll lend you my cap and eyepatch, if it'll make you feel any better.

JASMINE: I'm going to my room. (*She stands up.*) I'll cry my eyes out in the comfort of lonely solitude.

VERONICA: Go ahead. Have a ball.

JASMINE (*Dragging herself off left*): Oh, woe is me. Woe is me.

DONALD: She seems upset. Oh, well. You'll excuse me. I still have to finish soaking the flaming arrows in kerosene. (*DARKLY and WILLIE enter right, dragging shovels, etc., as DONALD exits.*)

DARKLY: Did someone call?

MAMA: No, but how about the mortgage?

DARKLY (*Seating himself*): Patience, Griselda. (*WILLIE trips over equipment, causing a loud clatter.*) Quiet, Willie! (*To MAMA*) I'll foreclose any time now.

VERONICA (*Stopping her work*): I wish you'd hurry up about it. We're almost ready to leave.

DARKLY: I thought I heard someone talking about treasure.

WILLIE: That was you and me, boss.

DARKLY: Quiet!

MAMA: Oh, that was only Donald. (*She sits next to DARKLY.*)

DARKLY: Your little boy? Isn't he the one who used to torture caterpillars?

MAMA (*Dreamily*): Oh, I'd almost forgotten. It's a shame the way the endearing traits of childhood fade from memory.

VERONICA: Donald's pretending he has a pirate treasure hidden out at the point.

MAMA: Harmless fantasy.

DARKLY (*Looking at map, then jumping to his feet*): Fantasy?

MAMA: You didn't believe that old legend, did you? (*Laughing*) I can see you did! Dupe Darkly taken in by an old wives' tale!

CONSTABLE (*Off right*): Open in the name of the law! (CONSTABLE *enters right, followed by* BELLISSIMA *and* STERLING.)

BELLISSIMA (*Pointing at* DARKLY): That's the rat, over there.

DARKLY: Bellissima, baby!

STERLING (*Pointing at* DARKLY): That's the man, for sure.

BELLISSIMA: Arrest him at once!

DARKLY (*Innocently*): Arrest me? But, why?

CONSTABLE (*Sternly to* DARKLY): The beautiful Miss Borgia turned state's evidence. We heard how you stole the map while she was looking at it in the sunlight.

BELLISSIMA (*Emphasizing*): *Innocently* looking at it.

CONSTABLE: And then you pushed her into the arms of Sterling Silverheart, to make the situation look reprehensible in the eyes of decent folk. You blackhearted devil, you! You're under arrest. (*As* WILLIE *backs toward the door*) And you, too!

DARKLY (*Shaking his fist*): Foiled again! This time by a dame!

WILLIE: Yeah.

MAMA: And we still have our mortgaged house.

VERONICA: A plague on you, Dupe Darkly.

MAMA (*Sighing*): Sterling, would you mind helping us take these things back to the attic?

STERLING (*As he picks up suitcases and moves left*): That'll mean another good deed for today. (*Exits*)

MAMA (*Calling*): We'll give you two gold stars and a lollypop.

DONALD (*Entering left wearing "Dracula" costume*): Stand back, everybody. I decided not to wait until Saturday. Meet Dracula!

MAMA (*Sweetly*): You look lovely, Donald.

DONALD (*Pacing about*): No more stupid pirate treasures for me. At least not this week.

VERONICA: It's a good thing, too. We're still left with this old barn to haunt. Sometimes I think we have no control over fate at all.

STERLING (*Re-entering with an old trunk*): Say, look what I found in the attic. It's filled with coins and shiny stones.

DARKLY: Let me see that!

CONSTABLE (*Grabbing DARKLY*): Oh, no, you don't.

MAMA (*Opening trunk; amazed*): Looks like pirate treasure.

DONALD: That's what it is, all right. (WILLIE *stumbles over the picks and shovels to get a closer look.*)

STERLING: Wahoo! A trunk of treasure, and it's all mine!

MAMA: Oh, no, it isn't.

VERONICA: You found it in *our* attic.

DARKLY: I was foreclosing. You have to save it for me 'til I get out of jail.

CONSTABLE: Not on your moustache.

STERLING (*Wrapping his arms around trunk*): It's mine, and I won't share it with anybody!

BELLISSIMA (*Stroking STERLING'S hair*): But what about me, Romeo? Remember those mandolins on the Grand Canal. . . .

STERLING (*Stamping his foot*): It's mine, mine, mine!

MAMA (*Astonished*): Why, you mean, nasty little boy.

VERONICA: That's exactly what you are.

STERLING: Finders keepers!

DARKLY: All my lovely foul play ending in disaster.

JASMINE (*Entering*): What's all the commotion? Can't a betrayed maiden be miserable in peace?

STERLING: Marry me, Jasmine. I've found a fortune!

JASMINE: I wouldn't be seen with you at a hog-callers' convention, you two-timing coyote!

MAMA: But, Jasmine! Sterling has been cleared.

VERONICA (*Happily*): He's turned out to be a greedy, selfish, scheming scoundrel!

MAMA (*Putting her arms around* STERLING): My son!

STERLING: Jasmine, my fortune is yours.

JASMINE (*Dipping into the treasure and giggling*): Do you mean it?

STERLING: Yes, provided you give enough to your mother to pay off her mortgage, and enough to Miss Borgia for a ticket to Hollywood.

JASMINE: Sterling Silverheart! My hero!

MAMA: Our hero, too. This place will be a blast to haunt, if we own it free and clear.

DARKLY: Curses on all of you!

WILLIE: Right, boss.

CONSTABLE: Come with me, you fugitives from a fractured flick.

DARKLY (*As he and* WILLIE *are led through door*): Revenge! Revenge on all of you! (*They exit.*)

VERONICA (*Watching* DARKLY): Oh, dear. There goes another chance for marriage with a sophisticated gentleman.

DONALD: Never mind, sis. I'm due to meet the Wolf Boy out at the point tonight.

VERONICA (*Delighted*): Wonderful! Donald, you really are thoughtful.

MAMA: I have an idea for a party game. Let's sit down and count our treasure.

STERLING: *My* treasure!

BELLISSIMA: May I stay and watch?

MAMA: Pull up a cauldron and sit down.

STERLING (*Counting*): One gold coin for you, two gold coins for me.

MAMA: Sterling, do you know how to shred bats' wings?

STERLING: Sure, and I have some great ideas about what to do with the rest of the bat. (*Gestures broadly*) Now three for me, and one for you, and four for me, and one for you. . . . (*Curtain.*)

THE END

Production Notes

THE REFORM OF STERLING SILVERHEART

Characters: 5 male; 5 female.

Playing Time: 35 minutes.

Costumes: Mama and Veronica wear dark, ghoulish costumes. Mama wears an apron over hers, Veronica's has "mod" touches. Jasmine wears a sweet, frilly dress with ribbons and lace; Donald a pirate costume, changing to a "Dracula" outfit at the end. Sterling wears overalls and a work shirt; Dupe Darkly a white shirt, dark trousers, and a black cape; Fraud Willie wears work clothes. Darkly has the traditional villain's hat and mustache. The Waitress and the Constable are dressed appropriately. Bellissima wears an overly glamorous, sophisticated dress.

Properties: Large map, picks, shovels, hoes, miner's helmet, tray, hot dogs, pie, pizza, large pocketbook, suitcases, boxes, trunk, coins, etc.

Setting: Scene 1: Old-fashioned kitchen, containing an old stove, black pot, chairs, and a table. Exits are left, to upstairs, and right, to outside. Scene 2: The malt shop, with tables, appropriately decorated with colorful tablecloths, salt and pepper shakers, etc., and chairs. Exits are at rear, to kitchen, and left and right, to outside. Scene 3: The same as Scene 1, with suitcases and boxes scattered about.

Lighting: No special effects.

Big Red Riding Hood

Characters

ROSETTA HOOD
MRS. HOOD, *her mother*
GRANDPA WOLFE, *President of Wolfe's Tasty Toasties*
SCHUYLER WOLFE, *his grandson*
GRANNY, *Rosetta's grandmother*
CHARLIE HUNTER, *a detective*

SCENE 1

SETTING: *Humble cottage of Mrs. Hood and her daughter, Rosetta.*

AT RISE: ROSETTA, *wearing a long, voluminous red cape with a hood, is busy loading an assortment of goodies onto a wagon attached to a bicycle. As she takes boxes from table and puts them into the wagon, she pauses to nibble on a goody from time to time.* MRS. HOOD *is pacing the floor and wringing her hands as she watches* ROSETTA.

MRS. HOOD: Such a load of goodies—such a load!
ROSETTA: Poor Granny's stomach is empty.

MRS. HOOD: Poor Granny's stomach is bottomless. And it will bankrupt me if I have to pay for all the goodies you bake to fill it. Rosetta, will you stop that nibbling? I told you people are beginning to call you *Big* Red Riding Hood, instead of Little Red.

ROSETTA: I have to nibble, Mother, to make sure the quality is up to poor Granny's standard. She has such a delicate digestion.

MRS. HOOD (*Pleading*): Rosetta, you're cooking us out of house and home with these goodies. We can't afford all this sugar and spice.

ROSETTA (*Coyly*): That's what little girls are made of.

MRS. HOOD: Just stop trying to be cute and tell me what Granny does with all these goodies.

ROSETTA: Why, she eats them.

MRS. HOOD: How *can* one little old lady eat macaroons, marble cake, ladyfingers, cheese bread, brownies, bagels, butter rolls, gingersnaps and vanilla wafers, all at one time?

ROSETTA: She eats them all, *one* at a time—all of them. And I wish you'd stop making it sound as if I enjoy baking all these goodies. I'd love to get out of the kitchen. I'm tired of greasy pans and egg beaters, of boiling and simmering and folding in gently.

MRS. HOOD: *You're* tired of it! (*Sitting*) If you're so tired of it, why don't you stop?

ROSETTA: But what will happen to Granny if I do? You don't care what happens to Granny.

MRS. HOOD: Of course I care. But I also care what happens to you. I want you to enjoy life while you're young. Go out on dates. Have fun. And besides, all that nibbling and sampling isn't going to do your figure any good.

ROSETTA: But Granny says my goodies are the only things that keep her going. You know how sick she's been . . .

sick and weak. (*Sniffling*) If I should stop baking them, she might . . . she might . . . pass on.

MRS. HOOD: I don't think she's quite ready for that big pastry shop in the sky.

ROSETTA: You're heartless. You'd let poor Granny kick the goody basket for want of a chocolate creampuff.

MRS. HOOD: Rosetta, I think that Granny may be putting you on. And while Granny stays thin as a reed, you have to hide your bulk under that hideous cape.

ROSETTA: This cape was a present from Granny.

MRS. HOOD: I think it's high time I had a talk with Granny. As a matter of fact, I think it's high time I gave her a piece of my mind. She has an awful nerve keeping you in the kitchen and sending us to the poorhouse just because she can't control her sweet tooth. (*Phone rings and* ROSETTA *answers it.*)

ROSETTA (*On phone*): Hello? . . . Oh, hello, Granny dear. How are you today? . . . Poorly? Poorly-er than yesterday? . . . I know I'm late with the goodies, Granny, but it isn't my fault . . .

MRS. HOOD: Give me that phone. (*Grabbing receiver*) Hello, Granny? . . . Now, listen to me. You couldn't possibly have gone through all the goodies that Rosetta brought you yesterday. . . . I'm getting awfully tired of having my little girl—all right, my *big* girl—work herself to death in the kitchen.

ROSETTA (*Straightening load on wagon*): I have to hurry.

MRS. HOOD (*On phone*): And we can't afford this any more.

ROSETTA: Granny's getting weaker.

MRS. HOOD (*On phone*): No, Granny, I don't think money is more important than your health, but there are certain facts of life you're not too old to learn. . . . Now, Granny, why don't you call Wolfe's Tasty Toasties and have them send you some goodies? They make home deliveries.

ROSETTA (*Looking at goodies still on table*): These won't all fit into the wagon. I'll have to make two trips.

MRS. HOOD (*On phone*): What do you mean—there are reasons why you can't call Wolfe's Tasty Toasties?

ROSETTA: Tell Granny I'm on my way. (*She pushes bike and wagon offstage, waving as she exits.*)

MRS. HOOD (*Calling after her*): Take care of yourself in the woods, Rosetta. (*On phone*) O.K., Granny. We'll manage somehow, I guess. Rosetta's on her way. *Please* get well soon. . . . 'Bye. (*Hangs up*) For a weak old lady, she certainly knows how to get her own way. (*She looks around room.*) I'll just bet Rosetta left the kitchen for me to clean up—again. (*Curtain.*)

* * *

SCENE 2

TIME: *Same day.*

SETTING: *President's office at Wolfe's Tasty Toasties, Inc. On rear wall are two charts with movable lines representing sales graphs. One graph, with line pointing down, reads* WOLFE'S TASTY TOASTIES; *the other, with a rising line, reads* GRANNY'S GOODIES. (*Note: Lines on charts can be manipulated from offstage.*)

AT RISE: GRANDPA WOLFE, *furious, stands watching the charts.* SCHUYLER WOLFE *stands by desk, downstage. Both wear half-masks of wolves.*

GRANDPA: Schuyler, look at that sales chart! Down, down, down, go Wolfe's Tasty Toasties. (*As he speaks, sales line on Wolfe's chart moves slowly downward.*)

SCHUYLER: I'd rather look at Granny's Goodies! Up, up, up, they go. (*Line on* GRANNY'S GOODIES *chart moves up.*) The competition sure has us beat, Grandpa.

GRANDPA: I will not stand by and watch my doughy empire being squashed to the ground by an upstart Granny. (*Pacing*) I have to find that sneaky old crone—steal her recipes—buy her off. . . . Somebody must know who she is and where she hangs out. Down with Granny's Goodies! (*He bangs his fist on the desk.*) Ow!

SCHUYLER: Grandpa, that gives me an idea.

GRANDPA: You've never in your life had an idea!

SCHUYLER: It's a piping hot idea. Phone the electronic sales chart company and tell the manager you'll cancel your subscription unless our sales go up. Try it—what do you have to lose? (GRANDPA *rushes to phone.*)

GRANDPA: I'll try anything! (*On phone*) Hello—hello—hello, operator? This is an emergency! Get me the Electronic Sales Graph Company, on Main Street. . . . Busy? They can't be busy when I'm calling. I'm Grandpa Marley Wolfe, of Wolfe's Tasty Toasties.

SCHUYLER (*Following line on Wolfe chart downward with his finger*): Going down, down, down.

GRANDPA (*On phone*): Hello, Electronic Sales Graph Company? Listen, you. If you don't show my chart going up, up, up, I'll cancel my subscription. . . . Who am I? I just told you! I'm Grandpa Wolfe, of Wolfe's Tasty Toasties. I want my sales to go up, and Granny's Goodies to go down, or else! I'll give you ten seconds, and I'll hold the phone. (*He watches, as line on Wolfe chart starts upward, and line on* GRANNY'S *chart moves downward.*) That's better. (*On phone*) See that you keep the charts the way they are. (*Hangs up*) Well, Schuyler, we've solved that problem.

SCHUYLER: Grandpa, you're losing your grip. You ought to

retire. Go back to Hoboken and look for that strawberry picker who was almost my grandma.

GRANDPA (*Gazing into space*): Good old Tilly, the greatest
little strawberry picker I ever knew. (*Roaring, pounding his fist on desk*) No, I'll never give up here, until I
make Wolfe's Tasty Toasties a living monument to my
business genius.

SCHUYLER: What are you so worried about? You have
enough doughnuts, pretzels and apple strudel to live on
for life.

GRANDPA: I won't be outsmarted by a doddering old
woman. Granny—the evil genius behind Granny's Goodies. I must find her and stop her. I'll hire a detective.
Yes, a detective. Call Charlie Hunter and tell him to
get here on the double! (*Before* SCHUYLER *can move,*
HUNTER *runs in double-time*) Hunter! Were you eavesdropping? (*Line on* GRANNY's *chart moves upward, but
no one notices.*)

HUNTER (*Continuing to double-time in place*): I'd never
do a thing like that! I just happened to be passing by.

GRANDPA: Stand still and listen to me. (HUNTER *stops.*
GRANDPA *paces floor.*) Hunter, have you ever heard of
Granny's Goodies?

SCHUYLER (*In stage whisper to* HUNTER): Better say no.

HUNTER: No. A thousand times no. (*Pauses and sees charts*)
Why, there it is, on that chart, going up, up, up.

GRANDPA: I'm surrounded by traitors. You *have* heard of
Granny's Goodies. (*Sobbing*) I thought you were my
loyal janitor, who never heard of anything but Wolfe's
Tasty Toasties.

HUNTER (*Patting* GRANDPA *on the back*): I promise I never
heard of Granny's Goodies till just now, when I saw the
sales graph going up, up, up.

GRANDPA: Stop torturing me. I have a job for you, Hunter.

Get yourself a Sherlock Holmes outfit and turn into a
detective. Find out where Granny's Goodies come from.
Find out where they are baked. Find the armored car
she uses to make her secret midnight deliveries. Find out
about the whole shebang before my million-dollar bake
shop turns into a heap of broken cookie crumbs—before
I'm just one more brokenhearted business man trudg-
ing to the poorhouse, ruined by a little old lady who
learned to bake a better bagel.

HUNTER (*Whipping out a notebook and pencil*): And
what's her name, sir?

GRANDPA: I just told you! Granny—Granny—Granny!

HUNTER (*Writing*): Name's Granny. Where does she live?

GRANDPA (*Heatedly*): You're supposed to be the detective.
You find out.

HUNTER (*Writing*): I'm the detective. *I* find out. (*Looking
up*) And what business is she in?

GRANDPA (*Choking with rage*): You—you—you numskull!

SCHUYLER (*In a stage whisper*): She's in the goody game,
Hunter.

HUNTER: Oh, yes, she makes and sells Granny's Goodies.
(*Pauses*) Grandpa Wolfe, sir, are you quite all right?

SCHUYLER: Nothing's wrong with Grandpa that Granny's
hide won't cure.

HUNTER (*To GRANDPA*): Sir, do you want me to skin her?

GRANDPA: Yes! Before she skins me.

SCHUYLER: He means, Mr. Sherlock Holmes, that Granny's
got the goodies on him and is flooding the market with
macaroons, marble cake, ladyfingers, cheese bread,
brownies, gingersnaps . . .

GRANDPA: Stop, Schuyler, stop! You're breaking my heart.
Hunter, it's up to you. As soon as you locate Granny,
call in on your two-way magnifying glass radio, and
Schuyler and I will take care of that brownie baker once

and for all. (*With a smart salute,* HUNTER *exits on the double. Curtain.*)

*   *   *

SCENE 3

TIME: *Short time later.*

SETTING: *Road through woods.* (*This scene may be played in front of curtain.*)

AT RISE: ROSETTA, *wearing her cape and hood, enters right, pushing her bicycle and wagon.* HUNTER, *dressed like Sherlock Holmes, enters left. He carries a big magnifying glass and examines ground closely through it, as he walks along. He meets* ROSETTA, *who has stopped at center, and looks through glass at her feet, then straightens up, until he is peering at her face through the glass.*

ROSETTA: Good afternoon, Mr. Hunter.

HUNTER: Curses! You recognize me.

ROSETTA: I sure do. You're Charlie Hunter, dressed up to look like Sherlock Holmes. Are you playing detective?

HUNTER: My dear girl, I'm not *playing* detective. Right now, I *am* a detective. Now, who might you be?

ROSETTA: Mr. Hunter, do you mean you don't recognize me? I'm Rosetta Hood.

HUNTER (*Incredulously*): Rosetta? Little Red? The Little Red I used to bounce on my knee?

ROSETTA: That's right.

HUNTER: Wow, kid. I never would have known you. I mean, they must be calling you—er—*Big* Red now.

ROSETTA: Now, cut that out, and just tell me why you're playing detective out here in the Big Dark Woods.

HUNTER: I told you I wasn't playing. I'm working on a case.

I'm trying to track down an old lady, bake her in her own batter, and save an empire.

ROSETTA: Big deal. You always were peculiar, Mr. Hunter. Well, I have to get to Granny's. (*Starts to exit.* HUNTER *stops her.*)

HUNTER: Did you say *Granny's?*

ROSETTA: That's right. What's wrong with a sweet young thing like me going to visit Granny?

HUNTER (*Suspiciously*): Er—nothing. Say, kid, what's in the wagon?

ROSETTA: Goodies, of course. For my granny. She's sick, you know.

HUNTER: That's an awful lot of goodies for one sick granny.

ROSETTA: She's very sick, and I still have another whole load at home. So I have to be going now, if I want to make a second trip today. (*Starts to exit again.*)

HUNTER: Hold on, Big Red. Mind if I have a taste?

ROSETTA: I ought to mind—Big Red, indeed!

HUNTER: Aw, you'll always be Little Red to me, Big Red.

ROSETTA: That's more like it. (*She reaches into wagon.*) Have two goodies.

HUNTER (*Tasting them*): Do you make these wonderful goodies yourself?

ROSETTA: Sure. Poor sick Granny depends on them. Do you think they'll make her well?

HUNTER: You're an innocent little thing, aren't you?

ROSETTA: Being innocent is part of my charm. Well, I really must be off. Granny's fate is in my hands.

HUNTER: By the way, where does Granny live?

ROSETTA: Just down the road. (*Starts to exit*) Good luck on your case.

HUNTER: Thanks, kid. But watch out. There's a Wolfe out to get you. (ROSETTA *stops and looks back.*)

ROSETTA: A *what?*

HUNTER: A Wolfe, a big, bad Wolfe.

ROSETTA: Oh, sure, there is. (*She hops on bike and starts to pedal off.*) Hang on, Granny. Your goodies are on the way. Here comes Little Red Hood . . . riding. (*She exits left.*)

HUNTER: Unbelievable! What a setup! Granny's Goodies baked by the former Little Red Riding Hood, and sold by Granny from secret offices in her cottage in the Big Dark Woods. Wait till the Wolfes hear about this! (*He runs off right, speaking into magnifying glass*) Hunter calling Wolfe, Hunter calling Wolfe. . . . (*Curtain*)

* * *

SCENE 4

TIME: *Short time later.*

SETTING: *Same as Scene 3.*

AT RISE: ROSETTA *enters left, wearily pushing her bike and pulling wagon, which is now empty. She reaches center and stops to rest.* SCHUYLER *runs in right, and stops abruptly when he reaches* ROSETTA.

SCHUYLER: Excuse me, please. I'm in a hurry.

ROSETTA: Take it easy. Everybody rushes around too much these days.

SCHUYLER: I can't stop. I have to find a little old lady who's out to ruin our business. Besides, little girl, didn't your mother ever tell you not to talk to strange Wolfes?

ROSETTA: Oh, sure. But you're not really strange, just a little peculiar. (*Starts to push bike right*) Well, I have to get home, pack up another load of goodies and get right back to Granny's.

SCHUYLER: Goodies? Granny's? (*Sweetly*) Say, your name wouldn't be Little Red Riding Hood, would it?

ROSETTA: No, it wouldn't. (*Bitterly*) I mean, it was, but it's Big Red now. And I'd ask if you're the big bad Wolfe I'm supposed to look out for, but that would be too much of a coincidence. Anyhow, I have enough troubles now without that.

SCHUYLER: I'd be glad to listen to your troubles. I have very sympathetic ears.

ROSETTA: Rather long and pointy, aren't they?

SCHUYLER: Quite aristocratic, I think.

ROSETTA: I don't have time to stand around and chat about your ears. Granny needs her goodies. Sometimes I think her stomach is a bottomless pit. (*Starts to exit*)

SCHUYLER (*Calling after her*): Red, I warn you, you're being victimized by that bottomless pit.

ROSETTA (*Pausing*): I never thought of it that way. (*Suspiciously*) Are you trying to turn me against that dear, sweet, sick old lady?

SCHUYLER (*Hurriedly*): No, no. I'm just looking out for your interests.

ROSETTA: That's sweet of you. I'll keep what you said in mind. 'Bye. (*She exits.*)

SCHUYLER: Well, I did what I could to stop Granny's source of supply. Now to find Grandpa and get to the brains behind the business. On to Granny's! (*He exits left. Curtain.*)

*　　*　　*

SCENE 5

TIME: *Later that day.*

SETTING: *Granny's cottage. On rear wall are two charts, identical with those in Wolfe's office. A bed is at one side, and on the other, a desk with a telephone.*

AT RISE: GRANNY, *dressed in nightgown and nightcap, is*

standing in front of charts, tracing sales line of GRANNY'S
GOODIES *with her forefinger.*

GRANNY: Boy! The Electronic Sales Graph Company is
going to have to give me a bigger chart. Granny's
Goodies are over the top! Wolfe's Tasty Toasties have
sunk to the bottom. (*Phone rings. She answers it in
weak voice.*) It's poor sick Granny talking. . . . (*In her
normal voice*) Who is this? . . . My stockbroker? . . .
How's the Dow-Jones average today? Up? Good, good.
Now, have you bought shares of all those stocks I
wanted? . . . Good. I'll come around to your office tonight about midnight in my delivery-mobile and leave
the cash under your door, as usual. Over and out. (*She
hangs up and takes a bundle of cash from desk drawer
and begins to count.*) Three hundred and forty, fifty,
sixty! Oh, you're a smart business woman, Granny! If
this keeps up, Wolfe's Tasty Toasties will be right where
I want them—on the brink of bankruptcy. (*There is a
knock at the door.*) Ooops! That must be Rosetta, back
with her second load of goodies. My, that was a fast
trip. (*In weak voice*) Just a minute, dear. (*She quickly
puts money in drawer, draws curtain over charts to hide
them, and jumps into bed.*) Come in, come in. (*Door
opens, and* SCHUYLER *and* GRANDPA *enter.*) Why, Rosetta
dear, playing Halloween, are you? And you've brought a
little friend to see your Granny.
SCHUYLER: This is no game, Granny.
GRANNY: What a deep voice you have.
SCHUYLER: The better to ask you where you keep the
goodies, Granny.
GRANNY: Goodies? Whatever do you mean?
GRANDPA (*Suddenly pulling aside curtain to reveal charts*):
Look—the old witch has charts just like ours.

SCHUYLER: Granny, the jig's up.

GRANNY: You have me confused with somebody else, sonny. Oh, dear. I feel I'm sinking rapidly.

GRANDPA: If you're not the notorious Granny, what's this chart doing on your wall?

GRANNY: That's not a chart. It's an abstract portrait of my dear, departed husband. He was a very mixed-up man. Sometimes he was down, sometimes he was up.

SCHUYLER: Come off it, Granny. We know you've been exploiting your poor granddaughter, Rosetta Hood, known to the trade as Big Red.

GRANDPA: Where do you keep your beat-up delivery wagon—the camouflaged job you use to smuggle Granny's Goodies into the supermarkets late at night?

GRANNY (*Hopping out of bed*): Beat-up delivery wagon? Why that's the newest, most souped-up model armored delivery-mobile on the market. (*Catching herself*) Oops. You trapped me, didn't you? Sly foxes.

SCHUYLER: Not foxes—Wolfes. Now, where do you keep that delivery-mobile?

GRANNY (*Sullenly*): In a secret underground garage. I don't watch television for nothing, you know. (GRANDPA *stands gazing at charts.*)

GRANDPA: I do see a certain resemblance in this chart to a fellow I used to know in Hoboken. He stole my girl, nigh onto fifty years ago.

SCHUYLER: Grandpa, I thought you were going to forget about Hoboken until we took care of Granny.

GRANDPA: You're right, boy. First things first. (*To* GRANNY) O.K., Granny, where do you keep the goodies?

GRANNY: I don't know what you're talking about.

SCHUYLER: We'll get the information from Big Red, Grandpa. Quick, let's tie Granny up. (*They start to tie*

up a struggling GRANNY, *putting a gag in her mouth.
There is a knock at the door.*)

ROSETTA (*Offstage*): It's me again, Granny. Rosetta.

SCHUYLER (*In falsetto*): Just a minute, dear. (WOLFES *push*
GRANNY *into closet.* SCHUYLER *puts on her nightcap,
and jumps into bed, as* GRANDPA *hides behind desk.*)
Come in, Rosetta. (ROSETTA *enters, pushing her bike
and wagon.*) Dear Rosetta, come to see her poor ailing
Granny. What have you brought me this time?

ROSETTA (*Going over to bed*): Well, Granny, I may have
brought you your last load of goodies. I got to thinking
on my way here that I've just about had it with the
goody-baking business. (*Looking closely at* SCHUYLER)
You know, my very own dear little Granny, I hate to
say this . . .

SCHUYLER: Then don't.

ROSETTA: But it's expected of me. My, Granny, what big
eyes you have.

SCHUYLER: Not really. I'm just nearsighted, and I can't
find my glasses.

ROSETTA: And what big, pointy ears you have.

SCHUYLER: Quite aristocratic.

ROSETTA: Haven't I gone through this bit before?

SCHUYLER: Do continue and see if I recognize it.

ROSETTA: And what big teeth you have. Not in very good
condition, either. You should see your dentist twice a
year and brush regularly after every meal. The trouble
is, I think, that you eat too many goodies.

SCHUYLER: I'll cut down. But one dainty morsel for now.

ROSETTA (*Handing him a cookie*): One dainty morsel.

SCHUYLER (*Eating it*): Mm-m-m. Delicious. Now there's no
doubt about it. (*He jumps out of bed, removing nightcap and calling*) Grandpa!

ROSETTA (*Knowingly*): My, my. Some kind of gag.

GRANDPA (*Jumping up from behind desk*): The gag's in your granny's mouth. (HUNTER *runs in*.)

ROSETTA: Very funny. I suppose you're in on this, too, Mr. Hunter.

HUNTER: Indeed, but it's not very funny for you, Big Red. Granny's kept you baking day and night while she's been marketing the goodies and hoarding the profits.

ROSETTA (*Delighted*): Really? How clever of her. (MRS. HOOD *rushes in*.)

MRS. HOOD: Where's Granny? I want a word with her, and I want it now. Where is she? (*She rushes about room, searching, finally opening closet door.* GRANNY *stumbles out*.) Well! I don't blame you for hiding, Granny. Playing some childish game, when we're supposed to believe you're on your death bed. (*Removes gag and unties* GRANNY)

GRANNY: Have to get my kicks somehow.

HUNTER: Hah! You get your kicks fattening your bank account by selling the goodies Rosetta bakes.

MRS. HOOD: Is that what you've been doing, Granny?

GRANNY: You don't think I could eat all that stuff, do you?

MRS. HOOD: I suppose not, but haven't you been a mean Granny to poor Rosetta?

GRANNY: Granny has been a smart business woman. Don't you Wolfes agree?

GRANDPA: How did you know who we are?

GRANNY (*Indicating* SCHUYLER): This young fellow told me the name, and besides, if I hadn't known right from the start, I would have screamed bloody murder. I wanted to show you Wolfes that Granny cannot be stopped!

MRS. HOOD: Granny, you should be ashamed.

GRANNY: Of what? Not of beating out Wolfe's Tasty Toasties.

GRANDPA: Please—you're ruining a wonderful old man's life's work.

GRANNY: You? Wonderful? That's not the word they used back in Hoboken.

GRANDPA: Hoboken? What do you know about Hoboken?

GRANNY: Well, only that you were the biggest skinflint in town. Why, I remember the last time we had a date, and you took me picking strawberries. Then I found out that there were five acres of the blasted things, and you'd been paid hard cash to get the crop in before the rains came.

GRANDPA (*Going to* GRANNY): Tilly! It's you! Oh, Tilly, you wouldn't want to ruin me, Marley Wolfe, your old beau.

GRANNY: Oh, wouldn't I?

ROSETTA: I think this is all pretty silly. Now that Granny's up and about, there aren't going to be any more goodies, anyhow. I quit.

MRS. HOOD: Thank goodness.

GRANDPA: Hooray! Hear that, Schuyler? We'll be back on top in no time.

ROSETTA: I mean, there aren't going to be any more goodies from me. I'll give Granny the recipes and she can take it from there. I'm not going to set foot in the kitchen for a long, long time.

GRANDPA: Please, Tilly, can't we make some kind of a deal?

GRANNY: Maybe. What do you have in mind?

GRANDPA: Wolfe's has the factory. We have the marketing facilities. You have the recipes, and you know the business. We'll work out a partnership.

GRANNY: Well, I already have a sort of partner . . . what do you think, Rosetta?

ROSETTA: It sounds dandy. As long as I don't have to work in the kitchen.

GRANNY: Nor me. I'm strictly the lady-executive type.

GRANDPA: Then it's a deal?

GRANNY *and* ROSETTA: A deal!

MRS. HOOD: And I always thought she used cake mixes.

GRANDPA: Why don't we all go down to the plant, and I'll give you the grand tour. We could pick out your new office, too, Tilly.

GRANNY: Fine. You get started, and Rosetta and I will be along in a minute. I want a word with her first.

HUNTER: Mrs. Hood, I'd be happy to escort you through the Big Dark Woods to the Tasty Toasties factory.

MRS. HOOD: Why, thank you, Charlie. You know, it's been years since you were around our place, bouncing Little Red on your knee. (*They exit.*)

GRANDPA: Come along, Schuyler. We'll wait for the ladies outside. (*To* GRANNY) Don't be long, Tilly. (*He and* SCHUYLER *exit.*)

GRANNY (*Giggling*): Well, Rosetta, we did it!

ROSETTA: At last. Another week of sugar and shortening, and I'd have gone bats. And this Red Riding Hood farce! (*She removes her cape and hood, revealing fashionable dress.*) This outfit always made me look like a balloon. I was getting pretty tired of having people call me Big Red.

GRANNY: It was the only red cape I could find. No harm done. And things are working out just as I planned. I learned a long time ago that it's one thing to have something to offer, and it's something else to make people appreciate it. To do that, you need a little publicity, a gimmick. That's what we've done with Granny's Goodies, and we've come out on top of the creampuff pile.

ROSETTA: We never could have done it, if you hadn't come up with this scheme, Granny. We've beaten the Wolfes at their own game.

GRANNY: The Wolfes, yes. Tell me . . . (*Coyly*) what do you think of Marley Wolfe? (*Without waiting for an answer*) He used to be quite the boy in his day. Has a nice grandson, too. You ought to keep him in mind, Rosetta. (*Businesslike again*) Now, about those recipes.

ROSETTA: Recipes? What recipes?

GRANNY: The Granny's Goodies recipes. Do you have them with you?

ROSETTA: Oh, the *recipes*. Well, it's this way. I take a pinch of this and a pinch of that . . .

GRANNY: Quite an artist, aren't you? Well, never mind. We'll feed the data into a computer. You have to be very forward-looking in business these days. Let's find Grandpa and Schuyler. (*As they start to exit*) Say, why not bring along the hood—just for luck?

ROSETTA (*Picking up cape*): I guess I should. It's kind of symbolic.

GRANNY (*As they exit*): Not only symbolic, but I have this great idea for an advertising campaign. We'll make your face and the red hood famous. . . . You'll look great on color television. Feels pretty good to be a tycoon, eh? (*Calling offstage*) We're coming! (*To* ROSETTA) And those Wolfe boys aren't bad . . . not bad at all. (*Curtain*)

THE END

Production Notes

BIG RED RIDING HOOD

Characters: 3 male; 3 female.

Playing Time: 30 minutes.

Costumes: Rosetta wears a red cape with a hood over a fashionable dress. Granny wears a long nightgown and a nightcap. Schuyler, Grandpa and Hunter wear business suits; Hunter changes to a Sherlock Holmes outfit. Mrs. Hood wears an ordinary dress. Schuyler and Grandpa wear halfmasks of wolves.

Properties: Boxes containing cookies, cakes, etc., notebook and pencil, large magnifying glass, stage money, bike with wagon attached.

Setting: Scene 1: Mrs. Hood's cottage. A table at center is loaded with goodies, and there is a telephone nearby. Scene 2: Grandpa's office at Wolfe's Tasty Toasties.

Grandpa's desk is at left, with a telephone on it. At rear are two charts with movable lines, representing sales graphs. The lines are manipulated from backstage. One chart reads GRANNY'S GOODIES and the other WOLFE'S TASTY TOASTIES. Scenes 3 and 4: The woods. Both scenes may be played in front of the curtain. No scenery is necessary. Scene 5: Granny's cottage in the woods. The same sales graphs as in Scene 2 are on rear wall. A bed is at one side, and a desk with a telephone on the other. A closet door is near desk.

Lighting: No special effects.

Sound: Telephone ringing, as indicated in text.